PENGUIN BOOKS

THE FOX IN THE CUPBOARD

Jane Shilling is a columnist for *The Times* and a book reviewer for the *Sunday Telegraph*, the *Evening Standard* and *The Times*. She lives in Greenwich with her son and hunts with the Ashford Valley.

The Fox in the Cupboard

A Memoir

JANE SHILLING

PENGUIN BOOKS

PENGUIN BOOKS

Published by the Penguin Group
Penguin Books Ltd, 80 Strand, London WC2R ORL, England
Penguin Group (USA) Inc., 375 Hudson Street, New York, New York 10014, USA
Penguin Group (Canada), 10 Alcorn Avenue, Toronto, Ontario, Canada M4V 3B2
(a division of Pearson Penguin Canada Inc.)
Penguin Ireland, 25 St Stephen's Green, Dublin 2, Ireland
(a division of Penguin Books Ltd)
Penguin Group (Australia), 250 Camberwell Road, Camberwell, Victoria 3124, Australia
(a division of Pearson Australia Group Pty Ltd)
Penguin Books India Pvt Ltd, 11 Community Centre, Panchsheel Park, New Delhi – 110 017, India
Penguin Group (NZ), cnr Airborne and Rosedale Roads, Albany, Auckland 1310, New Zealand
(a division of Pearson New Zealand Ltd)
Penguin Books (South Africa) (Pty) Ltd, 24 Sturdee Avenue, Rosebank 2196, South Africa

Penguin Books Ltd, Registered Offices: 80 Strand, London WC2R ORL, England

www.penguin.com

First published by Viking 2004
Published in Penguin Books 2005
2

Copyright © Jane Shilling, 2004
All rights reserved

The moral right of the author has been asserted

Set by Rowland Phototypesetting Ltd, Bury St Edmunds, Suffolk
Printed in England by Clays Ltd, St Ives plc

This book is dedicated to the memory of my grandfather, Percy Charlton, who loved stories.

'Falling in love is a desolating experience, but not when it is with a countryside'

T. H. White, *England Have My Bones*

PART ONE

Some time towards the end of the nineties I read an article, in *Vogue*, I think it was, about an American company that had begun to market a new range of scents. The thing about these scents, however, was that they weren't what you'd normally think of as scent. They weren't exotic blends of chypre and ambergris, orris-root, peony and vetiver; they weren't the haunting aldehyde avatars of these natural aromatics. They weren't even the innocent, uninflected distillations of single flowers: rose, violet, bluebell, jasmine.

They came packaged in small, quasi-medical glass and silvery metal bottles, labelled in the functional, faux-pharmaceutical typescript that was an idiosyncrasy of late nineties' cosmetic packaging. The labels were distinctly prolix, in a chatty, down-home style intended, I suppose, to persuade the prospective buyer that these essences, however unortho-dox, had a narrative: an aura if not precisely of glamour, in the expected manner of scent, then at least a kind of mystery – you could call it dirty romanticism, perhaps.

Anyway, if you picked up one of these little bottles and pressed the metal aerosol thingy on top, out came a squirt of colourless liquid and, a second or two of olfactory reaction time later, a smell. An intense and eerily accurate chemical repro-duction of something vivid and entirely unexpected: tomato, grass, gasolene, dirt (not filth, in the English sense of that word, but earth, in the American use of the term: a sharp, damp brownness that was the exact smell of digging as a child, when your nose is so much nearer the earth than an adult's, with a toy spade in the garden on a spring day after rain the night before).

The oddest thing about these scents – once you'd got over the sheer weirdness of the notion of some laboratory full of parfumiers labouring to extract the fugitive, tom-cat essence of ripe tomatoes, was their extreme solipsism. By and large, people wear musk or carnation or civet for the same reason that musk oxen or carnations or civet cats do, to send out intimations of sexy availability. But these sharp elemental extracts were something different. Trapped in a bottle and sold for £30, they were the commercial essence of nostalgia, than which there is nothing more idiosyncratic or more private.

For everyone, there exist certain smells, the effect of which is to slash open a window in the impermeable membrane of the present, through which the past then floods. But the magic is particular, not transferable. Is face powder the smell of comfort, or of loss? Does coffee smell of anger or of sex? The sharp reek of newsprint – essence of excitement, or a desolation of tedium? And what about the metallic tang of railway stations? The coal-flavoured iciness of falling snow, which you taste, rather than smell? Crumbly old sun-warmed brick? Yew trees? Apple bark? Seawater drying on warm rocks when the tide has gone out? A myriad smells; an infinity of notional little glass bottles, every one of them containing, for someone, the scent of memory.

The house in Greenwich is small. A nineteenth-century river-worker's cottage in the still slightly slummy fringes of little roads that splay along the southern bank of Greenwich Reach as the Thames curves round the Isle of Dogs on the last stage of its journey towards Tilbury, Gravesend and the sea. Flat-fronted, built of yellowish London brick, it looks like a doll's house: a neat, square box with a door in the middle and five sash windows (two up, two down, and an extra, narrow one on the landing above the front door); the repository of quantities of dampish memory, no doubt, if one began to dig for it.

Inside, the house has the reverse Tardis quality of seeming even more cramped than it does from the outside. Each of the two-up, two-down windows on the outside has a very little room behind it, built as though for a smaller race of people than ordinary humans – Borrowers, possibly. Or then again, perhaps merely poor, undernourished and rather sickly, thanks to the damp rheumatic vapours that sink to the bottom of the river valley and hang there. (If you climb to the top of the hill in Greenwich Park, where the Observatory stands and the tourists straddle the Meridian Line, you can look out and see them at dusk and in the early morning: a ravishing shimmer of iridescent, mother-of-pearl toxins.)

The front door opens disconcertingly on to a blank: a white-panelled rectangle that looks as though it should be another door, but isn't. To the left there is a room for which no adequate modern term exists. It is ludicrously undersized for a drawing room, and too prim for a living room. What it is, is a parlour. It contains a steel grate capable of accommodating at most three lumps of coal, two narrow sofas, evidently not meant for sitting on (they are covered in cream brocade of a forbidding pallor, with a pattern of green and pink flowers and butterflies), and a shrunken upright cottage piano whose foreshortened expanse of yellowed ivory keys and sticky black lacquer case were manufactured on the same diminutive scale as the house, at about the same date.

To the right of the front door is the room where the living gets done. Part dining room, part study, part office, part thoroughfare to an exiguous, stone-flagged corridor of rear extension containing the kitchen, bathroom and a sort of all-purpose scullery full of brooms and garden forks, half-empty bags of fish, blood and bone meal and ancient packets of unsown larkspur and nasturtium seed (Best before 1992), it is the junction box of the house.

This room is an echo chamber for a cacophony of smells from all over the house. Here a peppery drift of scent from the tulips and daffodils on the parlour mantelpiece collides with the domineering citrus stink of the kitchen detergents. A pile of ironing, waiting for someone to take it upstairs and put it away, sits in a localized cloud of lightly scorched cotton, mixed with the artificially compounded whiff of morning freshness that some scientist has identified as signalling cleanliness to the noses of diligent housewives. The smells of last night's roast chicken and this morning's toast and coffee waft alternately from the kitchen.

Underpinning this comparatively wholesome domestic mixture are a couple of less savoury base notes. An expert might identify the intermittent, ominous taint of the slow-moving sewer, built by its Victorian engineer on not quite enough of an incline, and imperfectly sealed by the rusting manhole cover just outside the back door. Then there is the musty miasma of mice, rising from a small gap in the skirting board just by the fridge where the cat sits patiently, his front paws and tail disposed in comfortable curves, indicating that he intends to stay there for as long as it takes.

And then if you follow the track like a rabbit-path, where the stain on the floorboards has been worn away by the constant traffic of feet between the front door and the kitchen, at the halfway mark, just where the shabby blue cupboard stands, another smell leaps out and grabs you. Not a hint, this one, or a whiff, but a powerful, nose-grabbing reek of stables – of straw, sweat, horse-dung and leather. Where is it coming from, and why? What business has a front room in a Greenwich terrace to stink of a stable-yard?

The source of the smell is a jacket, slung on a dry cleaner's hanger and hooked half out of sight on one side of the cupboard. It is a heavy jacket, single-breasted, with a full skirt and a single pocket flap on the waist seam. It is made of dense navy wool, like the stuff of a pea-coat, and the body is lined with finer-weight wool – cream-coloured, with a Tattersall check of navy and yellow. Inside the coat skirt, a black cotton lining opens into an enormous pocket, big enough to put a rabbit in.

Beside its sharp animal smell, the garment shows signs of violent wear. Of the three buttons on the front, two are loose and the bottom one is entirely missing. A cuff button hangs by a thread, and there is a chip and a deep scratch on one of the two buttons sewn at waist level on either side of the single back vent. Coat, buttons and lining are all thickly encrusted with gobbets of dried mud. A sprinkling of coarse white hairs clings to the navy nap on which there are greenish, shiny smears of something else that is not mud, but looks like snail trails mixed with grass.

Coiled round the metal hook of the hanger, falling half-hidden inside the coat, hangs something else: a short, stout stick, covered in worn brown plaited leather. At one end the stick is finished with a silver collar and a crooked stag's-horn handle in creamy bone-colour, worn shiny with half a century of handling. The other end is whipped with fine cord and ends in a stiff flap of brown leather with a slot through which is threaded a tapering, yard-long, plaited brown leather thong, ending in a short, knotted lash of muddy blue cord. It is a hunting whip. The coat is a hunting coat. And the animal smell that rises from it is the smell of fox-hunting.

As to what the coat is doing, slung on the side of the china cupboard in the front room of the house in Greenwich where I live with my son, who is 12, and ambivalent about hunting – I can explain. It is in transit between the last day's hunting and the next, waiting for the mud to be brushed, the grassy horse-slobber to be sponged, the buttons sewn back on and the whole thing hung in the bathroom with the shower running in order to steam it back into respectability. It can't spend the time between meets in the wardrobe, or the cupboard-under-the-stairs where the other coats of the household are kept, because it infuses everything near it with its clinging, insistent aura. And so on its days off it hangs about the place, a palpable presence in the household, administering small electric jolts of flashback memory of the last day's hunting and the one before, and the one before that; each like a video clip a few seconds long, only more vivid, more pungent than anything trapped behind the two-dimensional flatness of a TV screen could convey.

The letterbox rattles. On my way to pick up the post I pass the coat and am gripped by a dizzy echo, the full version of which came on a Saturday afternoon late in the season, when we turned away from the huntsman, who was determined to hunt on until he could no longer see his hounds. The sky was a cold, ethereal blue and you could feel the dew sinking chilly through the air, ready to become frost as soon as the sun went down. Skirting the edge of a wood we saw a little wooden post-and-rail fence into the next field and hopped it. Except that on the other side, the ground wasn't level, but fell away and away, so the expected rhythm of approach, take-off, flight, landing and recovery into the lullaby three-time of canter failed to materialize; replaced for some fractions of a second by the appalling vertigo of riding a runaway lift on an uncontrollable plunge down a shaft.

Or this, from the start of the same day's meet, when we turned off the metalled road into dense, low-growing woodland and suddenly were transformed from the orderly cavalcade of hounds, huntsman, whippers-in and, at a respectful distance, the field, trotting neatly along the high road like a print on a pub wall sprung into animation, into a wild herd, veering blind through the trackless forest after the sound of the hounds and the huntsman cheering them, bent low to avoid being swept off by bare whipping branches and sinewy, neck-high nooses of honeysuckle in breaking leaf, face pressed hard into the horse's neck, eyes tight shut to avoid having a contact lens poked out (the country is sequinned all over with the transparent discs of my lost contact lenses, and cobwebbed with my hairnets).

Or this, from mid-season, when the field was told by the Master to stand along the edge of a spinney and keep watch. The covert was sparse and leafless, long and quite narrow. You could see straight through it and out the other side, where more of the field were waiting. Behind me was a steep grassy bank on top of which were gathered a couple of foot followers: watchful men with waterproof gaiters and stout sticks who know the country (whereas I never have a clue, and might as well be hunting the Russian steppes or the American prairies when it comes to having any sense of where I am, or have come from, or might be going to next).

There was a lot going on inside this little clump of trees and underbrush: the high yelping wail of hunting hounds and the throat-music exhortations of the huntsman cheering them on, by voice, mainly, though with occasional notes of his horn. First nothing was visible, then a trickle of hounds – pale, elegant, cream-and-caramel animals, plunging intently through the dull brown underbrush like figures on a tapestry, but on a rising note of excitement. The lead hound checked, faltered, turned back on the line and then they all turned away and disappeared back the way they had come. As soon as they'd gone, the fox came barrelling past: small, bunched up, dark reddish-brown.

Time slowed. The foot followers would be bound to have seen him. They never missed a thing. Why didn't they shout? Was this not the hunted fox? I glanced behind. The foot followers were trying to light a cigarette in the wind. It was the hunted fox, I was sure of it. Should I scream, or not? It depended whose side I was on, the hounds' or the fox's. Generally, I was far enough away from the action not to have to take sides; my role purely that of a spectator, happy if hounds caught their fox, and just as happy if he got away. This time I was part of the narrative and whatever I did would have a consequence. If I stayed silent, he might get away. If I screamed, they might catch him. I had to decide. The foot followers were still bent over their flickering Zippo. A moment or two had passed since I caught sight of that fox and he was moving fast. With no sense of making a conscious decision, I opened my mouth, and out came a scream.

Was I right to do it? I've thought about it a lot since, and I still have no idea. The huntsman would say yes (as long as it really was the hunted fox, and not just one of his friends, out for a risky stroll at an inopportune moment). My brain and my heart say maybe, but neither of them was engaged when that scream came roaring up from my lungs and into my mouth. Pure instinct squeezed it out of me. Which is odd, in itself, since there is no hunting in my background: no horses, no hounds, no foxes; no kennels or meet cards, hunt coats, hip flasks or ancient, dusty fox brushes. I was in my late thirties when I first put the toe of my newly acquired riding boot into a stirrup iron, and two years older than that before I first followed hounds. That instinct was either very late-blooming, or very deep-rooted. But now it has me gripped.

The other thing is this. The smell of hunting is not for me the scent of nostalgia; it is not the bottled essence of my past, but of my recent present. Nevertheless, the rent in time's membrane is there, and the present and the past flow back and forth through the breach, each permeating the other, for this reason: that the country over which I now hunt is the country of my childhood. I thought I knew it well, but now it seems like a different realm, a landscape of known contours, seen in a dream, where everything seems at once familiar and unrecognizably strange.

When I was little, I knew exactly where I belonged. My name was Jane Elizabeth Shilling and I lived at 117 Bell Road, Sittingbourne, Kent. I had a mother, a father, a sister and a Siamese cat who was older than me, because someone had given him to my parents as a wedding present. He was fond of balancing high above the kitchen sink on the narrow metal ledge of the kitchen window, squinting proudly down his long, chocolate-brown nose at us like an eagle from its eyrie as we sat around the kitchen table, a parent and a child on either side, eating our bacon and eggs in the mornings before school.

The house stood on ground that had once been an orchard. All the surrounding land had been orchards, so there were apple trees at the bottom of the garden; but the apples that grew on them were Bramleys – large, sour green cookers, often pitted with brownish scabs, or with the scattering of brown granules around the star-shaped bit on their bottoms that meant there was a worm living inside. We had to pick them up a lot, when they fell off the trees in the autumn and lay rotting in the long grass, but I never remember eating them, even cooked.

Under the apple trees was a spiny thicket of gooseberry bushes into which my guinea pig, Flora, once disappeared. We had a series of insipid white guinea pigs with ruby eyes, and rather more engaging hamsters, but never had much luck with them. If they didn't run away, the cat generally got them.

Outside the kitchen window was a huge cherry tree with wrinkled dark brown bark that sometimes dripped a sticky golden gum that looked like solid honey. I licked it once, but it tasted horrible, like earwax. One end of the washing line was tied to this cherry tree. On washing days, rows of white pillowcases and handkerchiefs hung on the line, snapping in the wind. The cherry tree had white flowers in spring with a sweet, elusive, almondy scent, and you could lie on the grass looking up at the blue sky through the black branches and the white flowers and the flapping squares of hankie, surrounded by the smell of cherry blossom and clean laundry, which is what I was doing one day when my mother came out of the kitchen in a state, saying that someone called Bobby Kennedy was dead.

We didn't have a car to begin with, but sometimes my father hired one to take us on holiday, when my parents were very keen on visiting Stately Homes. I formed the impression from these visits that 117 Bell Road might also be quite Stately in its way. It had two approaches, a steep, narrow path to the front door, bounded on either side by brick and flint walls which started quite high at the pavement end, and dwindled steadily to the height of a single brick at the house end. The great dare was to jump off the steep end without falling over and grazing your knees. On the other side of the front garden was a wider, asphalt drive that led to the black-painted double doors of what would have been the garage, if only we had had a car. My father kept his woodworking tools in it instead: a long bench with a vice on it and ringlets of golden shavings on the floor, and rows of chisels, from huge to tiny, hanging in rows on a big brown board punched with little holes that covered the whole of one wall.

The house was built of reddish brick and on the front of it, where my bedroom was, the brick was laid in a zig-zag herringbone pattern and there were three thick beams of wood. It was these beams that gave me the impression of stateliness, together with the front door, which was made of massive varnished wood with curly black iron hinges, like the ones I had seen on castle doors, and a square pane of glass in the middle of it just too high for me to look through, not flat, like ordinary glass, but thick, like a Fox's glacier mint, and ridged in a circle shape as though someone had tried to melt it, with a fat glass bobble in the middle.

Indoors the floors were made of wooden bricks, arranged in the same herringbone pattern as the bricks on the outside. My mother used to polish them on her hands and knees, pushing *The Times* ahead of her and reading as she polished. All the paint on the doors and bannisters was dark brown, and so were the floors and most of the furniture, so downstairs at least it was a very brown house.

Upstairs was a degree more colourful. There was a long corridor with a bathroom at the end of it, papered with green wallpaper that had orange and black fish on it, swimming through trailing fronds of weed. On top of the bathroom cupboard was a large china ornament of two swimming fish, a big one and a little one, with rippling fins and thick parted lips. They were purplish-blue, very shiny, with a sheen like the colours on bubbles, and I thought they were beautiful. My mother said they were hideous, but a wedding present, so couldn't just be done away with.

In my room, the wallpaper was yellow and the bed was pushed up against a big window that looked out over the front garden and the road, and was divided up into lots of small rectangular panes, each framed in a strip of soft grey metal. There was a street lamp just outside and the curtains were thin, so it was possible to carry on reading even after you had been told to switch off the light.

My father had made me a doll's house, painted yellow, with a red roof and black-and-white chequered paper like tiles on the floor, and also a treasure shelf where I kept a collection of glass animals – a swan, a black cat with an arched back, a purple duck, a small yellow dog with black spots and a broken front leg, and miniature Limoges china cups and plates with turquoise, pink or crimson borders picked out in gold, and tiny vignettes of flirting shepherdesses with bows on their crooks and barefoot boys in ragged breeches.

The other thing my father had made me was a bookcase. It was screwed to the wall above my bed and I was afraid that it might fall on me in the night and I would be crushed to death by an avalanche of books. I had a reputation as a bookish child and was often given books as Christmas and birthday presents by my friends and relations, although really I much preferred dolls and in particular should have liked a doll called Tressy, which had a hole in its head through which you could pull out or wind in, by means of a screw mechanism in its flesh-pink plastic midriff, a thick lock of glittering hair.

Nevertheless, the fact was that I didn't have a Tressy doll, but did have an enormous library of children's classics, many of them in the handsome, large-format Everyman editions with beautiful illustrations. I had books by Beatrix Potter, Alison Uttley, Rosemary Sutcliff and Cynthia Harnett. I had *Black Beauty*, *Peter Simple*, *The Children of the New Forest*, *The House at Green Knowe*, *Mary Poppins*, *My Naughty Little Sister*, Laura Ingalls Wilder's *Little House* series, *Ballet Shoes*, and a great many other books by Noel Streatfeild, including a not very good one about a vicarage, described by my mother as a 'pot-boiler', the whole *Swallows and Amazons* series, which I loathed energetically for their cold-water heartiness, and all the E. Nesbits, of which I veered between liking *The Wouldbegoods* and *Five Children and It* best, because of the marvellous naughtiness of the Wouldbegoods, and the extreme crossness of the mythical psammead, which I found oddly comforting.

It is noticeable in retrospect that most of these books were in some way about belonging to places: belonging somewhere and then having to go away and learn to belong somewhere else, like Laura and Mary leaving the Little House in the Big Woods because their Pa had taken a notion to live in a Little House on the Prairie instead. Or the Beverley children, Edward, Alice, Humphrey and Edith, who became the Children of the New Forest after being forced out of their ancestral mansion because their father was a (Wrong but Wromantic) Cavalier who opposed the (Right but Repulsive) Levellers.

Then there were the children who didn't seem to belong anywhere at all and had to carve a place in the world to accommodate them, like Rosemary Sutcliff's orphan in *Brother Dusty-Feet*, cuffed from gatepost to shippen by his horrible aunt until he fell in with a band of strolling players and ended up eventually in Logres, in Arcady, in the land at the Rainbow's End – that is, in Oxford, the pale gold city of infinite learning and heart's desires fulfilled that his father had once told him about.

Or the three oddly assorted children in *Ballet Shoes*, Pauline, Petrova and Posy Fossil, vaguely collected up like a trio of archaeological curiosities by their eccentric old guardian and deposited by him in Kensington, from where they went to ballet school and became, in their different ways, marvellous. I myself went to ballet school, at Miss Thompsett's, in Park Drive. But although she had remarked on my high insteps and admirable sense of rhythm, I felt pretty certain that this was not where I was going to belong.

Downstairs, in our extremely brown dining room, was the thing that I regarded as the ancestral hearth: an immense fireplace with purplish-brown glazed tiles and a massive wooden surround. It had a solid overmantel shelf, just at a little girl's head height, and at the back of the shelf was a big circular carved inset of birds with scaly legs and cruel hooked beaks, grasping and tearing at a background of knobbly berries. This, I reckoned, must be our family crest.

Besides the crest, we had a thumping family bible with a

flaky brown leather cover, a penetrating, sweetish, musty smell and thick, creamy pages that didn't lie flat like the pages of a modern book but described a series of gentle undulations and clung together when you tried to turn them. All the 's's were printed as 'f's, which showed how old it was. And at the back of this bible was a list of names – Shillings and Hinges, with their dates of Birth and Death in faded, thin, loopy writing of unearthly regularity. The last name was that of my grand-mother, Florence Ellen Jarrett, born Dec 22nd, 1895. I took a pen one day and wrote my name and my sister's after hers, but my ink was bright blue, not brown, and I couldn't do the spidery writing. It didn't look right, and I wished afterwards that I hadn't done it.

Only half the family was accounted for in this bible. The other half, my other grandparents, were Charltons and Bachelors, and the reason they didn't have a family bible of their own, I imagined, was that one of them, my grandfather, didn't have any ancestors to write in it. His name was Percy Charlton, and he had that name because he had been found as an infant by a policeman, name of Percy, in Chalton Street (the 'r' crept in a bit later on, my grandfather said), just behind King's Cross station in London.

From Chalton Street he went to the St Pancras workhouse, and from the workhouse to a foster home in Bishop's Stort-ford, and from the foster home into the Navy, which became his family, and he travelled all over the world on fighting ships with strangely frivolous names borrowed from flowers, drinks and shepherdesses: *Bluebell, Curacao, Phoebe*. And although he married my grandmother and had her and my mother to come home to, it wasn't to the same house every time, but to rented lodgings in different ports with landlords, obliging or disobliging, and other people's furniture, and restrictions as to the use of the front room, or the frequency with which baths might be taken.

Some of the storybook children I read about lived in houses where their parents had been born, and their grandparents and great-grandparents, in the same bed, in the same bedroom, looking out of the window over the same piece of land, on which, year after year, generation after generation, the leaves came out, the hedges blossomed, the migrating birds arrived from hotter places on the same date, to build nests under the same bit of eaves. These children knew their surroundings by heart, like a nursery rhyme, or scripture; the cadences of it beating in their blood almost before they were conscious; the deep structure of the landscape embedded in their minds like language.

Then there were the other children, the ones like Laura and Mary Ingalls or the Railway Children, who lived somewhere for a while but then, because of misfortune, danger or simply because their parents said so, had to leave the things that they knew – the curve of the bannister rail that their fingers traced each morning, the tree in the garden with the branch low enough to swing on – and move to somewhere else, to a different house with doors in unexpected places, the church bells chiming the wrong tune on the quarter hour, to grassland instead of woodland, the trickle of a stream instead of the drag-and-slap of the sea on the pebbled shore.

I could see that I, in my brown ancestral home with the cherry tree, the fishy bathroom and the treasure-shelf full of glass animals that I rearranged every week, was like the first lot of storybook children. And my grandfather was like the others. He made himself at home wherever he happened to fetch up – Chatham, Glasgow, running away from the Germans across occupied Norway during the war, on a ship in the middle of the ocean with no land to be seen at all. And he did this by telling stories about those places, with himself at the centre of them.

By the time I knew him, he had come to rest in Cumberland. That was where he went to work when he came out of the Navy. He and my grandmother lived in a rented house called Roseneath, in gold letters on a half-circle of glass above the front door. But one day they came to stay with us at Bell Road and my grandfather said that they were building a bungalow quite nearby. He drove me to look at the place where the house was to be built in his car, which was pale blue with silver trimmings and an orange indicator that flicked up and clicked irritably when he forgot to turn it off, which was often.

I sat in the front seat, an unusual privilege, and we set off down the long, dull, straight Roman road that led out of Sittingbourne, through Teynham and Ospringe to Faversham. The windows of the houses on either side of the road were dirty with the greasy grey dust the traffic threw up. We passed garages, fish-and-chip shops, zebra crossings with Belisha beacons, and all the time the road stretched out straight ahead of us, glittering greyly into the flat, dull distance.

At Faversham, my grandfather turned on to a smaller, narrower road with meandering twists and kinks at each of which he tooted his horn twice. On either side were corn-fields, then a church, a cricket pitch with houses around the edge of it, more fields, a long avenue of ancient beeches, then a pub with a tiled roof and an outside covered in overlapping white-painted boards. After the pub, we came to a piece of scrub ground with weeds growing on it, piles of bricks, a heap of gritty sand, a cement mixer and a tabby cat crouched under a straggling rose bush on which some loose red roses were blooming half-heartedly. 'This,' said my grandfather with a flourish, hauling on the handbrake as though heaving in an anchor chain, 'is Greenways.'

Greenways was not yet a house. It was a series of trenches filled with lumpy grey concrete and a set of plans on springy intractable rolls of crackly blue tracing paper. The grandparents were retiring to Kent. For the first time ever, they would live in a house that belonged to them. The sailor was home from the sea.

Week after week my grandfather and I made the journey to see how Greenways was growing. First there were foundations, then walls, then wooden frames where the doors and windows would be, then a pale gold ribcage of wooden roofbeams and finally a tiled roof. Part of the front was given a coating of some stuff with the texture of hard-cooked scrambled eggs, painted pale green. The rest was sharp-edged red bricks which weren't crumbly, like the bricks in our house, but looked somehow raw, like the meat in the butcher's window.

The bungalow windows were strange: rather high and slitty. They gave the place a shut-up, unfriendly look behind its new hedge of leggy adolescent beech saplings. But it had a fish-pond with green and pink crazy paving, flowerbeds with scalloped edges and a front garden of raked earth on which a fine fuzz of blades of new grass was beginning to show, and my grandfather was enchanted with it, his little place in the country.

Not that grandfather was a countryman. Apart from the fostered years he spent at school in Essex between being found on a city pavement and sent off to sea, the earth had never been his element. But when at last he found himself lodged in a Kentish hamlet, with a pub and a general stores at one end of the sparse scattering of houses, and a Victorian chapel with a parlour organ and a single cracked bell at the other, he set about turning himself into a villager with characteristic vigour.

He bought a flat tweed cap and accumulated a collection of knobbly walking sticks. He attended both the Victorian chapel and the much grander flint church in the bigger village a mile or so away. (This church contained a fascinating white marble statue, life-sized, of two Victorian children of about my age. They had crisping carved curls and leaned together over a story-book with their heads confidentially inclined. A stone battledore and shuttlecock were tossed onto the ground by their barefoot marble toes, which I used to try and warm with my own pink fingers.)

My grandfather belted out the hymns in his tone-deaf hoot at services here on alternate Sundays, and took the collection in a pointy brown leather bag with a wooden handle. When he took up woodcarving as a hobby, using odd lumps of tree that he picked up on his rambles and my grandmother's vegetable knife, he made several ambitious attempts on religious subjects and donated the results to the church. There was a St Francis of Assisi holding a small, lopsided dove that made its way into the children's corner, and a life-sized head of the Virgin, painted like a ship's figurehead in hectic shades of pink and blue household gloss. A picture of him hacking at St Francis with grandma's kitchen knife appeared in the local newspaper, above the caption, 'Mr Percy Charlton, merrily chipping away'.

When he was not merrily chipping he sat on the parish council and made a nuisance of himself to local landowners on the subject of footpaths. He and my grandmother had always been great ones for elaborate picnics at beauty spots, involving folding chairs and large Thermos flasks and once an apple pie in a Pyrex pie dish that slipped from my grand-mother's grasp as she was handing it from the front to the back of the car and disappeared in a welter of sugary crumbs and collapsed apple slop beneath the front passenger seat. Now they became keen ramblers, netting their newly adopted terri-tory with an invisible skein of footsteps; superimposing its geography on their own personal landscapes.

I didn't ramble. I was too small to keep up with their stately march in boots and gaiters, properly kitted out with OS maps in waterproof covers and pairs of wirecutters. Instead I wandered. To begin with I went only as far as the wilderness just beyond the scalloped flowerbeds. It had been someone's cottage garden once and now was the private domain of a couple of cats, who lounged like little lions through the long grass and the abandoned raspberry canes.

On hot afternoons, when I climbed over the sagging fence that separated my grandfather's sparse lawn from the wilderness of tumbledown apple trees and garden flowers gone wild, I would look up from my book and bag of toffees in the nest I had made among the dry grass and meet the blank, glassy stare of one of these cats, frozen in the act of stalking a blackbird along a lilac branch, or poised as though in a game of musical statues, with a limp little body, still twitching feebly, in its mouth.

There was a dark and pleasantly sinister wood behind the grandparents' bungalow. It rose up in a conical mound and provided a gloomy backdrop to the well-tamed domestic view of forsythia and rose bushes. From the shipshape galley of my grandmother's kitchen the woods looked like the sea: a billowy scribble of different shades of green, swaying and rolling for as far as you could see until they met the sky. You could reach them in five minutes by turning left out of the fancy wrought-iron garden gate whose latch made a sweet glockenspiel ping as it shut behind you. Past the liver-coloured Victorian chapel and down into a sloppy little lane whose rutted surface turned into rivulets of mud whenever it rained.

Over time the lane had worn lower and lower and now ran like a miniature ravine between two steep banks on either side that were crumbly and carious with rabbit diggings and the more ambitious earthworks of some larger animal. Nut trees grew on top of the banks and closed overhead to make a green aisle of twigs. At the bottom of a downwards slope the banks fell away into a mess of clods and nettles and the lane began to rise steeply towards the woods between loose hedges of sloe, wild rose and bracken, with a cherry orchard on one side and the jostling mast-and-halyard architecture of a hop garden on the other.

The earth of the hop garden was thickly sown with flints – large, gnarled tubers with chalky-white outsides smashed to show glittering, adamant innards. Once my grandfather bent down and picked up an elongated flint triangle, with a narrow rounded end flaring into a flattened blade like an axe-head.

At the top of the hop garden, on the edge of the wood, stood the hop-pickers' huts: a row of single-roomed black shacks made of corrugated iron, fitted with wooden stable doors. Inside some of them there clung scraps of the patterned wallpaper with which the hop-pickers had tried to make them homely. A strip of harsh china blue with cream and orange paisley commas squiggling inside a chocolate-coloured oval; a mottled patch of milky tea colour, spangled with thorny moss roses in expiring purple with tight, carmine-tipped buds.

The shacks lay empty and abandoned now, some with piles of straw on the floor; good for playing house in, with stick fires and meals of blackberries and green cherries on leaf plates. On one of the piles of straw I found a dead robin, the fragile head with its shut eyes flopping in limp disarticulation from the plump, light body; the claws like dead leaves; the breast feathers a lifeless dull orange, already harbouring, I noted disgustedly, the blind, furtive movements of other sorts of life.

In summer the margin of the wood was a shoulder-high filigree of bracken and blackberry bushes, giving way to the dense, arching mass of tree trunks – beech, oak, sweet chestnut and forestry pine for felling. The point of entry was a stile at the top of the cherry orchard, overhung by a holly tree that had grown or been cut into a hollow cave, like a church porch at the margin between the orderly rows of pruned fruit trees, the hop-poles strung with cord like an enormous harp, and the secret disorder of the wood's green gloom.

From the stile the land falls away in graceful, rhythmic contours, rising and falling under its fur and skin of cropped grass and plough like the breathing flank of some huge sleeping animal. Sheltered under the dark porch of holly I could see to the limits of the known world – not the one where I lived my daily life, but the one I inhabited with my grandparents. The neat pattern of squares of green and brown and gold, each with its edging of darker green hedge, stretched away to the far distance where the sky and the land dissolved into water, at the Channel's margin, where seagulls stabbed at the piles of nets lying in tangled heaps outside the black fish houses and we sometimes went to fetch herrings and a pint of prawns for our tea.

As a child of ten, a furious teenager of 17, and at intervals ever since, I sat on that stile, with the wood at my back and the world spread out like a map in front of me, swinging my legs, wondering what was to become of me, and when it would begin.

What happened when I was 17 was that my grandfather died, very suddenly. It was the end of September, a few days before he was to have driven me to begin my first term at Oxford, where it had been his idea that I should go. Lacking education himself, he had an autodidact's keen sense of its value and had been looking forward with relish to the glory of seeing me installed at the college to which he had also sent my mother. As it was, I turned up at the gatehouse in a taxi, lugging the movable elements of my new life in a horrible black vinyl suitcase, and began a separation from his last landscape, my known world, that was to continue for almost 20 years.

Two decades after my grandfather died I formed an attachment to a man who collected houses and land in the way that some other people collect furniture, or stamps, or first editions. Some of the time he lived in a black-and-white manor house with low ceilings and gaping fireplaces which stood among vast, flat fields of kale, maize, rape and flax, and plantations of spindly saplings that would mature in time for his great-grandchildren, perhaps, to enjoy them. At the back of the house he had planted a cowslip meadow in which we stood one night of sparkling darkness, straining to decipher Halley's comet from the curving net of stars overhead, a spangled shawl slung over a cosmic birdcage.

Far to the north this man – we will call him Robert – had a huge, hideous, comfortable, square Victorian shooting lodge in which everything, from the cavernous doorways to the glass-eyed heads of antlered beasts, staring down from the walls with expressions of silly astonishment, was built on a slightly greater than human scale. The taps of the coffin-shaped bath gushed with a tide of what looked like boiling tea. The bath itself was like an exceptionally roomy sarcophagus: so capacious that when you got in, you had to cling to the taps with your toes to avoid floating away. The plug wasn't a little black rubber stopper – naturally not – but a massive, gurgling brass cylinder of marine engineering.

In the bedroom, a curtained bed was moored on a calm sea of carpet: a galleon at anchor in a harbour bobbing with smaller craft – cheval glasses, *bonheurs-du-jour*, chests of drawers artistically hand-painted with blue bows and wreaths of pink rosebuds. From the window was a view as pure as cold water: a pale arc of sky, the rising swell of a hill, an expanse of flat, cropped lawn on which, waking one morning at dawn, I found a herd of deer, branchy heads bent towards the dewed grass, still as the moment before some mythic catastrophe.

In France there was yet another house, in a village square

perched high above an estuary on the great northern plain where every place name is the name of a battle. A wrong turning on the way to the nearest big town would land you at Agincourt, or at the strange, melancholy cemetery containing the remains of 900-odd fallen members of the Chinese Labour Corps. Once or twice Robert, who was restless and could hardly bear to arrive in a place before longing to be off again, deposited me at this house, an eccentric, bow-fronted confection of nineteenth-century rose-coloured brick, then drove away at speed, leaving me to play house on my own.

I took to the small-scale rhythms of pretend housewifery with dreamy enthusiasm, hardly leaving the village, but learning its shape by heart; walking every day down the steep stone-paved lane that led from the church square, through the shopping street, a model of respectable small-scale prosperity, with matched pairs of butchers, bakers, greengrocers, haberdashers and *charcuteries*, each presumably in fierce competition with the other, as well as a newsagent's and a surprisingly expensive jeweller's, down to the boardwalk that skirted the edge of the salty, ambiguous reach where the estuary ran into the sea. At the end of this stood a small art gallery, run by a young man dressed with crumpled sophistication in a white linen shirt and black linen suit, who sold watercolour postcard views of the harbour with a disappointed air of hoping for something better.

This house was the least finished of Robert's projects. It wasn't quite derelict, but shabby enough to make his ancient next-door neighbour, who subscribed to the French bourgeois code of housekeeping standards, shake her fist whenever she saw him. The building had played a bit part as a Gestapo headquarters in a Second World War television drama and had a fantastical air of faintly menacing charm. It had hot water and electricity, so it wasn't uncomfortable to live in. I grew very fond of its seedy elegance and used to flick around the barley-sugar twists of its interminable brown-stained staircase with a canary-coloured feather duster.

On my second visit, I grew more ambitious and used to sit, sipping my bowl of breakfast coffee in the morning-room, where the light streamed in over the glittering water, thinking how well a nice Chinese yellow would look on the walls in there. And perhaps a watery blue-grey in the bedroom a floor above, so that when the shutters were opened to the screams of the estuary birds, the great walnut *lit bateau* would seem to float between the sky and the sea. The front room, on the other hand, which gave on to the square, and passed the day in the stony shadow of the church, would show to better advantage in French grey and rose madder . . .

Soon after I began to think along these lines my little love affair withered, as these pretty diversions tend to the instant a girl's mind turns to thoughts of interior decoration. It had sprung unexpectedly from an old friendship, into which it was reabsorbed without much drama. Nevertheless, it had taken me away from my own territory, which seemed when I returned to it oddly cramped and shoddy, as if the house in Greenwich had lost its ability to charm me in the same instant that I had lost the power to charm my lover.

When I bought it, I was adrift with an infant and nothing to hold on to, and the house, with its shrunken proportions that were just big enough for a woman and a baby, felt both magically safe and slightly removed from the world from which I was in retreat. The boundaries of our new landscape were sharply delineated. We lived inside a rectangle of a few acres, bounded by the raffish walk along the river path in front of the old Royal Naval College, the flower garden at the top of the park, where Greenwich shades into Blackheath, and the children's playground at the bottom, where mothers sat on the grass or round the edges of the sandpit, sopping up the sunlight in a companionable stupor of dazed exhaustion while their babies explored the maelstrom of new experience that a swing, a slide, or a flowerbed full of French marigolds, squirrels and worms offers to a person of a year or so old.

For a long while, this was all I felt I wanted. And now I'd spoiled it. I'd strayed outside the boundaries of the place where the charm was effective, and returned to find that it didn't work any longer. I was bored, restless, confined. The house felt insubstantial, as though a good slam to the front door would bring the whole thing down with a patter of bricks and sandy mortar.

The building had no foundations, I discovered one day, prising up a floorboard to retrieve the bits of jigsaw that it was my son's new game to post down the cracks between the boards. There was nothing under the floor but bare earth. It wasn't dug into its position, merely resting on it. If it had had hen's legs, like the hut belonging to the witch Baba Yaga in the fairy stories, it could have stepped off the pavement one night when we were asleep indoors, and strolled away down the street to somewhere new. A pity it couldn't, really. A change was what we needed. I could feel it gathering, but didn't know where to look for it, or in what form it would appear.

Saturday 22 February – The Kennels, Hothfield

It is getting on for half-past five on a late February afternoon. We met at the kennels this morning at eleven and have hunted round in a great circle. Now we are almost home again, and it is still just light. At any rate, the sky ahead shows pale blue above the twiggy black silhouette of the wood towards which we are headed. Behind us, though, it is darkening to mauve. A single bright star is visible overhead, and a pale segment of moon. In the far distance, beyond the fields and the unseen road, there is a lurid orange flicker that means the street lamps of Ashford are lighting up.

The huntsman is set on drawing one last covert. I shall come out only once more this season, and had meant to stay to the end. But as we pass a turning that leads across the fields towards home, I feel suddenly overcome with cold and tiredness. The mare reads my mind, or has the same idea, and half-turns her head in the direction of her stable. 'Good night,' I call. 'Good night,' comes wavering back from the handful of bitter-enders. The mare skirts the edge of the first field at a trot, brisking now that she knows she is nearly home. As we turn towards the metalled road and the lit windows of the first house, there floats towards us the cry of hounds beginning to hunt the last fox of the day.

The change, when it came, arrived in the form of an unlikely image. I dreamt one night about the dolphin heave of the fat round quarters of a pony I'd once had a ride on at a school fête. I'd had my pony phase as a little girl – an unsatisfactory, theoretical period of galloping up and down the garden, switching my own bare leg with a twig from the apple tree. I asked for a horse for Christmas and got one: it arrived in my Christmas stocking, two inches high, and made of brown plastic. My sister eventually got as far as riding lessons, but I didn't. The only time I got anywhere near a real horse was on that pony ride, between the laburnum bush and the yew tree in Colonel Lumley Webb's front garden. And I didn't like it at all.

For one thing, when I got up there, it felt much too high to be safe. And there was all the lurching about when it moved. It was nothing like the feeling I had imagined when I cantered up the garden, or thought myself into the skin of little Laura Ingalls and her wild cousin, racing bareback in skirts for miles across the prairies with their fingers twisted into the manes of

their mustangs; their bare kn[...]
sides.

This pony was plodding, not raci[...]
was a shiny leather saddle, the same glossy [...]
with a leather safety strap at the front to hold [...]
arrangement was comically sedate but still con[...]
incredibly precarious. The saddle looked absurd st[...]
the pony's fat body, like a howdah on top of an elephan[...]
when they lifted me up there, it felt hard and shiny, like t[...]
pews at church and I was sure I would slip off.

I was not a brave child, and I had a vivid imagination. The
distance to the ground seemed immense. In my head I could
feel the thud as I hit the ground, the snapping of my bones,
the jagged ends piercing flesh. I had been on a camel ride
once, at London Zoo. They made me sit on its neck with my
legs dangling, because I was the lightest. The harsh camel
smell and the feel of the matted pelt under my bare legs, the
rolling articulation of its vertebrae beneath me and a dim
apprehension of the terrible pathos and tedium of a life spent
patiently ambling back and forth along the same few yards of
trodden earth with a clinging cargo of children had appalled
me at the zoo, and now the feeling came back. 'No,' I said. 'I
don't want to. I want to get down.'

My grandfather, who had queued for some time in the hot
sunshine to provide me with this longed-for treat of a first
pony ride, and was dying for a sit-down in the tea tent with a
nice cup of tea and a butterfly bun, was not pleased. The lady
in charge of the pony helped me get off, smilingly contemptu-
ous, and I trailed after my grandfather towards the tea tent,
weeping drearily at having made him cross and spoiled the
treat, and with shame at my own cowardice.

I don't know why that pony came to revisit me in my dreams
in such an inconsequential fashion, but I am literal-minded

his image in my head,
den grass, the leather,
yew leaves, I didn't
m about riding.

ks' holiday coming up
take any more time off
ring those three weeks,
and they fell during his
how not to squander the
the idea for a project. I
hree a week, which would
ments – and see where that

ndon, though. I'd seen the
drooping   rses slouching along Rotten
Row, their riders flopping   t on their backs like half-filled
sacks of grain dressed in jeans and fleeces. That wasn't at all
what I had in mind. What I wanted, I couldn't exactly say,
but I thought I should know it when I saw it. I drew an
imaginary circle around my grandparents' old bungalow, made
a shortlist of the British Horse Society-approved riding schools
that fell within it, and booked lessons at three of them. As in
the story of *Goldilocks and the Three Bears*, one place was too
small and childish, one too slick and grand, but the third,
Rooting Street Farm Riding Centre, run by a Mrs Rogers,
was just right.

How did I know it was right? I'd never properly sat on a
horse, never been inside a stable, never visited a riding school
before that three-week holiday. How could I possibly judge
what I wanted? It wasn't the look of Rooting Street that sold
the place to me. It was neither glossy nor picturesque, but
workmanlike, spartan, even rather ugly. The paddocks were
fenced with electric tape and a clutch of trailers and horse
lorries in various stages of disrepair stood in the potholed,

beaten-earth car park through which you approached the stables.

The yard itself consisted of a couple of fenced outdoor arenas, one with a surface of black shredded rubber, the other of sand. To one side of the sand school was a large, dark barn and a row of stables, from whose open upper half-doors came sounds of stamping, crunching and whickering, emitted by the bulky shadows that could dimly be seen turning and shifting within. There was a purposeful litter of pitchforks and battered wheelbarrows, buckets and shallow black rubber skips with hoof picks attached to their handles by loops of bailer twine, coiled lead ropes, head collars and discarded whips. And there was Mrs Rogers.

Mrs Rogers was a compact person in faded purple breeches, a padded waistcoat and half-chaps. She had short, desiccated fair curls, blue eyes, a pink-and-white complexion, a Roman nose and a brisk manner. She must have been a pretty girl, and was now, probably in her late 40s, a handsome woman with a fine profile, like a goddess on a Roman coin, or a more feminine version of the Duke of Wellington. Her profile, I later found, was not the only characteristic she shared with the Duke. I hadn't really come across leadership qualities before, having dedicated much of my life from school onwards to avoiding being led anywhere by anyone. But I recognized them without difficulty in Mrs Rogers. This, I thought, was the woman who would teach me to ride. For some reason, she thought so too.

Strictly speaking, the Rooting Street yard wasn't a riding school, but a livery yard (that is, a sort of boarding school for horses whose owners lacked the land or the time to look after them themselves). Mrs Rogers said that she didn't generally teach novices, but would see what she could do for me. I signed up for a lesson the following week and was given a card with spaces in which to mark six lessons at a time. I got the impression that it would probably take more than three weeks to master the basics.

Saturday 15 February – Halden Place, Rolvenden

This is one of our best meets. I have been looking forward to it all season. But so far, it is not going well. To begin with I discover, once we are in the horse lorry several miles down the road on the way to the meet, that I have left my hard hat at the yard. 'I hope you're not going to cry,' barks Mrs Rogers, when I tell her, in a whisper. 'Not if you say not,' I say, though I was thinking about it. 'But if I had a gun, I might just do the decent thing and shoot myself.' 'There's one in me bag, just under me boots,' says Boyd, the knackerman, who is driving the lorry.

The hat is retrieved and we set off again to the meet, which is picturesque in the extreme – a balustraded courtyard in front of a large, many-windowed house, a convivial tangle of hounds and horses, people on foot hailing people on horse-back, stamping, snorting, cries of recognition and greeting. The only thing is, I don't seem to be able to find very much to eat or drink. This is grim for a couple of reasons. When I got up at 5.30 this morning, a cup of tea and a little bowl of cereal was all I could manage. But now it is 11 a. m., the first terror of the day – that of getting the horse and myself ready and loaded on to the lorry without being shouted at – is over, and I am ravenous.

Almost worse, though, is the drink shortage. When I started doing this, the idea of consuming quantities of whisky or cherry brandy at 11 in the morning seemed impossibly racy and exotic. But now I have rather come to rely on it, if I know there will be jumping later. (It is possible to get this very wrong. At one meet I sank, with the swift efficiency that is a necessary technique for consuming coloured liquids if you are sitting on top of a fidgety white horse, an enormous glass of something tawny that I took to be whisky mac, only to discover, once it was on the way down, that it was neat whisky. There followed a gentle day of wandering through the woods, a very contemplative, peaceful, watercolour sort of hunting, entirely without heroics – the sort of day that generally I love, except this time I spent it growing steadily more savage as the superfluous jumping fuel raced irritably round and round my system.)

As far as I am concerned there is a two-fold relationship between drink and hunt jumps. The first thing is the straight-forward injection of artificial courage that strong doses of alcohol provide. The second is the helpful blurring of reflexes that takes the edge off my novice tendency to stiffen every muscle at the mere sight of a jump, and thus become an unbalancing impediment to the process – a sort of badly packed rucksack wobbling about on the mare's back – instead of a smoothly integrated participant in the movement.

Eventually a thimble of port appears, we drink it gratefully and set off towards a field in which – I remember it from last year – there is a little fence, followed by another little fence at a sharp angle. The mare and I manage the first fence all right, then wheel rather raggedly towards the next one. When the mare reaches it, she braces her forelegs and we skid to a stop just in front of it.

'No one saw, it doesn't matter,' I mutter to myself (though of course it does matter, and if I don't get a move on, lots of people will see). We turn, retreat, approach again. I can feel the mare planning to stop and kick wildly. She hesitates, thinks about it, cat-leaps from a standstill and I fly over her head into a soft landing of mud and leaves, from which I am rescued by half a dozen kindly people, all of whom have managed this baby jump, despite the fact that most of them are either half or twice my age. There is a large slash of telltale mud across my shoulder. One of the buttons on my jacket has snapped off, exposing an indecent expanse of checked waistcoat, and I have also managed to rip the thong off my hunting whip. 'Yes, thanks, perfectly all right,' I snarl, in answer to everyone's concern. I am almost speechless with rage and humiliation, stamping about on the muddy ground in my no longer immaculately polished boots.

And there is further humiliation to come, because I know I can't get back on the horse from the ground. ('You're very thin, but you're not very athletic, are you?' one of Mrs Rogers's girl grooms once said to me, in mild astonishment that anyone could be so feeble.) In the end, someone has to shove the mare up against a bank and someone else has to hold her head, while I let the stirrup leather down as far as it will go and heave my trembling leg back over the saddle.

Some way ahead, I can see Mrs Rogers. Her back is turned to this squalid scene and has been throughout, but I know perfectly well that she hasn't missed a thing. At home, when my son wonders how I found out about some childish mis-demeanour that he thought he'd covered up, I tell him that my Seeing Finger knew about it, as it knows about everything he does, whether or not I am there when he does it. Mrs Rogers has the Seeing Finger, big time. It tells her about everything that happens, everywhere. With her back turned, she has registered every incompetent moment of this incident. And she hasn't liked it. It is a fair bet that there will be an indefinite period of Rat Week when we get back to the yard.

I jauntily assumed that I was going to be a natural at riding, so it was a fearful shock to find out how bad I was. I hadn't been as bad at anything since abandoning organized sport at the age of 16, when I finally came up with an unassailable excuse (a chronic but mysteriously undiagnosable kidney condition) after years of savage, irresolute skirmishes with the games mistress.

No doubt the school curriculum is different now – broader, more Baccalaureaty, more interested in forming the Whole Person, rather than turning out lots of bulging megabrains tottering about on tiny vestigial legs. But I was shaped by an education system that favoured – indeed, doted on – swift specialization. At 16, I secured a string of pointless O-levels (13 of them, actually) and at once forgot everything I had ever learned about maths, physics, chemistry, biology, history, geography, German and the rest of it.

These days, if I find myself in need of some elementary piece of general knowledge, I rattle at the handle of the mental store cupboard in which the feast of information that is the legacy of my O-levels should be stored. But when the cupboard opens, there is hardly anything inside: a few stale verbs; a rancid rind or two of vocabulary; a couple of mouldy dates, but nothing with any richness or intellectual nourishment in it.

From the first term of the sixth form, all my effort of learning was concentrated into three sharply focused areas of knowledge: English, French and Latin – with even the connections between them left unexplored. There were treasures to be had here, easily discernible, even by the pallid light shone on them by my teachers. But there wasn't much room in the timetable for anything other than conscientious excellence. Very little opportunity for trying things out, or making mistakes, let alone falling off things, or learning to look ridiculous and not mind too much.

It perhaps didn't help that, apart from my grandfather, we were not a family much given to playfulness or experiment. It wasn't actually carved on the overmantel underneath the wooden cartouche of predatory birds that I mistook for the family crest, but 'You're not here to enjoy yourself' was definitely our family motto.

The list of things we didn't go in for in our house was long and startling: comics, cheap sweeties, telly (to begin with. We got one eventually, passed down from the Shilling grand-parents. The screen took ages to warm up into a reluctant black-and-white image that was volatile and prone to dissolving into a firework burst of fizzing white sparks, or a slow, seasick roll. It was housed in a massive wooden cupboard of highly polished mahogany veneer, which fitted right in with the prevailing dark-brown decor.) Where was I? Oh yes – roller skating, pop music, circuses, funfairs, Enid Blyton, make-up, high heels and hanging around the Recreation Ground after school with unsuitable friends.

I went to the cinema exactly once, when a friend's mother took her and me to see *Bambi* at the Odeon on Sittingbourne High Street, an excursion about which I remember two things, neither of them to do with the film, which I gather is harrowing, though I've never seen it since. What registered was a) the luscious magnificence of the red velvet curtains that swooshed apart when the movie was about to begin, and b) the fact that the cinema, with its showy Art Deco exterior and lavish use of mirror glass and gilt, was clearly a very common building, of a sort that I would not generally be encouraged to enter.

'Suitable' was a key word in our vocabulary. Suitable activities included reading, and playing quietly with your toys, both of which I did a lot of. My favourite toy was the doll's house that my father had made me. Superficially it didn't much resemble the house we lived in, since it was built to a cheerful, open-plan Swedish design, and painted an ebullient egg-yellow with a nice red roof. But the interior decorations had a certain familiarity. The kitchen was green with mottled linoleum, just like ours. The dining room was papered in a brown doll's wallpaper, with more paper, printed to resemble miniature parquet flooring, on the floor. And in the bedroom, where the walls were covered in a soothing grey and white stripe, there was some fuzzy crimson stuff underfoot that was clearly a junior relation of the blood-red carpet that seeped up our stairs and spread all over the landing and into my parents' bedroom.

Downstairs, the house was furnished with a marvellous matching suite of wooden furniture, grained to look like Jacobean oak and lacquered to a high shine: a table, a sideboard and writing-desk with doors and little drawers that really opened when you pulled on the red-painted metal pins that served for handles, and a grandfather clock with a long, narrow door in its body that opened to show a pendulum inside.

There were four people in the doll's-house family: a father made of pipe cleaners, dressed in grey flannel bags, a navy felt blazer, a checked shirt and a tie made from a strand of hairy green wool. He had a faded face made of painted silk and wispy, receding grey threads of hair. His wife and daughters were altogether more robust: podgy, German-made dolls, moulded from a kind of soft rubber that had the translucency and yielding firmness of human flesh. The mother had articulated legs and arms and shiny brown moulded rubber curls; the two children, one dark and cheerful, one fair and melancholy, had moving arms but rigid legs. They all had the tight pot bellies and bracelet creases at wrist and ankle of toddlers. Their arms ended in balled fists with little clenched fingers, and their legs in white moulded ankle socks and red or black Mary Jane shoes, an effect that left them looking weirdly overdressed at doll's-house bathtime.

I played endlessly with these dolls, all the way through primary school, and all the way through secondary school as well, a fact that I kept well hidden from the unsuitable friends of my teenage years, who were generally keener on the New

York Dolls than doll's houses. The doll's-house game was a kind of rolling soap opera, except an awful lot more soap than opera. I lacked a child's doctor-and-nurse instinct for high drama and the macabre. There were no incidents in my doll's house, no domestics, no house fires, no lost children or broken limbs. The most exciting thing they did in that house was the housework.

Father was packed off first thing to do some kind of unspecified 'work', and then mother and the two children (the dark one was called Emily and the fair one Charlotte) would get down to an orgy of cleaning, moving every stick of furniture out of the house on to my bedroom hearthrug, dusting and sweeping with their mouse-sized brooms and dustpans, mopping with their tiny looped string mop and tin bucket, then putting everything back where it had come from with infinite tidiness and precision: making up the beds with sheets sewn from half-handkerchiefs, folding garments the size of postage stamps into matchbox drawers; ranging inch-high glass storage jars full of hundreds-and-thousands along the kitchen shelves. It was a world as tight and safe as the inside of a nutshell.

When I was 12, something happened to crack it. Not a bad thing, but a treat. I went on an exchange trip to visit my French penfriend, a glossy, brown-haired girl called Anne, a little younger than me, whose family was mad about skiing, and were going to take me straight from the airport to their house in the Jura for a week's skiing holiday.

The build-up was tremendous. My mother and I went all the way to London, to Simpsons of Piccadilly, to buy ski clothes – a pair of navy stretch nylon pants with tapered stirrup legs to which were attached, just below the knee, a couple of extra bits of fabric to give a daringly modish bell-bottomed flare effect. In the shop these, worn with a royal blue waterproof jacket with elastic shirring all over the back, produced an effect of dazzling cosmopolitanism, quite in keeping with the journey to come, in which I was to fly to Geneva as an Unaccompanied Minor.

The flight – my first ever trip on an aeroplane – was a miracle of international sophistication: my new cream imitation-leather suitcase with a pale blue silk lining the envy of the baggage carousel, my schoolgirl French miraculously understood by my designated stewardess (who spoke perfectly good English, but that was hardly the point. I had never, until now, thought of French as a means of communication with anyone other than our French teacher, and was entranced by the novelty of the idea that there were people who spoke French all the time, just like I spoke English).

I felt the odd twinge of homesickness, the first night. But it wasn't until I got on to the nursery slopes that things really went wrong. It was the snow that was the trouble. I couldn't get on with it. I was small, underweight, short-sighted, unco-ordinated and felt the cold terribly. I was put in a class of French seven-year-olds who sneered in an unmistakable cadence of French contempt, even though I couldn't understand the vocabulary, in the intervals of scooting competently down the slope and stopping in a showy spray of powder at the end. When I wasn't rooted to the spot because one ski had some-how got crossed over the other, I fell over continuously, and every time I did, my glasses (NHS, with swoopy Dame Edna rims in sapphire-blue plastic decorated with a small gilt fleur-de-lis) fell off too and someone had to find them for me, because I was too short-sighted to do it myself.

The humiliation was so complete as to have something almost mystical about it. For some reason it didn't strike me that the sneery French children had probably done this before, and that if I persisted, I too, by the end of the holiday, might also be able to slither down a nursery slope with my bottom in the air, even if not as stylishly as the French brats, and without their enviable shiny brown hair, mirrored sungoggles and metallic silver salopettes . . . Instead I took to weeping in a hopeless sort of way. I cried on the slopes until the tears froze and made my face hurt. I cried into my food at mealtimes, I cried in bed until the pillow was all wet. I cried as steadily as Alice in Wonderland, shedding pools of tears big enough to drown a mouse in after she had grown to nine foot tall.

My hosts were bemused, worried, irritated and scornful in varying degrees. In the end, M. Clerc, the father, had a happy inspiration and bought me a present. It was a book – a magnificent hardback with a great many watercolour illustrations. Inside it he had inscribed it: 'Pour un petit oiseau perdu dans les neiges, pour le rechauffer un peu', which made me cry a bit more, once I'd worked out what it meant.

The book was called *Le Grand Meaulnes*, and it turned the whole trip around (for me, that is. It is possible that the Clerc family don't look back on it with unmixed affection). Every day the Clercs went off to ski, and I sat in the warm sunshine, well away from the snow, and puzzled out the story of Meaulnes, who had once stumbled into a lost realm of light and grace where people seemed happy and affectionate, and then spent the whole of the rest of his life trying to find the place again. I liked the story very much. It reinforced my taste, already well developed, for the literature of yearning, and underpinned my conviction that the best place for experience was safely confined within the covers of a book.

I had forgotten all about the skiing disaster when I began my new life as a horsewoman at Rooting Street. I fancied the idea of myself on a horse. I was taken with the thought of my legs in breeches. In fact I'd admired the whole horsey look (or what I thought was a horsey look – though I fairly soon realized that my notions were more Ralph Lauren than Musto; more *Vogue* than *Horse & Hound*) for years, and never had the excuse to wear it. Well, here was my chance. I bought a pair of black jodhpurs and in these, with my new black leather jodhpur boots and black velvet crash cap, plus a navy polo shirt in a sort of aertex material (Good grief. I hadn't owned an aertex polo shirt since the days I used to have to change into one for netball, in the disgusting, sweetish, underarm miasma of the school cloakrooms) I reckoned to look neat but not showy. In particular, I was anxious to avoid the comic effect of looking like a novice who had just gone out and spent a fortune on brand-new kit.

Somehow I had also contrived to shuffle to the back of my mind the memory of my abortive early encounter with a pony. Before my first lesson at Rooting Street, I had a clear mental vision of how things would go. I would arrive, get on and at once my natural affinity with horses would emerge. A smooth progression of expertise would follow, from walking, trotting and cantering to whatever you did after cantering. At some point, probably towards the second of my three weeks of leisure, I supposed I would start learning to jump. I'd sometimes watched the showjumping from Hickstead on the television and admired the glorious, effortless, intoxicating energy of it (only Harvey Smith made it look like hard work). I wanted to do that, too.

On my first visit to the Rooting Street yard, I had noticed an air of contained energy about the place. Arriving for my lesson, I was struck by it again. One girl was mucking out a stable with a fork and a wheelbarrow; another was leading two horses in head collars down from the yard towards a distant paddock at the end of a track of rutted mud. No one was hurrying, but the atmosphere was intensely purposeful.

Just inside the barn, tacked up and tied by a length of rope to a loop of orange baler twine attached to a metal ring on the wall was a fat, shaggy brown pony. Up close, he looked absolutely enormous: a massive, elephantine presence with huge carthorse feet, a bulging barrel belly and a long, sagacious, pachyderm face with drooping fleshy pink lips. His eyes were half shut. The saddle perched like a toy on top of his hairy back. He seemed as fixed and immovable as a statue.

'This is Herbie,' said Mrs Rogers, materializing suddenly on the opposite side of the great horse-mountain. 'He's a nice, quiet cob, and you'll be riding him today. So I'll just walk him round to the mounting block and we'll get you up on him.' She gave a sharp tug to the end of the rope that attached Herbie to the baler twine. The complicated knot fell apart. Herbie raised his drooping eyelids and lumbered sleepily out of the barn towards the wooden mounting block.

'Always lead a horse on the left,' said Mrs Rogers, alarming me slightly – surely I was here to learn about riding, not leading? 'Now, stand on the block, gather up the reins, left foot in the stirrup and swing your right leg over.' Concentrating furiously – left foot in stirrup; right leg over . . . But to what point exactly were you supposed to gather up the reins? – I did as I was told and flopped down hard onto the saddle, which was several inches further away than I had been expecting. And now Mrs Rogers was talking again. And – Oh, Help! – the animal was moving.

'Keep your hands down,' said Mrs Rogers. 'Allow the reins to pass over your little fingers, and turn your wrists so your thumbs are on top. Heels down. Don't draw your leg up. Sit up, and squeeze alternately with your legs to keep him walking on. Don't look down.'

I couldn't help it. The ground seemed miles away; the pitch and toss of the pony's burly quarters exactly as I remembered the feeling from 30 years before. The graceful partnership between horse and woman of my imagination evaporated in a welter of straining and sweating. If I stopped for a moment, so did Herbie. Much of what Mrs Rogers was telling me to do seemed physically impossible. 'Squeeze with your left leg to turn him across the school,' she shouted. But how did you squeeze with one leg? It was like being told to clap with one hand. If you didn't squeeze back with the other leg, wouldn't you just fall sideways over the edge?

Then there was this heels down business. I knew all about that. I'd read about it somewhere. And all over London were statues of bronze horsemen – very senior and heroic Cavalrymen, on the whole, with a scattering of martial Royalty – with their lower limbs articulated at extraordinary, grasshopper angles – toes pointing skywards at 45 degrees to their shins. But I'd imagined that to be some formal convention of equine sculptors – a kind of military ideal, to go with their clenched jaws and blank-eyed, thousand-yard stares. At any rate, not the sort of thing that living bone and ligament could be expected to reproduce.

'Heels down,' said Mrs Rogers, sounding a bit fierce, I thought. I tried. 'Imagine you have a breeze block tied to your ankle,' said Mrs Rogers. I tried some more. 'Hmm,' said Mrs Rogers. 'Take your feet out of the stirrups and let your legs hang loose. Now rotate your ankles. Good. Now lift your right leg sideways away from the saddle.'

She couldn't be serious. The human leg is not meant to be lifted sideways when you are sitting astride something. It isn't how hip joints work. And in any case, I was already doing something like a full splits, just to get my legs to hang down on either side of Herbie's monstrous mid-section. I made an effort. Nothing happened. 'Go on,' said Mrs Rogers, with some asperity. I gave my right thigh a mighty lateral heave. It moved about half an inch from the surface of the saddle. Somewhere, far within the ball-and-socket workings of the joint, I felt a plangent twanging sensation, like the sound of a breaking violin string translated into feeling.

'All right?' asked Mrs Rogers, who seemed to have

registered my silent grimace of anguish, although she was facing the other way. 'Good. Now do the same with the left leg. OK? Feet back in the stirrups. Heels down. Better. Much better. Walk on.'

Better. I was better. I was going to be a brilliant rider after all. I was going to thunder around – well, I wasn't quite sure what I was going to thunder around, but something big, like a moor, or the seashore – with the wind in my face and my toes pointing skywards. I was going to be Lucy Glitters and tackle huge bullfinches – whatever they were – with frightening competence. I was . . . 'Next time,' said Mrs Rogers, 'we'll see how you get on at the trot.'

With difficulty, I swung my right leg over Herbie's back and dropped heavily to the ground. My polo shirt was sodden with sweat and so was the inside of my crash cap. My legs were twitching palsiedly and felt as though they had been moulded to Herbie's barrel shape. There was a large blister on the outer side of each of my ring fingers. 'I'd get a pair of gloves, if I were you. See you on Thursday, then,' said Mrs Rogers, suddenly switching the full beam of her attention off me and vanishing into the dim barn with Herbie plodding heavily behind.

I felt most peculiar, driving home. Shaken and trembly as though in the aftermath of an accident from all the unaccustomed exertion. And at the same time exhilarated, as though I'd been caught up in the drama of some kind of game or performance, the structure and rules of which I only partly understood. Not that there was anything dramatic about Mrs Rogers's manner. It was brisk, straightforward, friendly enough, but with a fine, steely edge to it that had made me keep very quiet about my twanging hips and blistered fingers. Though she had noticed those anyway.

At any rate, I'd come to her interested only in learning how to ride a horse. But now I began to feel curious about the mechanisms of that yard. Those little figures busily engaged in their routines of cleaning out the stables: did they throw all the straw away, or just some of it? Where did it all go? And where did they get the new straw from? And what was the difference between straw and hay? Did the horses I'd seen being led down to the paddock spend their days in the field and their nights in the stables? Why were some of them wearing rugs and some not?

And what were the uses of the various mysterious bits of equipment that I'd seen through the open door of what must be the tack room: the collection of whips propped in one corner, from short switches to things like fishing rods with long, trailing thongs; the racks of saddles, all different shapes and sizes; the snaky tangle of leather straps and looped bundles of inch-wide, dun-coloured webbing, and the astonishing collection of bits – an infinity of variations on the theme of a bar and two side pieces?

There were straight bits, bits with a plain joint in the middle, or two joints with a link between them. Others had a curvy hump in the middle, or were made of rounded links like a chain, or with loose rolling pieces like cylindrical beads along their length. There were bits made of shiny white metal, or dull brown metal, black rubber, banana-coloured plastic, with soft rubber discs at the side, or sticking-up pieces of metal, or in one case a pair of curving S-shaped bars. There was even a bit with a metal loop that looked as though it went all the way around a horse's muzzle, like a scold's bridle.

So how did you know which bit to use on which horse? And why were there so many different kinds in any case? Between the deeply rutted mud, the muck-heap, the wheel-barrows piled with dirty straw and the dark barn full of the smell and sound of horses on the one hand, and the painstaking calibration of saddles, bridles, bits, whips and pieces of equip-ment whose name and purpose I did not yet know on the other, was some intricacy, some fusion of chaos and precision that wasn't what I had been expecting.

Saturday 25 January – The Rose and Crown, Mundy Bois

One of the many difficulties of hunting in the south-east is the unboxing arrangements. Almost always the meets are too distant to hack to from wherever your horse is stabled, so you have to load it into a lorry or trailer and drive it across country to some obscure farmyard, the directions for which, taken down over the phone in a hurried, illegible scrawl on the dog-eared back of a torn envelope, read like the instructions for a dead-letter drop in a camp old spy movie. 'A28 Tenterden. At end of high street (before ruined gate house) Down Hill. Along A Bit. Up Other Side' reads one such crumpled note, removed from my waistcoat pocket by the dry cleaner at the end of the season.

Often the instructions lead you to some bleak farmyard, full of huge, menacing bits of machinery, bristling with fearful, rusting spikes, and split bales of musty hay on which grass has begun to grow. Sometimes there is a barn full of sheep or young cattle who canter about in contagious alarm as their yard begins to fill up with the nervy clatter of horses who know they are about to go hunting, and the nervous chatter of their riders.

Once, at the end of a rather large, commodious farmyard, there was an eccentric little building – a green-painted wooden hut on stilts, reached by a steep wooden ladder, like an old-fashioned signalman's cabin. There was a picturesque tangle of bushes around this charming folly – an ideal place, I thought, to disappear into for a moment before we moved off. (Six hours or so in the saddle, and the fact that I daren't get off, for fear of not being able to get back on again and getting left behind in some unknown bit of country, tended to fix my mind on my bladder to the detriment of the hunting as the day wore on.)

I went round to the other side of the bushes and there I discovered, squatting in a dignified row with their breeches round their ankles, a trio of hunting ladies (I didn't know their names, but the dandelion-yellow hunt collars on their black coats announced that they were Somebodies), all gazing off into the middle distance with the detached expression of a cat having a pee in a flowerbed, or the Queen watching a display of music and movement by a group of inner-city schoolchildren.

On this particular day, however, we hadn't a farmyard, not even a squalid one, to unbox in, but must do it at speed by the side of the road, then lead Mrs Rogers's horse to the meet while she drove the horse lorry to wherever we planned to finish the day, after which she would have to get a lift back to the meet.

The lorry draws up on the verge at a T-junction, in the centre of which is a triangle of grass with a signpost in the middle of it, pointing to Pluckley, Charing, Egerton Forstal and Mundy Bois. We are meeting at Mundy Bois. 'Get your hat and gloves on. We'd better get you up first,' says Mrs Rogers to me, in the special clipped voice she saves for hunting mornings, the sound of which makes my insides shrivel to icicles and dead leaves every time I hear it.

After a season's practice, I have learned a fair fluency in the rough ballet of loading and unloading horses from a lorry. Shove the locking bar towards the lorry to release the pressure on the clip; push the clip up and flip it towards you. Pull the bar back and turn it away to the side of the lorry. Heave on the ramp until it starts to come down, then get out of the way while it crashes to the ground. Undo the partition doors and clip them back against the bars so that they don't flap about and frighten the horses. Give a shove to the horse nearest the doors, which is now all excited by the prospect of release and struggling to climb out backwards while still tied up. Untie its lead rope, point its head towards the ramp and lead it out at a sedate pace. Try not to fall off the side of the ramp while doing this. Tie it to the bit of string dangling from the side of the lorry and repeat until all the horses are unloaded.

Then you have to unwrap them. You remove their rugs and the padded travel boots that look like ballerina's leg-warmers. You tighten the girth, unbuckle the reins, thread them through the rings of the martingale (a leather strap intended to discourage the horse from getting its head in the air and rushing out of control across country) and buckle them again. Then you unbuckle the head collar, take a firm grip on the reins, lower the stirrups, get your foot in the stirrup iron and begin the *pas-de-deux* of hopping on one leg (you) and skittering round in little circles (the horse) that is the ceremonial preliminary to getting into the saddle. Once you are up, you look round in satisfaction at everyone else still struggling on the ground, and realize that you have forgotten to take off the tail bandage. So then you have to get off and repeat *da capo* until you are sorted out and back on again.

On a good day, with plenty of time and a calm friend in charge, I can manage all this quite competently. But Mrs Rogers in a hurry has the power to turn me into an instant imbecile, unable to tell my right glove from my left. She and Boyd spring from the lorry like members of the King's Troop manhandling a gun carriage. As I dither with my hairnet and gloves I can hear them rattling the horses down the ramp, and by the time I step out of the lorry into a sucking puddle of liquid mud my mare is stripped of her rugs, looking slightly stunned and very tidy – the girth fiercely tightened and every impertinent flapping strap lying meekly subdued within its keeper ring.

'I'll give you a leg-up,' threatens Mrs Rogers. 'No, no, no, please don't,' say I in a panic. 'It's quite all right, I can get up from the ground these days.' It isn't strictly true. I still have to let the stirrup down and find something to stand on. But it is less risky than a leg-up, in which, even when not seized with pre-hunting nerves, I occasionally get out of sync with the one-two-three heave, and leap just before the heave, or miss it altogether and kick the unfortunate heaver in the chest.

I sidle off round the back of the lorry and scramble into the saddle, trying to keep my muddy boots clear of the mare's pale flanks, at least until the mud has had time to dry a bit. I've wiped the worst of it off on the grass, but the high polish that I spent the best part of an hour last night raising on the black leather is utterly ruined.

In the murky Ashford Valley country you can be certain that you and your horse will be spattered with mud within minutes of moving off from the meet, but it is still a matter of honour – or rather, of something deeper than honour; a matter of something elemental, like religion or superstition – to arrive at the meet in a state of dazzling, almost ostentatious neatness. Your boots have to be polished, your hair netted, your hat and coat brushed, your gloves mended and your stock tied in a crisp stranglehold about your throat, with the gold pin piercing it horizontally, not vertically, which is how the pro-fessional hunt staff wear theirs. The horse, meanwhile, has to have its mane plaited into a row of knobbly love-knots (which gives it, to my inexpert eye, an oddly naked look, like a skinned rabbit) and its hooves oiled until they match the shine on your boots.

Not everyone who hunted with the Ashford Valley was always as fastidiously turned out as this. One girl came to a Boxing Day meet in a white polo-neck sweater and a jockey cap with a silk patterned with large pink stars, and not only did the sky not fall in, but no one said a word. And not everyone plaited their horse's mane. But if you came from the Rooting Street yard, no variations were permitted to the basic uniform, for you or your horse.

Once, early on, my hairdresser cut my hair too short to coil into a bun, so I came up with what I thought was a brilliant alternative – a small crocheted snood with a jaunty blue velvet bow, into which I stuffed the bristly ponytail which was all that remained of my long hair. It wasn't a success. Mrs Rogers spotted it just as we were getting into the lorry. 'Get that thing off Jane Shilling,' she screamed to a minion, as though anyone with the criminal inclination to wear such an outrage in the first place couldn't be trusted to remove it without supervision.

Now, in the middle of getting two other horses unloaded and ready, organizing Boyd, on his own horse, to lead her hunter, Camilla, to the meet, and raising the ramp on the horse lorry again before setting off to drive it to whatever bleak and distant farmyard it is supposed to be left in, she suddenly appears by my stirrup leather with a towel in her hand and begins scrubbing at my leg. 'Can't have you arriving at the meet with muddy boots,' she says, quite kindly. I am mortified. Possibly not quite as taken aback as the Apostles must have been when Christ started attending to their grubby feet with a bowl of water and a flannel, but nearly.

'Oooh, Jillie,' I squeak. 'It ought to be me doing this for you, not the other way round.' 'Hmph,' snorts Mrs Rogers, and bustles off to give Boyd's boots a scrub, too. There is something about all this that feels faintly familiar, but I can't quite catch hold of the elusive memory. Suddenly it comes to me. Here we are, Boyd and me, well into middle age, reduced to the condition of a couple of messy toddlers whose mother is scouring their chocolatey faces clean with a spat-on hanky.

My new relationship with Herbie progressed in halting fashion, like an arranged marriage in which the parties are well disposed towards one another, but not ideally matched. Herbie, despite his monumental looks, was apparently capable of astonishing feats of athleticism. Once, at a meet, when his blood was up, he had jumped over an old lady in a wheelchair, according to Mrs Rogers. So far, I had not discovered the key to stirring up Herbie's blood. There were moments, usually towards the end of my lessons, when something would happen quite sweetly. I would make a circle that was circular, rather than egg-shaped, or triangular, or a wavering, no-shape blob.

For an instant or two – it was never more than a few seconds – I would relax into a state of being that was weirdly different from the highly verbal, analytical frame of consciousness in which I ordinarily existed. At these moments my heels would sink, my shoulders go back, my wrists and elbows become extensions of the reins' contact with the horse's mouth, and all without the constant anxious checking of my brain that everything was doing what it was supposed to. And then I'd remember who I was, and where, and it would all fall back into the habitual cramped, effortful, self-conscious struggle between me and the pony that was the raw material of my lessons.

The brief moments of glory were bought at heavy cost. Generally I found it impossible to forget that I was sitting on a horse, doing riding. The knowledge contracted my muscles, fixed my gaze on the floor, locked my wrists, knees and pelvis to stony rigidity, clamped my fingers on the reins and my knees on the pony's sides. The ferocious concentration that I brought to the task of riding shut down entire areas of involuntary muscular reflex. 'Breathe!' Mrs Rogers would shriek from the centre of the arena, and I would let out a huge sigh, not having noticed until then that I had been holding my breath.

Herbie's was a disposition of uncomplicated amiability, but he responded in kind to the prodigious snarls of muscular tension being woven by me in the act of sitting on top of him.

Never (except in Mrs Rogers's stories about him) exactly swift, he grew slower and slower and slower. It was like a clock winding down, except the harder I wound, the slower he ran. One day, after I'd been walking him around for a few minutes at the beginning of a lesson, and was trying to kick him into a trot, he simply stopped. I squeezed and kicked and chirruped, but I might as well have been chirruping at a little brown car with no petrol in the tank. He was quite mild and neutral about it all; not hostile or even particularly unwilling. Simply immobile.

'I'll ride him up for you,' said the groom who was keeping an eye on me until Mrs Rogers arrived. She jumped on and with some imperceptible contraction of her muscles gathered the pony first into an alert, forward walk, and then into an elegant, springy trot, his drayhorse legs bending and extending as smoothly as pistons in a display of energy of which I could hardly believe him capable. Round and round the school he went, and I stood in the middle, turning to watch him until his legs became a blur and I began to grow dizzy.

'There you are,' chirped Emma, a cheerful girl with a nice round face who didn't seem to find it especially odd that I couldn't manage a basic walk-to-trot transition. I scrambled back into the saddle and tried again. I could feel the difference as he started to move: a fizz of energy and direction that rose through the saddle and up my spine. But then the fizz went flat; I could feel the energy leaking away as though a plug in the saddle had been pulled out. I knew that sensation: it was the feeling of failure.

What I really couldn't get over was the unfairness of it. I'd been used, on the whole, to a simple equation governing the things I wanted to learn: the amount of success you got out was in direct proportion to the effort you put in. So if you worked hard, your mastery of whatever it was could be expected to increase by steady, perceptible increments. A little patch of colour would appear on the vast, opaque expanse of ignorance that was Latin or French or whatever. And by degrees, as you continued to work, the detail of the map was filled in and the journey became steadily less baffling.

It was true that the graph, if anyone had plotted it, of my efforts to learn to drive would not have described this kind of elegant upward curve. It had taken three goes and something like 50 lessons between the ages of 17 and 26 before I passed the test – and my last teacher, a furious Irishman whose foot hovered angrily over the dual controls as I hopped and slewed my way around the thoroughfares of Clerkenwell and Bloomsbury, had looked a broken man at the end of it all. But I didn't really count driving in the category of things I wanted to learn. It was a boring necessary skill, like typing (which I eventually mastered) or shorthand (which I never did) and all I cared about was a basic competence, enough to get by.

Riding, though, I found I passionately wanted to do well. But the process of learning seemed as fluid, impalpable and changeable as weather. One lesson I could trot an efficient serpentine, looping back and forth across the school in a shape like an adder on the move. The next, all clarity and precision had vanished and my brain's ability to transmit its intentions to my muscles was as blurred and fitful as the sound from a badly tuned radio. For the horse, being ridden by me must have been like being shouted at in a foreign language by a distraught person with a loudhailer.

Normally, this was the point at which I would give up. I'd done what I could. It wasn't working. I lacked conspicuous talent – or even moderate ability – so I'd banish it from my life, along with maths, geography, chemistry, hockey, skiing and the rest of the stuff I wasn't much good at. But I didn't. I was too interested to stop.

Mrs Rogers was not especially encouraging. Very rarely,

she might say 'good'. The rest of the time, I couldn't read her at all. She had the knack of making you feel at the start of each lesson that anything was possible: that today might just be the day when – sit up, look up, outside leg behind the girth, tap-tap-tap on the girth with the inside leg – you pulled off a beautiful, effortless trot-to-canter transition, as smooth as the ones I sometimes saw her do when she was schooling in the arena.

If I'd been inclined to mythologize the forks and wheel-barrows and dusty bundles of lunge reins that hung about the yard when I first saw it, she was adept at encouraging the tendency. There was a complicity about the lessons: a sense of being drawn into a secret that she was sharing with you. Once, when I had graduated after some months from Herbie to Flossie, a chestnut mare who gave the faint, alarming impression that at any moment her nerves might give way and cause her to go off into an equine fit of hysterics, Mrs Rogers suddenly said, 'That mare goes better for you than she does for her mummy.' (All the horses in livery at Rooting Street had mummies, I noticed. Long before I learned the owners' names, I recognized them, exactly as I did the women in the playground at my son's school, as Flossie's Mummy, Thomas's Mummy, Savannah's Mummy and so on. Mrs Rogers herself owned several horses – Sam, Maxi, Charles, Camilla. She was not, however, a mummy to any of them.)

I fed ravenously on this tantalizing scrap of praise. How did she go better for me than for her mummy? What was I doing that mummy wasn't? Was it a chance coincidence of temperament (Flossie and her perpetual borderline hysterics was certainly closer to my own nature than Herbie's Mogadon calm), or something more useful that I could carry over to some other pony? But when I tried to ask her, Mrs Rogers shut up with a snap like a tapped mussel, and when I arrived for my next lesson, quivering with readiness to build on my unexpected rapport with Flossie, I found her in the tack room with a sponge, a bucket of saddle soap and a rack full of dirty saddles. 'I thought we'd have a stable management lesson today,' she said. 'You can help me clean this lot.'

Ouf. My vivid party balloon of excitement and unexpected new competence deflated with a sad little pop. Was this a reproof for getting cocky over Flossie? Apparently not. While I began to sink into a sulk (not to mention a fastidious spasm of disgust over the revolting pail of slimy grey bits of torn-up towel and foam rubber into which I was now expected to plunge my hand) Mrs Rogers embarked on a lecture about the science of proper tack cleaning, then segued smoothly into the Naming of Parts. 'This is the cantle, this is the pommel, this is the skirt . . .' Hang on, hang on, which is the cantle and which is the pommel? 'You've got too much water on that sponge. It should be almost dry. If white foam comes off when you rub the leather, the sponge is too wet. These are the cheekpieces, this is the brow-band and this is the throat lash. Now, if you would just pass me the breastplate . . .' The what?

Another day it was the Grooming of the Horse. 'Just come in here for a moment,' said the voice of Mrs Rogers invisibly from inside the barn. I went inside and still couldn't see her, but the door to one of the stalls was a little way open and inside there loomed something black and huge. 'How big is it?' I asked, startled. 'Seventeen hands,' said Mrs Rogers, popping out from behind him. 'Just start to brush him off, left side first, and I'll be back in a moment.'

I began to dab at the Horse of the Apocalypse with the little brush she'd handed me, keeping well away from its teeth, hooves, front end, back end and so on. The stable seemed very cramped, suddenly – just big enough for him to trap me against one of the walls and break all my bones with a couple of savage movements; not large enough for me to hide or flee. Dab, dab, dab. How far were you meant to go with this brushing? Did you just do the sides, or were you supposed to do its underneath as well? What about its legs, and its head? I wished Mrs Rogers would come back.

'Try to lean into each stroke, so it's like a massage for the horse. Like this,' said her voice from the other side of the animal. I could see her legs, but the rest of her was blocked from view by the black cylinder of its body, which was now juddering rhythmically towards me with the force of her brushstrokes. Thump, thump, thump, went Mrs Rogers on her side, like a housewife bashing the dust out of an old rug with a carpet beater. Dab dab dab, went I on mine, in a gesture more like the patting of a nose with a powder puff. After a bit, though, I began to get the hang of it. Swipe with the brush along the horse's side, then rasp the brush across the curry comb, a sort of metal cheese-grater affair on a red wooden handle, meant for scraping scurf and hair off the body brush, but which could also take the skin off your knuckles in one graceful movement, if you didn't watch it. Swipe, rasp. Swipe, rasp. In the semi-dark and soothing horse smell of the barn, the rhythm was hypnotic and my mind began to wander.

Looked at from one perspective, all this washing and saddle-soaping, brushing and scraping (and what next? mucking out?) seemed very much like housework, a necessary skill, no doubt, but one in order to learn which the making of a weekly round trip of 100 miles from Greenwich seemed a trifle excessive. Then again, my current bedside reading was a biography of Caroline Blackwood in which the novelist was described by her sister Perdita as a 'front-door rider'. 'She didn't like all the work that was involved – the grooming, the caring for the horse,' the biographer quoted Perdita Blackwood as saying. 'She liked the horse to be brought round to the front door so she could mount, and then be taken away afterwards.'

Shake the kaleidoscope once, and I was a front-door rider: a silly townie in the process of being put to work by Mrs

Rogers, perhaps even to fill in for the unexpected absence of a girl groom, and paying a pretty steep fee for the privilege. Shake it again, though, and a different pattern appeared. Slowly, painfully, a good 30 years after most people who have anything to do with horses begin to learn these things, I was now being formed into a horsewoman, of sorts. The trouble with this second pattern was that it was infinitely receding. Whatever I learned, it didn't seem to fill in a corner on a map of knowledge. It was more like opening a door into a room full of more doors, each opening in its turn into another full of yet more doors.

Grooming, saddlery, feeding, worming; dressage, show-jumping, cross-country, affiliated and unaffiliated; gymkhanas, hunt shows, junior shows, clinics for various disciplines, toll rides, sponsored rides – pastel-coloured leaflets and lists of instructions about these various activities fluttered like prayer flags on the noticeboard in the office. The thought of the infinite possibilities contained within this papery herbaceous border of pink and primrose, mandarin, pale green and blue made my spirits droop every time I passed it. The sickly colours seemed like a jaunty reminder of the infinity of things I didn't know about horses and the magnificent completeness of my ignorance – so total that I couldn't even judge the extent of what I didn't know.

Misgiving shimmered constantly at the edge of my mind. I was too old, I'd started too late. I simply hadn't the muscle power for what I was trying to achieve, at a rate of one lesson a week. I kept thinking of poor, mad Zelda Fitzgerald and her loopy attempts to train as a ballet dancer, years after it was too late to begin. In any case, if I did eventually master the basics (as presumably I should at some point, even given my snail's rate of progress), what then? What did I think I was learning to ride for? I was too restless to be content with ambling about the toll rides, however pretty, on the back of a borrowed horse, and not good enough to do anything else. The combination of an excess of temperament with limited ability was a tricky one. I'd had trouble with it before and knew how it could leak a faint, sour taint of disappointment into the whole of life. Perhaps I should give up, before that started again.

In a way, it was the constant flirtation with the idea of failure and giving up that made it possible to carry on, despite a lack of evident progress. Here, at least, was something that I could give up if I chose to. The other bits of my life – going to work, running a household, bringing up my son – were non-negotiable. Only death or some other catastrophe could get me out of those. Not, most of the time, that I wanted to get out of them – but most people need a little superfluity in their lives, and this was mine. 'Smile!' Mrs Rogers would order, from time to time, exasperated by my combination of intensity and incompetence. 'You're supposed to be having fun!'

Fun was a concept that flickered in and out of focus on my afternoons at the yard. It was sharpened by a successful lesson, an approving word from Mrs Rogers or one of those rare, marvellous moments when the gears linking me and the horse suddenly meshed and I caught a distant echo of what it must be like to ride really well. But then a bad lesson, the feeling that I'd ridden clumsily, that I couldn't make myself or the horse do what I wanted, that the animal was feeling as fractious and disconsolate as I was myself, and any notion of enjoyment dissolved as swiftly as sugar crystals in hot water.

The most infuriating thing of all was the lability of these alternate emotions. Every lesson was like a phone call at the start of a new love affair: if it went well, everything was marvellous, perfect, the sun shone, flowers came out, birds sang, tweet tweet tweet. And if it didn't, the world froze to a wilderness of sunless ice. Until the next week . . . I did think it a bit peculiar that I didn't seem able to conduct the learning process in a more temperate emotional climate, but concluded that violent physical exercise (about the psychological effects of which I knew next to nothing, having never voluntarily done any until now) must just lead, through some coarse manipulation of the consciousness by a mind-altering cocktail of hormones and enzymes, to this slightly undignified triumph-or-disaster mentality.

I'd started learning in August. By the time spring came and the bare branches of the pussy willow that grew by the rubber school were covered in scuts of silky grey and Easter yellow fur, I knew it was growing into something more than a hobby. There was something secretive about these lessons, almost like an assignation. The yard was a closed world – it sometimes felt like an imaginary world – of my own, where nobody from my London life could reach me (most of them didn't even know it existed). I liked the oddity of having found this place, full of a busy life that was entirely strange and different from anything I knew, on the borders of what once had been my own familiar territory.

After the first few dozen times of doing it, I even began to like the drive back and forth from London. With repetition, which you would think would be dulling to the perception but actually proved the opposite, the journey began to reveal a pattern, a kind of tidal rhythm as the pebbledashed shoreline of the city blurred into the receding expanses of open land. From outside my front door, the journey was a steady progression through the grim, respectable expanses of the south London suburbs, past untidy urban scrublands, fenced with concrete posts and wire, where cow-headed, piebald ponies grazed in meadows spangled with scraps of bright litter. But then, astonishingly close to the city, with the glittering obelisk of Canary Wharf still almost visible in the rear-view mirror, the motorway begins to gash through an incongruous pastoral vista of low, undulating escarpments, flint and brick barns and cottages, white-capped oasts (converted now into homes for commuters – the hop-gardens of Kent these days are mostly for show) and apple orchards, fields of wheat, barley and rape, sheep-grazed meadows hedged in hawthorn, blackberry, hazel and wild rose.

It isn't showy countryside, which is why you don't really notice it at first. It is not emphatically pretty, like the Cotswolds, or dramatic, like the rural landscapes much further to the west or north. At a careless glance it just looks like a tape-loop of non-specific greenness on the way to nowhere in particular. If your French or American cousins were coming over on a visit and you wanted to show them a piece of our island home at its best, you probably wouldn't start with the view from the M20 between Sidcup and Ashford. Yet it is a landscape of intense, modest Englishness, whose settlements of brick and flint seem to grow from the earth on which they stand, a place of muted colours – infinite permutations of brown and grey, watersoaked blue, pink-white, a mist of green in spring darkening to duller green and gold as summer wears on. You learn by degrees to see its beauty. It lodges in the heart gradually, like friendship, rather than overwhelming it like romance. Or so I found. Though I was perhaps already disposed to love it.

Saturday 22 February – The Kennels, Hothfield

It is the beginning of the Kennels Meet, and for once we are hunting over country that I know quite well. It is the land that lies all around the yard and I have ridden and driven around it often enough to feel a vague sense of familiarity with my surroundings. It isn't the prettiest of our meets, but it has a certain naive domestic charm. And although I don't necessarily need to know where I am all the time, once in a while is nice. In a bit, I expect, we'll be moving on to hunt the ghastly quarry-cum-tip, a vast and sordid funnel-shaped depression in the ground, full of brambles, the dumped carcases of old fridges and washing machines and, in the autumn, rotting, cidery heaps of the season's discarded apple crop. It is heaven for foxes, and reeks of them so pungently that you could follow the scent quite nicely all by yourself, no hounds required. But for the time being, my friend Lesley and I are sitting quietly on our respective horses, Big Molly and Little Molly, at the top of a rise, watching hounds work below us.

It is late in the season. You can feel the gathering strength in the pale spring sunshine. The branches are still leafless but the buds are fat and there is a sense of energy and expectation in the air. By this time next week, the caramel outsides of the sticky buds on the chestnut trees will have cracked open to show the marzipan green of young leaves inside and there will be celandine, anemone and primroses underfoot.

'The scene . . . has a sort of classical quality, with its fold upon fold of wooded or open slopes, studded with kilns and red roofs . . .' wrote Richard Church, the poet and writer on Kent, of the landscape around Bedgebury, only a few miles from where we are now. More than half a century after he wrote that, you can still see exactly what he meant. The pasture falls away from below our feet towards woodland in a gentle curve, like the soft vortices that draw you into one of Claude's ideal landscapes. You wouldn't be very surprised to see some elegant peasant in tawny classical drapery, with a staff and a wide-brimmed hat come plodding across the valley bottom, driving his bleating flock ahead of him along the line of the stream. Or even a little ambiguous goat-footed creature dodging between the trees, with horns and a shaggy brown pelt, a malicious smile on an almost human face and a set of pipes between its sunburned fingers.

'Goodness,' I say to Lesley, 'isn't it pretty.' 'Mmm Hmm,' says Lesley, on a rising note of sardonic doubt. She raises one eyebrow, glances behind her and we start to laugh. Behind us is a very different scene. The urban sprawl of Ashford – also looking rather beautiful, from this distance, but decidedly more Modernist than Classical – glitters with chunks of metal and structural glass and pale slabs of concrete like a synthetic city of the future, with shining ribbons of traffic snaking around its perimeter. In the foreground rise the pointed white sails, like a great ship blown aground, of the Ashford Designer Discount Outlet which, since it is now mid-afternoon on a fine spring Saturday, will be swarming with busy termite life – too small for us to see from here – hectic with the fraught excitement of shopping for pleasure and the triumphant beep, beep, beep, of the tills swallowing up the cash.

'Well, I don't care,' I say. 'I think it's good for us to hunt within sight of the Designer Discount Outlet. It makes it real – doesn't it? – to be hunting within sight of people getting on with their ordinary lives. Who wants to hunt in a picture postcard?' I am thinking of a Devon Master of Foxhounds I met the previous summer, at the hound show at Ardingly, who said with great charm, 'We think it's so marvellous, the way you keep on going in the south-east. Such an example to the rest of us.' He meant to be entirely kind, no doubt, but having spent almost all my brief hunting life in the Ashford Valley, I got into rather a huff at the tone of deathbed sympathy and the implication that south-eastern hunting was conducting a doomed struggle against such incapacitating disabilities that it was a miracle that it managed to stagger on at all.

The obstacles to hunting in Kent include, it is true, roads, railways, the sale and subsequent break-up of farms, meaning that the hunt country encompassed almost no single large estate, but a multitude of owners of smaller parcels of land, each of whom had to be contacted for permission when setting up a meet; shooting, the steady transition in farming from pasture to arable and above all the inexorable creep of sub-urbanization. From my reading, I had realized that the Ashford Valley's style of hunting was not the stuff of classical hunting mythology. It offered none of the five- and seven-mile 'points' that are (no doubt) so wonderfully exciting to ride, but so fabulously dull to read about in the great musty pantheon of hunting literature. Occasionally someone would say that they'd had a 'good run', but these good runs always seemed to happen on days when I wasn't there.

On the days I hunted – usually once a week during the season, generally on Saturdays, rarely on Wednesdays – the meets tended to take one of two forms. Some were rather urban, with a lot of trotting from covert to covert on metalled road ('I call you lot the tarmac harriers,' said Gary, the farrier, grumbling at the state of Molly's shoes) and lining the road once we'd arrived at the covertside to prevent hounds rushing to their deaths under the wheels of a car. These could be cold, lonely and exquisitely dull. But the majority were in country that still seemed startlingly wild and remote, given how built-up Kent seems when you drive around even the more rural bits of it.

Here the country was generally well wooded and the pattern usually was that the huntsman would disappear with his pack into some dense thicket – often dismounting in order to do so – into which we would follow him when it was possible. When it wasn't, we would stand around in knots at the covertside, the people who were interested in houndwork trying to keep in touch with what was going on in the wood by the sound of hounds and the huntsman's voice and horn, everyone else gossiping. And then at a signal from the master we would canter off to the next covert or, more alarmingly, find ourselves improving an idle moment by making a detour over some horrible course of cross-country jumps. Not once did I find myself caught up in the drama of pursuit – a fleeing fox, with a pack of hounds in full cry behind, followed across country by the huntsman and the field – that is the traditional image of hunting.

The absence of open country is the reason for a snobbish prejudice against hunting south of the Thames. 'It must be allowed, even by the most deeply engrooved fox-hunter, that some districts do not consort suitably with fox-hunting,' wrote Sir William Beach Thomas in 1936, in his book *Hunting England*. 'The market-garden lands . . . are of this nature. So are the Kentish orchards . . . Close cultivation of fruit or poultry or what not does not suitably accord with the pursuit of the fox or even the hare. Kent is known as the Garden of England and cannot well be a great hunting district.'

But I reckoned that if Kentish hunting was sufficiently interesting to captivate Siegfried Sassoon, it would do well enough for me. I should have liked, just once, to see what hunting in the Shires was like. But I loved the domestic scale of the Ashford Valley – the comparatively small fields and lack of grandeur, combined with the unobtrusive excellence of the huntsman and his hounds. They seemed to inhabit their country in a particularly ingenious and inventive way, adapting their style of hunting to accommodate its quirks while keeping the impetus and character of the hunt fiercely alive among the field as well as the people directly concerned with the business of fox-catching. Despite the snobbish disdain of Sir William Beach Thomas, I felt proud of our ability to hunt within sight of Ashford.

Besides, I had learned that the minor key was a popular strain among hunting people. If you believed them, there had been a golden age of hunting, quite within living memory – within their own memory, in fact – but unluckily for you, you'd arrived just as a terminal decline of country, sport, hounds, mastership, the field and everything else had really begun to gather momentum.

In 1906, says Raymond Carr in his history of the sport, *English Fox Hunting*, 'the huntsman of the Old Surrey complained that some of his best country was given over "not to hunting but to bricks and mortar".' Almost a century later, the threat of bricks and mortar pressed hard on the Ashford Valley. The Janus-faced view that I loved for the comic tension of its contrasts – the preposterous perfection of the sylvan pastoral in front of us, and the brutally prosaic urban vista behind – was about to disappear.

Looking out from that most beautiful of vantage-points, the back of a horse, over the landscape where Richard Church had walked before the Second World War, I could still see—what he saw; a vista changed, but not obliterated. But the day on which Lesley and I paused at the top of the rise in Great Chart was just a few weeks after John Prescott, the Deputy Prime Minister, had made public his document, 'Sustainable communities: Building for the future', in which he announced plans to invest about £164 million in building new housing in four growth areas in the south-east. Ashford, which was one of these, was expected to receive about £30 million of investment towards the creation of 31,000 new homes by 2031. The population of the town was predicted to rise to about 130,000 people – more than double the existing number of 55,000 inhabitants.

The expansion of the town would devour the surrounding villages. Charing, five miles away, could expect to become a suburb. As for Great Chart: if someone should come in 100 (or even 30) years' time to the point where we now stood, it was certain that nothing would be left of what we could see ahead of us. There would be no hounds, no huntsman and no covert. The tense ambiguity of the scene – busy urban life in a state of fragile coexistence with the living survival of an older

England – would be shattered. The grassland, the stream, the ancient woodland that looked such an ideal habitat for satyrs and herdsmen would be gone forever; vanished like the water-cress beds and sheep meadows around Hampstead, where John Keats used once to wander.

I thought, when Mrs Rogers said that we were going to spend a lesson hacking out, that she wanted to talk about selling me her fierce little dark-brown pony, Maxi. He was a compact, muscular, headstrong animal; dark brown, the colour of very good cooking chocolate. He looked as though he would taste sweet if you licked him. He had a small, choleric, rolling eye and a bristly hogged mane. When you walked down the line of stables that ran between the farmhouse and the stableyard, a row of horses' heads poked out, some watchful, some bored, some kindly, some impassive. Right at the end was Maxi, handsome, furious, ears back, as though permanently spoiling for a fight.

He was not as alarming to ride as his ferocious manner threatened. He used to toss his head irritably during lessons, which I privately interpreted as contempt for my tentative riding, but he was brisk and willing, responsive to my blurry, indecisive leg aids and sporadic contact with his mouth, and there was a springy, resilient feeling about him, and a kind of solid poise to the muscular arch of his neck that gave me a sense of being braver and more competent than I really was. I liked him very much, and when Mrs Rogers remarked into the air one day, while I tried unsuccessfully to pick up the canter, that she was thinking of selling him, for a non-negotiable figure of just over £2,000, my mind began to work.

I hadn't thought about owning a horse before. My riding was so remote, so contingent, so apart from the rest of my life that it felt almost as though I were impersonating someone else when I put on my boots and breeches. If I happened to catch sight of myself in the huge mirrors placed around the sand school, so that you could check your position, my reflection never gave me the little jolt of recognition that the image of your own face generally causes. I always felt I was looking at a stranger in a crash cap. The notion that I might make a commitment to a horse, to the extent of becoming its owner, seemed almost too outlandish to absorb properly.

Various disconnected half-thoughts bounced around the inside of my head like unstrung beads when she said he was for sale. For a start, I couldn't afford it. I'd never spent £2,000 before, except in instalments on the car and the house, and those were necessities of life, not bizarre extravagances. In any case, buying a horse at my level of competence seemed a bit like being a novice driver and buying a high-performance sports car full of knobs and dials, each controlling some sensitive function that was too subtle for your lumpen levels of mastery to comprehend.

Suppose I did buy the pony. Who would look after it? Would it be able to stay at Rooting Street? How much would that cost? When would I be able to visit it, and what exactly would I do with it? What did people do with their ponies when they had them, apart from take lessons? Up to this point, my lessons had given me a series of finely detailed glimpses into a world that was not my own. The smells, the chores, the craft and skill that went on at Rooting Street were little once-a-week mini-dramas, as perfectly framed by the limits of each 45-minute lesson as the view through a keyhole into a brightly lit room. The drama over, I retreated from the keyhole, back into my own familiar territory. But now the door had swung ajar and I could walk in if I chose. Except, of course, that it was out of the question. This wasn't where I belonged.

Just then the pony unexpectedly made the transition from trot to canter. I'd been so busy thinking about the impossibility of owning a horse that I'd forgotten to nag him and he'd done it quite smoothly, all by himself. 'I think,' I said, 'that I might be interested in buying Maxi.' 'Really?' said Mrs Rogers, with a beautifully calibrated blend of interest and surprise. 'Well, you have a think about it, and we'll talk about it next week.'

After my lessons were over, rather than climbing straight back into the sealed pod of the car that would transport me from one of my worlds to the other, I had taken to pausing on the journey, like a diver anxious to avoid the bends. About three miles from Rooting Street was Charing, a pretty village with all the usual signs of a healthy community supplemented by some thinly coded evidence of serious prosperity. Beside a primary school, several pubs, a couple of butchers, a green-grocer, ironmonger, post office and general stores, the hand-some high street of medieval cottages with elegant later additions supported an estate agency and an interior design consultancy whose shop windows were filled with Osborne & Little drapery and handsome bits of antique furniture, all arranged in strenuously perfect *World of Interiors* taste.

I'd never been inside the interior designer's, but I knew the ironmonger's well. This was where we used to come when my grandfather needed a handful of nails or some screws for one of his reckless attempts at DIY (even he used to describe them as 'lash-ups', the sailor's universal term of amused con-tempt for a botched job). While he and the man in a brown dustcoat who served behind the counter were talking bolts and washers, I used to poke about in the rest of the shop, which was a cornucopia of unexpected treasures: daffodil bulbs, balls of hairy string, fly swatters, enamel pie dishes, rolls of passepartout and brightly-patterned sticky-backed plastic (they spoke of little else on *Blue Peter*, but this was the only shop I ever found that actually sold the stuff), shoelaces, reels of lamp wick, night lights, hurricane lanterns, mousetraps and cellophane packets of jampot covers.

It was the only shop of its kind that I knew, and I loved it. We didn't visit very often (it was a dozen miles from Greenways, and Grandpa's fits of domestic fervour were intermittent, in any case) but the glamorous availability of mousetraps and sticky-backed plastic lent Charing the mysterious allure of the Land of Lost Content.

Now I took to drifting into the village on the pretext of some errand that I needed to accomplish before going back to London: a newspaper, a few eggs and a scrap of something for supper from the butcher, or a bite of lunch at the pub, the Royal Oak, where the beers changed according to the season and an unseen chef sent out platesful of steak and kidney pie, with a nicely crimped pale gold crust afloat on a savoury brown puddle of meat stew, or leathery pink aprons of gammon steak prettily veiled in a creamy, green-flecked parsley sauce, and lemon meringue pie or apple crumble with two round scoops of vanilla ice cream for afters, all looking like pictures from a 1950s cookery book.

After I'd done my errands or eaten my lunch, I would wander aimlessly up the main street, turn into the churchyard, read the parish notices, then walk back towards the car, stopping at the newsagent's window to read the advertisements for unwanted furniture in good condition, rabbit hutches, hay at so much a bale, aromatherapy, council house swaps, handyman to help about the house or garden, good homes wanted for tabby kittens. In the window of the estate agent's opposite, alongside the substantial brick farmhouses with several acres of garden at half a million apiece, or the centrally-heated 1960s four-bedroomed family houses with outlooks over farmland, there were generally a couple of two-bedroomed Victorian cottages for sale, either in Charing itself, or in some neighbouring village.

The interior photographs of these places often looked strangely poky, an uneasy alliance of weathered old brick and gingery pine kitchen units. And they seemed amazingly expensive for their size – almost as much as I'd get for my own house in Greenwich if I sold it. Still, if living in a place was the same thing as belonging in it, it would be easy enough for us to come and belong here. A sale, a purchase, an hour's trip down the motorway in a pantechnicon full of furniture, and that could be the end of the journey I'd begun when I left Kent for university, 20 years before. I'd be back where I'd started from – though in a condition rather like that of Rip van Winkle or any other of those odd leftover characters in fairy stories who find themselves returning as strangers to a place that once they knew intimately, and have spent years thinking of as journey's end – only to discover, when they finally arrive, that their elusive destination is no longer where they left it, but has drifted gently, implacably just beyond the borders of their known world.

This particular day in midsummer I arrived early to find the narrow main street full of cars and the churchyard busy with people. Outside the jagged knapped flint ruins of the fourteenth-century Archbishop's palace was a row of trestle tables, set out like a plant stall at a village fête, with a spry person in a quilted waistcoat selling pots of lemon balm and apple mint, pink and purple fuchsia, sprawling spider plants and a bucket full of bunches of fleshy dahlias in magenta, lemon, shrimp-pink and a marvellous black ruby colour, to a genteelly competitive throng of old people in comfy shoes. It was a Women's Institute market. I hadn't seen one since the baby and I used to go on dreamy, solitary seaside holidays to Bideford, and I'd thought of them as a holiday thing, like rock pools and clotted cream for tea. It hadn't really struck me that they went on all the time in real life, when I wasn't there to see them.

Behind the stalls was a narrow flight of brick steps leading to a low door which opened on to a cupboard-like kitchen with a draining board covered in neat rows of upturned jamjars and a gaggle of long-legged kitchen stools. On two of these perched a couple of ladies in pinafores nursing mugs of coffee. They smiled vaguely when I peered in, as though I were only partly visible. To either side of the kitchen were low-ceilinged rooms with stalls around the sides. One was crammed with fancywork: corn dollies, embroidered traycloths, ruched tea cosies, sausage-shaped holders for plastic carrier bags made out of Liberty print remnants, crocheted matinée jackets with matching hats and bootees in shades of coconut ice and sherbet yarn. There were photograph holders made from pressed flowers trapped between sheets of perspex, notelets with Kentish scenes in pencil and watercolour, memo boards with a mother duck and a troupe of yellow ducklings ambling across the top of them and the legless torso of a full-bosomed plastic glamour puss with a platinum blonde nylon chignon, firmly stitched into a crinoline of spangled pink satin for popping over the top of a spare loo roll.

On the half-landing was a produce stall selling bunches of herbs and spring onions, clusters of shallots with their ends neatly plaited, trusses of tomatoes, harlequin-striped in red and yellow, punnets of blackcurrants, raspberries and gooseberries like hirsute jade beads and clutches of eggs, arranged in size like the illustrations in old bird books: little transparent white bantam eggs, brown hens' eggs, smooth or flecked with speckles of darker brown, greeny-blue ducks' eggs and great, glaucous goose eggs. I'd had a goose egg once before. It was a thirteenth birthday present from my grandparents' friend, Mrs Kennett, who was even shorter than me, though an adult. She had a farmhouse with very low doors through which only she and I did not have to fold ourselves up to pass, and lived in a kind of perpetual low simmer from her white hives of humming bees and the hissing flock of geese that patrolled the borders of the garden, beaks gaping to show a pointed tongue and the sharp orange-pink serrations that they had instead of teeth.

On the other side of the half-landing was a room full of sugary teatime stuff: jam tarts, gingerbread, date and walnut cake, sultana loaf with a gritty demerara crust on top. A lone cellophane packet of cheese and Marmite straws stabbed a sharp, dissenting spike of salty masculinity into the overpowering billows of cakey female sweetness. A glass rampart of pots of jam in thrifty, domestic-science combinations – rhubarb-and-ginger, strawberry-and-gooseberry – glowed garnet and orange tawny by the window. My hands were full by now – sweet peas, raspberries, goose and bantam eggs, a pot of lemon thyme – but I added a jar of rhubarb-and-ginger to the pile and carried it all off to the car.

It was lunchtime now and the market was closing. The stallholders were packing the leftover plants into cardboard boxes and dismantling the trestles, the shoppers walking slowly back towards the high street with their heavy bags. They were mostly quite old, moving with an effort on bony legs encased in flapping trousers or wrinkled skeins of brown nylon stocking, leaning on knobbly wooden walking sticks with solid black rubber ferrules.

Somewhere among the slow-flowing stream of crisply curled iron grey or lavender hairdos, the tortoiseshell-framed bifocals and flat tweed caps now parting around me and closing again on the other side, was surely someone who would remember me, messing about on the floor in the ironmonger's with the feather dusters and the mousetraps. It was like a task set by a spiteful magician, to discover which among this bobbing mass of severe old faces was the one whose deeply incised downward-turning wrinkles would all curl upwards into a smile of recognition if I said I was Percy Charlton's girl.

There was no way of telling, though, so I got in the car and drove off to Rooting Street for my lesson.

All week I had been distracted by the thought of what I might be about to do. The nearest thing to what I was feeling was a sensation I'd had once or twice before buying some inexcusably expensive dress or pair of shoes: a dream-like illusion of falling at gathering speed down a steep slope with no handholds, like the game we used to play as children of rolling down the grassy hill in the park. Maxi, I realized, cost almost the same as an Hermès Kelly bag. The thing was that with a life as London-based as mine, the Kelly bag would certainly be a more sensible purchase.

On the other hand, this story had begun in the first place because I was restless with the life I already had. It was true that I wouldn't have any idea what to do with a horse if I bought one. But then, I hadn't had any idea what to do with a baby when I'd unexpectedly got one of those, and we'd managed all right, on the whole. You could retreat into the safety of the accustomed, when these things came along. Or you could step out and meet them. By the time we were ready to begin our hack out, I was already thinking of Maxi as mine.

'Tighten your girth and shorten your stirrups,' called Mrs Rogers, leg cocked in the air as she hauled up the girth strap around the middle of her elegant bay mare, Camilla. We set off down a grass and rubble track that ran down past the paddocks to I'd no idea where. It was rare for me to be riding outside the arena like this. To the left of us, in a little wild overgrown orchard of stunted apple trees, the blossom was over. Dog roses arched from the hedge with innocent, flat-faced pink and gold flowers and cruel jade thorns. Ahead, the wheat grew in greeny-gold waves, following the undulating lines of the earth. Along the field margin grew a scruffy frill of little weeds: scarlet pimpernel; speedwell with three pale blue petals and one of darker blue; purple and yellow hearts-ease. Years ago I used to pick bunches of these for the doll's house vases, pinching their thready stalks between my fingernails.

'All right?' called Mrs Rogers, striding ahead on Camilla. All right? was a question requiring the answer yes, so I took a firmer grip on Maxi's fidgety head and said it. 'Good,' said Mrs Rogers over her shoulder. 'We'll have a little trot here, then.' I didn't even have to lay my leg on Maxi's side. He was waiting for this. The hazel, hawthorn and black-thorn in the hedge, the overhanging canopy of beech, chest-nut and oak, the lazy slope of the ground ahead all began to bounce rhythmically up and down as Maxi burst like a cork, first into a vigorous bobbing trot and then – Ooh, help! – an energetic canter. He was evidently determined to catch up with Camilla, who was drawing effortlessly ahead on rangy, thoroughbred legs.

'Sit back, sit back,' called Mrs Rogers, as we caught up with her, and then, more sharply, 'Keep off the crop!' I hadn't noticed we were on it. My eyes were screwed up against the whipping twigs of overhanging willow and my hat had tipped forward over my nose. 'Get your leg off him,' hissed Mrs Rogers. Peering out from beneath my hat brim I could see a narrow gap at the top of the field between two stout wooden posts, a horse's width apart, and beyond them the road. There was a froth of foam on Maxi's espresso neck. With an effort of will I unclamped my gripping knees and heaved on the reins. In midair, it seemed, the inexorable forward momentum of the canter resolved itself into a steady trot and then a walk.

'We'll walk along this bit of road,' said Mrs Rogers, 'and then have another little trot on the way home. Now, about Maxi . . .'

I was fizzing with exhilaration. I had been for a canter, in the outside, without being run away with or falling off. That must surely mean I was on the way to becoming a competent rider. When Maxi was mine, we could do this all the time. Already I had begun to notice how different the world looked from the back of a horse. You could see over hedges and garden walls. You were at head height with the roses and the lower branches of trees, and the birds hopped and flirted at eye level when you passed. Then there was the pace at which you travelled: swift by comparison with the dreary trudge of human footfall, but still slow enough to catch the looping flight of a woodpecker and the wriggle and scurry of a rabbit in the roots of the hedge. What's more, the horse seemed to cast a spell of semi-invisibility as far as other animals were concerned. They didn't notice you. Or at any rate, you didn't startle them as much as when you were on your own feet, unequivocally human. Soon, when Maxi was mine, I'd be finding out a lot more about this . . .

'So the thing is,' Mrs Rogers was saying, 'there is another lady interested in him, just a bit more experienced than you. He's quite strong for you, and we don't want to start you on anything too sharp. We can look for something a bit quieter, to build your confidence.'

'Oh,' I said. 'Oh no. But I love Maxi, and I thought . . .' 'Well,' said Mrs Rogers, her voice like the shutting of a door, 'he needs a rider with just a little more experience. Don't worry. We can find something else for you, if that's what you want.'

I didn't want something else, though – some shadowy, unknown, imaginary future horse. I wanted this one, whose bristly neck was arching in front of me, whose ears were, for once, not laid back along his skull, but alertly cocked, who was now walking smartly along, emitting the snorts that I had thought were signs of fury, until Mrs Rogers explained they were a noise of contentment.

'I've got a bit of news,' said Mrs Rogers into the gloomy

silence as we turned back into the yard. 'I'm going to be quite busy from now on. I'm going to be an MFH.'

In the pause that followed this statement, the bright chaos of jagged mental fragments that were my reasons for learning to ride whirled rapidly, then settled into a pattern with a dry, decisive, kaleidoscope click.

'So if I learn to ride eventually,' I said. 'I mean, if I ever learn to ride properly, could I come out with you, one day, hunting?' 'Of course,' said Mrs Rogers, as though there were nothing at all odd about this idea, and vanished into the barn.

PART TWO

If you look up the Ashford Valley in *Baily's Hunting Direct-ory*, where it is the fourth entry, sandwiched between the Albrighton Woodland and the Atherstone, you find, after the listings of Masters, chairman, joint Hon. Secretaries, hunts-man, whippers-in, kennels, meets, subscription and cap, the following description: 'The country is a mixture of arable, grass and woodland and offers a great variety of fences includ-ing timber, hedges, ditches and dykes, but it is always possible for non-jumpers to negotiate the country. The ideal horse is a half to three quarter bred, capable of handling trappy situations . . .

'The country was hunted for many years by the late J. C. Buckland as a Harrier country, hunting fox whenever they found one. In 1922–23 the pack was officially recognized by the MFHA as the Ashford Valley Foxhounds under the Mastership of J. C. Buckland. The kennels were moved from his home . . . in 1948 to Cowlees, Hothfield, the home of A. Chester Beatty jun . . .'

All hunting is a matter of strong emotion and if you know the key to decode it, the eloquent concision of *Baily's* formula tells a story whose bitter clash of old tradition and new money would have fascinated Anthony Trollope, though he would probably have been tempted to write a neater and happier ending than the one devised by real life to the opening chapters of the Ashford Valley's history.

The story of a hunt – any hunt – is like the story of a family; a dynastic saga in which the good, the clever, the shrewd and the kind are thrown together, hugger-mugger, with the bad, the mad, the destructive and the stupid, with whom they must somehow contrive to get along, because above the battlefield fog and din of everyday life in a family or a hunt, there somehow persists the ideal of the institution itself as essentially benign, no matter what ignoble shenanigans its individual members may sometimes be getting up to.

The fortunes of hunts, as of families, tend to rise and fall in undulating generational waves. The alchemy of a successful hunt is almost as difficult to anatomize as that of a happy family. But combine a lucky blend of characters within a joint Mastership; harmonious relations between the Masters and the committee by which a majority of modern hunts are run; a talented huntsman who commands the trust and respect of the Masters and is allowed by them to do his job without undue interference and you might, with the addition of good country, well foxed, with friendly farmers, have the makings of the combination of sport and fellowship that attracts the field, draws in the subscriptions and builds the morale that gives a successful hunt (which may be, but is not necessarily, the same thing as a fashionable hunt) the sleek lustre of a football club at the triumphant end of a winning season.

But the balance between the elements of such complex social organisms is alarmingly fragile and easy to disrupt. A broken fence, a careless remark overheard at a puppy show, an accidental (or calculated) discourtesy, an old grudge revived, and hey ho, feelings are bruised, feuds spring up like weeds, factions form, resentments simmer, fellowship vanishes and subscriptions with it, resignation letters are written, hunt servants put their names on the transfer list, country that was once open becomes closed to the hunt.

And in the space of a few seasons an entity once well maintained and glossy with self-confidence becomes poor, nervous, apologetic, resentful and sad; its coverts and hunt jumps overgrown, its hound breeding programme abandoned, chilly gusts of neglect blowing wisps of straw around the half-empty kennels and rattling the stable doors on their rusty hinges. Until there appears some benefactor with a taste for costly and thankless projects, rich enough in money, energy, knowledge and time to ensure that the cycle of growth, flourishing and decay begins all over again.

In many hunts this process has been repeated over the best part of two centuries, with the result that, at a certain point of historical distance, the details begin to soften and grow vague, blurring into a stately list of more-or-less eccentrically named representatives of the nineteenth-century gentry, the lineaments of whose characters and deeds are as vague as the half-effaced names on weathered monuments in a country churchyard.

The fascination of the Ashford Valley is, in a way, its lack of a misty ancient past. The history of its emergence as a fox hunt is still crisp and new enough to be the stuff – though only just – of living memory. As William Scarth Dixon wrote in a pamphlet history of the hunt published in 1940, its development 'has taken place under our eyes and we may safely point to it as a modern example of what has happened at a more or less remote period in every county in Great Britain where "the sound of the horn is heard on the hills", or for the matter of that in the vale.'

The Ashford Valley's story is, in short, the hunting equivalent of that mesmerizing staple of television wildlife programmes, the time-lapse life cycle, which compresses into a few moments the emergence and flourishing of a new life that in real time takes place over an entire season. A pair of crumpled cotyledon leaves at the end of a ghostly frail stalk press blindly upwards through cracks in the earth towards the light. They open, expand, shoot out more stems and leaves. Buds form and unfurl in an instant into flowers that bloom, fade, then swell into ripening fruit. At this artificially high speed, the familiar process seems strange: at once prosaic and exotic – a brace of adjectives that describe exactly the quality of the Ashford Valley's early years: a vivid and eventually explosive mixture of Kentish yeomanry and American entrepreneurs, record-breaking international horsemanship and the juggernaut properties of financial clout.

Perhaps the beginnings of all hunts are essentially the same. Opening *Baily's* at random you find this, describing the origins of the Percy: 'During the latter part of the eighteenth and nineteenth centuries numerous gentlemen at different times had small packs of hounds, and hunted what is now the Percy country . . .' The Percy is an aristocratic hunt in the north-east of England. The Ashford Valley is a farmer's pack in the south-east. Still, you might begin its story in almost identical terms. During the latter part of the nineteenth and early twentieth centuries, numerous gentlemen at different times had small packs of hounds, and hunted what is now the Ashford Valley country.

There were four gentlemen in particular: Sir John Honeywood, Alfred Swaffer of Bethersden, near Ashford, Mr Blackman of Stone, in the Isle of Oxney, and Charles Witherden, all of whom kept private harrier packs in the eastern part of Kent and hunted hare in the mid-nineteenth century, both on foot and mounted. In 1848 John Carey Buckland was born at Goldwell Farm, Biddenden. He was Charles Witherden's nephew and he inherited Witherden's passion for hunting. As an infant he was carried out hunting, mounted behind a farmhand called Browne. Once he had learned to ride independently he began to act as Witherden's whipper-in and later as huntsman of his hounds.

The fact of a child's performing such a role, with its heavy burden of responsibility and its complicated freight of symbolism and ritual, seems remarkable, even rather disturbing, in the way that child prodigies, whatever their specialism, do disturb the ordinary rest of us. To hunt hounds is to put on a public performance, as horribly exposed as all public performances are, and a successful performer requires not merely an unusual combination of talent and composure but technique as well. To see all these qualities perfectly combined in an adult, whether on the concert platform, the football pitch or the hunting field, is an exhilarating experience, even if you don't fully comprehend the fine detail of what you are watching. But to find a child with a mastery of them is eerie. It reverses our sense of the normal order of things, which is that a subtle and accomplished authority over the external world is one of the privileges of adulthood.

Perhaps most adults' first, subliminal reaction to the spectacle of a prodigiously talented child, albeit suppressed so quickly that one scarcely has time to register the feeling before astonishment, pleasure and admiration kick in, is that it isn't fair. The mass of people – the audience – defers to performers as unacknowledged legislators; as a secular combination of priest and magician – as shamans, even. It is unnerving to encounter a shaman in short pants. Moreover, the Buckland family didn't look especially shamanic, with their wiry, horsemen's physiques and shrewd, knobbly Kentish faces in which the features looked as though they had been dabbed on at random. Nevertheless, the hunting gene ran strongly through the family and showed itself early. John Buckland's son, Harry, who plays an important part in the Ashford Valley's history, began whipping-in to his father at 11, and first hunted hounds at the age of 12.

In 1873 the four private harrier packs were amalgamated and became the Ashford Valley Harriers. John Buckland undertook the Mastership. It was a subscription hunt, which meant that its members contributed a certain amount of money annually towards the cost of running it, but any shortfall must be met by John Buckland himself. His pack was made up of blue-ticked old Southern harriers and dwarf foxhounds, and his control over them was the stuff of the well polished legends, rubbed smooth and opaque in the retelling as pieces of seashore glass, that are a vital element of the tribal activity that is sport.

'John Buckland had a wonderful way with hounds,' wrote the anonymous author of *A Master of Hounds*, a biography of Buckland's son, Harry. 'He was quiet but severe with them ... and loved his hounds as a Master should.' The hounds seem to have loved him in return. There is a story of his taking a terrible fall one day when hunting. He jumped a high drop fence, but his horse took off too close to it and leapt vertically, flinging Buckland against the pommel of the saddle so hard that he fractured his pelvis. Hounds were running, but they are supposed to have stopped and turned back to where Buckland lay, forming a mournful circle around their master.

Perhaps they really did do this. Or perhaps some of them kept on hunting while others turned back to guard the stricken huntsman. In a way, the precise degree of truth scarcely matters. The important thing is that John Buckland was a man around whom legends formed, and so was his son, and enough of the stories are verifiable to make the rest seem possible. There are no photographs of Jacko, the pet fox who is supposed to have lived on friendly terms with the hounds in kennels, but there is a picture of the tame deer belonging to Harry's sister, which used to go out on exercise with hounds and is shown sharing a bucket of food with two foxhounds.

And there are a great many pictures of Harry Buckland doing extraordinary things on horseback. Here he is jumping a strand of barbed wire on an Australian horse called Twinkle, the horse looking straight ahead, ears pricked, hind legs neatly tucked up, while Harry, wearing a soft hat with a dented crown and a turned-up brim, peers down at the wire. And here he is again, in tweed coat, gaiters and the same squashy hat, jumping a hitched waggon on Marmion, the Irish horse on whom at half-past midnight one day in 1909 he jumped 7ft 2in to win the World's Championship High Jump at the Olympia International Horse Show.

At a dress rehearsal for Olympia, a couple of weeks previously, he had jumped a dinner table laid with white linen and bottles of Champagne, and a burning five-barred gate, though no one seems to have taken a camera to record these feats. Marmion's fate was horrible but characteristically exotic. He was competing in Russia when the First World War broke out, was requisitioned by the Russian army and killed while being ridden by a Cossack officer in a cavalry charge on the Polish marshes, a world away from the little streams and hawthorn hedges and apple orchards of the Ashford Valley.

It is hard now, when hunting has become an issue that it is impossible to discuss neutrally; a wearisome subject, the mere mention of which comes automatically permeated with some strong, disturbing emotion – disgust, defiance, anger, boredom, sorrow, dread – to imagine what a glorious thing it must have been to be an MFH in the days when hunting was at its triumphalist height. The comparison with football is hard to resist: something like the airy pneumatic cushion of fame and adulation that buoys a star footballer at the marvellous height of his powers evidently floated beneath both Bucklands at the apex of their mastering careers.

Though their version of celebrity was local rather than global, it seems nevertheless to have had something of the bold, charmed, lawless quality of modern football stardom, with the same magical, cavalier sense of living just outside the rules that shackle everyone else. The biography tells a rather horrible story, of a dispute between the Ashford Valley Harriers and a local farmer (the biographer gives him the dismissive alias of Bloggs) who refused to allow the hunt over his land. One day in 1886 the harriers met at Bloggs's neighbour's farm. They found a hare, which ran – inevitably – straight on to the forbidden territory of Bloggs's land, followed by John Buckland and most of the field.

Summonses for trespass followed. Prosecuting counsel said that the issue was whether Mr Bloggs had rights over his own property, or whether the hunt might enter it with impunity. The defendants, John Buckland, the Hunt Secretary and Bloggs's neighbour, on whose land the offending meet had been held, had engaged a London QC who conducted a sneering cross-examination of Bloggs, in the manner of Edward Carson toying with a more stolid and less epigrammatic Oscar Wilde. Had he ever hunted with the Harriers? Yes he had. Had he ridden on other people's land? Yes. And had he been summoned for trespass as a result? No. And was this, suggested the QC, 'because the other landowners are Sportsmen?' No answer from the goaded Bloggs.

The case hung on the Harriers' purpose in entering Bloggs's land. If they had been led there by their Master in pursuit of game, they did so under the protection of the Game Laws and no offence had been committed. But if they had gone in search of it, their entry was illegal. The bench found that Buckland and his field had been in pursuit of the first hare, but had then remained on the land in search of other quarry and had therefore not committed a trespass by initially entering Bloggs's land, but had done so by hunting on after their first hare was lost. They were fined £1 each.

Bloggs left the court and walked a lonely route to the railway station to catch a train home, surrounded by a hostile demonstration of hunt supporters. At the railway station, one of them ('whose picture is reproduced in this volume,' notes the anonymous biographer, hinting perhaps that the picture is also that of the author) seized a live fish from a basket being carried by a porter and struck Bloggs in the face with it through the carriage window. 'The good old boisterous days,' comments the biography complacently, as who should sigh for the good old days of Heysel.

The only photograph of a member of the field reproduced in the book shows a podgy little man in a loud, checked ratcatcher coat and a curly bowler hat, astride a stocky mare with a short tail. He has tiny ears and small currant eyes, deep-set in a pale, doughy face with a little black moustache. The hedges and fields of the valley roll away behind him. He looks like a pocket Oliver Hardy. You can easily imagine him undertaking a bit of comic business with a flapping fish on an unsporting farmer.

Soon after the conclusion of the court case, the new flagpole on the gable of Bloggs's house was sawn off. It was a further spiteful example of the violent, moralizing strain of argument that thrives in hunting between the pros and the antis, each side convinced with a quasi-religious fanaticism that its position is the only virtuous one. Bloggs refused to allow the hunt on his land; therefore he was no sportsman, which was the same thing as a man of no virtue; thus he deserved the bullying ridicule, with its frank overtones of sexual humiliation, of the slap in the face with the wriggling fish, and the abrupt truncation of his flagpole. 'It may be said,' wrote Anthony Trollope, 'that in a real hunting county active antagonism to hunting is out of the question. A man who cannot endure to see a crowd of horsemen on his land, must give up his land and go elsewhere to live . . .'

It is a mistake to think that hunting, even at the height of its popularity as a pastime, was ever quite carefree. The ethics of chasing animals for entertainment, rather than necessity, has troubled people since the practice began. Nevertheless, for the infant Ashford Valley Harriers the 1880s, despite the onset of an agricultural depression that was to last for two decades, were evidently a golden time. The roads were un-metalled and free of cars, the hedges unwired, the quarry plentiful – the Harriers would turn out as willingly for a fox or a deer as a hare and once hunted a deer 25 miles from Woodchurch, on the edge of Romney Marsh, into the sea at Seasalter – and the company both congenial and local.

Fashionable hunts with famous names, long histories and grass country – the Grafton, the Fernie, the Belvoir, the Pytchley, the Quorn – attracted huge fields and hordes of visitors from beyond the country, including such exotic birds of passage as the brave, beautiful and improbably thin Empress Elisabeth of Austria who hunted obsessively in the Shires during the 1870s. This sort of thing lent hunting a particular kind of edgy social mystique: in effect, a rural version of the urban glamour that now surrounds an especially fashionable gallery or bar or couturier's *atelier*, with the same unforgiving sartorial imperatives, crucial to the insider, invisible to the outsider.

The hunting field was one place in nineteenth-century society where a kind of meritocracy prevailed. 'One of the best features of hunting,' wrote Otho Paget in 1900, 'is that it gives all classes a chance of meeting on terms of equality. In the hunting field all men are equal with the exception of the Master and the huntsman – they should be absolute autocrats. The peer must take a back seat if a butcher with a bold heart can pound him over a big fence.' This was only true up to a point – once the hunt was over, the peer would be unlikely to invite the bold-hearted butcher back to his place for dinner.

But it was true that access to hunting was remarkably free. Queen Victoria even went so far as to commend its democratic qualities to her son, Bertie (making an unfavourable comparison with what she regarded as the unfortunate social exclusiveness of the shooting that he preferred). 'Hunting,' as Mrs Rogers remarked to me at a particularly quarrelsome Ashford Valley AGM, 'brings together all sorts of people who otherwise wouldn't be friends.' It was as true in the nineteenth century as it is in the twenty-first. You could be an Empress or a harlot and as long as you rode bravely at your fences, people would admire you – for the duration of the meet, at any rate – just the same.

No Empresses came from across the sea to hunt with the Ashford Valley, and no harlots either (or at any rate, not celebrity ones like Skittles, who hunted ferociously with the Quorn and afterwards lent some of her adventures to Surtees's engaging heroine, Lucy Glitters). It was a resolutely local farmers' pack, without social pretensions and far enough from London, even by rail, not to be the first choice for Cockney sportsmen like Jorrocks, who thought Euston and the Great Northern Stations 'the two best covert hacks in the world'.

The interesting, hermetic, fiercely local nature of the AVH was astonishingly long-lived. In defiance of what Max Hastings once gloomily described as the 'urban monoculture' the Ashford Valley, even when I hunted with them, 130 years after the amalgamation of the four privately owned harrier packs under John Buckland's mastership, was intensely local: not merely Kentish, but local to its particular bit of Kent. Much of the field (apart from me, the London bird of passage) was born and bred within the country. If they weren't born there, they lived and worked there now. What seemed to me an astonishingly high proportion of the hunt followers had scarcely been to London – other than to go on the Countryside Alliance marches in support of hunting. Even the accent was specific. 'This is a Wealden accent,' said one man to me as we leant on our sticks and chatted during a long, uneventful passage in an evening's autumn hunting, keen that I shouldn't confuse the tones of someone born and bred in High Halden with any old hybrid Estuary rubbish.

Still, the hunt was not without its exotic passages. In its early days there came two separate infusions of a culture that was disturbing, invigorating and not Kentish at all. The first of them came in the person of Walter Winans, an American citizen of Belgian extraction, born in St Petersburg in 1852. He was an Olympic medallist and a co-founder of the Royal Horse Show at Olympia. Of all the places in the world where he might have come to rest, he settled eventually at Surrenden Park, Pluckley, in the heart of Ashford Valley country, where he kept a deer park, a pack of draghounds and a stable of 120 show horses. He used to shoot deer from the back of a horse and once shot at a ghost (Pluckley is a notorious haunt of spectres) but succeeded only in hitting the wall.

This was the man for whom Harry Buckland rode in the show ring for 16 years, from 1898, when he was 19, to 1914. Apart from winning the World Championship's High Jump on the horse Marmion, which the Bucklands themselves had found in Ireland, schooled and sold to Winans, Harry won the Grand Cross Country Race at Spa in Belgium twice in successive years, the second time (in 1904) on a mare called The Hind, which had cost £20. Out of the show ring he hunted and rode point-to-points with an eerie, intuitive success (though his father would never let him enter the Grand National, which Harry minded).

Between 1909 and 1913 Harry was honorary huntsman to the Mid-Kent Staghounds, in which character he appeared in Siegfried Sassoon's *Memoirs of a Fox-hunting Man*, thinly disguised as 'Harry Buckman . . . who was well known as a rider at hunt races all over the country . . . I gazed at Buckman with interest and admiration when he tit-tupped stylishly past me at the meet with his velvet cap cocked slightly over one ear. Buckman was a mixture of horse dealer and yeoman farmer. In the summer he rode jumpers in the show ring. His father had hunted a pack of harriers, and it was said that when times were bad he would go without his dinner himself rather than stint his hounds of their oatmeal.'

Sassoon's account of his day's stag-hunting with the

'Coshford Vale Stag Hunt' – that is, the Mid-Kent Staghounds – is mildly ironical. And in fact stag-hunting, in the version practised by the Mid-Kent and in other places where deer were no longer indigenous, does seem a very odd kind of distraction – nearer to the dangerous party game that is drag-hunting than anything more wild and elemental. The quarry was a 'carted deer' – that is, a deer kept in a paddock some-where nearby the kennels and driven to the meet in a van kept for the purpose. These deer were given nicknames, sometimes comic or admiring. The Buckland biography mentions The Catch of the Season, The Bart, Stalisfield Lass and a hind called The Hawk, who was famously swift. Mrs Rogers remembered one called Elusive Lucy. The deer was uncarted, given a head start, and then hounds and field set off in pursuit. The sport consisted in the chase, which could go on for exhausting lengths of time and distance – four, five and six hours, over twenty miles or more at a time.

'Provincial stag-hunts are commonly reputed to be comic and convivial gatherings,' wrote Sassoon, 'which begin with an uproarious hunt-breakfast . . . But the Coshford sportsmen . . . were businesslike and well-behaved; they were out for a good old-fashioned gallop. In fact, I think of them as a some-what serious body of men. And since the field was mainly composed of farmers, there was nothing smart or snobbish about the proceedings.'

The huntsman's aim was to prevent the deer from being killed when hounds caught up with it, an object accomplished, as Sassoon records it, with a certain jovial lack of regard for the feelings of the hunted animal. In the same passage Sassoon records another extraordinary piece of riding by 'Buckman' – when he jumped a set of railway gates with the 'paradoxical but humane' purpose of saving The Hawk, which had jumped them ahead of him, from hounds.

Harry was well known in Ireland, both as a buyer of horses

and from his riding at the Dublin Horse Show, and in 1913 he was invited to take up the Mastership of the East Galway Foxhounds for a season. The country was quite different from what he was used to: mostly old pasture, with gorse coverts ('mixed rough walls, open ditches, drains and banks may be encountered,' says *Baily's*). There was less plough and woodland here than in the Valley; far fewer human obstacles in the form of roads, railways and settlement, and the characters were more eccentric and less inclined to the solid seriousness that Siegfried Sassoon noticed among the Coshford farmers.

There is a picture of a meet of the East Galway in 1913, showing Harry flanked by a couple of Hunt dignitaries. It is hard to tell whether they are standing indoors or out. There is brickwork visible between the open French windows in the background, and what looks like raked gravel or short turf underfoot. But a line of bow-legged dining chairs with brocade cushions curtseys along the wall, and there is what looks like a grand piano off to one side. The two Irishmen are self-consciously magnificent in silk hats, brass-buttoned hunt coats, white stocks, glassily polished boots and soup-strainer moustaches. One glares fiercely at the camera, a half-smile twitches the ends of the other's walrus whiskers. He is so stout that two of his five shiny buttons have sprung from their buttonholes.

Between them, half a head taller than either, stands Harry in a huntsman's velvet cap, his horn thrust into the breast of his coat. He, too, is looking straight to camera, with his chin lowered and his head slightly bowed, so his face is all long, crooked, broken nose and watchful eyes peering from beneath the peak of his cap. He looks lean, beaky, diffident, slightly farouche. But the faintly improbable pairing of Kentish Master and Irish hunt seems to have worked. Harry found he preferred hunting foxes to hares. And at the close of the season he had killed sixteen-and-a-half brace of foxes and marked twelve-

and-a-half brace to ground. When he returned to the Ashford Valley, the East Galway told him they hoped, if he ever became a Master of Foxhounds, that he would adopt their yellow collar.

In the spring of 1914, Harry returned from Ireland to Kent and a year full of endings. In July he was riding Walter Winans's hunters and showjumpers at the Richmond show when he had a terrible fall in the pairs class at the water jump. He collided in the air with his pair and his horse fell on him, fracturing his skull and his arm. He was unconscious for three weeks, and in this time Walter Winans suddenly decided to sell his showjumpers – Marmion, the high jump champion, Twinkle, who could jump barbed wire, St Olaf, who jumped the dinner-table, and all the rest of them. When Harry came to and learned what had happened to the horses with whom he had worked so closely – horses whose potential he had often spotted beneath unpromising looks, whom he had made, trained, worked with and trusted – he said he would never ride in the show ring again.

And then the War came. Harry Buckland was 35 and his dreadful catalogue of riding injuries made him unfit for active service. Within earshot of the guns across the Channel he trained remounts and helped his father on the farm at Little Chart. John Buckland kept his harrier pack going, feeding them on fallen stock collected from the surrounding farms and taking them out occasionally with a field of soldiers on home leave and girls from the Remount Depot at Pluckley. As the war went on, hares became scarce – shot or snared for food – and the Harriers, who had always been inclined to hunt a fox when they found one, evolved by degrees into a fox hunt.

When the war was over, Harry, who had taken over the management of the hunt from his elderly father, replaced the dwarf foxhounds with some drafts from Lord Leconfield's pack at Petworth (some of whose names – Crimson and

Damsel, for example – survive in the Ashford Valley pack today) and introduced some Welsh sires, though he preserved the Southern strain, descended from Gascon hounds, brought to England in medieval times. The Southern hounds were large, deep-throated, steady, disinclined to riot, patient at working out the scent. In 1922–3, the Ashford Valley was officially recognized by the Masters of Foxhounds Association as a fox hunt, with John Buckland as its Master. For the first time, they began to hunt in red coats, with the yellow collar of the East Galway. The evolution of the four private harrier packs into a fox hunt had been done in 50 years, under a single mastership.

The formalization of the Ashford Valley into an officially recognized fox hunt meant a change in the nature of its hunting, from the fluid spontaneity of John Buckland's harrier pack, which might turn its attention to a fox or a deer when it suited him, to something much more formal, regulated and accountable. In this the Ashford Valley was following the lead of the Shires. There, fox-hunting had long since stopped being the private concern of the Master and his particular circle of friends, and become a mass public entertainment for anyone who could afford to join in. The railways had brought a day's hunting within easy reach of people who lived far outside a particular hunt's country, and that easy accessibility had a huge effect on the mass appeal of fox-hunting.

With popularity came a need for a different kind of organization. The informal arrangements of mere neighbourliness were not enough if more than half your field consisted of hard-riding strangers on hirelings. Regulation was required; properly set boundaries, a recognized governing body to settle disputes; a degree of professionalism. Until 1881 disputes in fox-hunting (which were quite frequent: where there is passion, as there invariably is in matters of sport and land ownership, there are bound to be rows) were settled by a marvellously amateurish device: an informal grouping of MFHs who also happened to be members of Boodle's and met to deliver judgement over hunting squabbles in the congenial surroundings of that club.

In 1878 a fearful row over some Quorn country proved too Balkan for the agreeable clubmen of Boodle's to handle. To their dismay, their genial authority seemed not to work its magic on a particularly intractable collection of Leicestershire farmers. The idea of hunting conducting its quarrels in the unseemly milieu of the public courts (with, perhaps, a nationwide repetition of the grotesque wet-fishery that resulted when the Ashford Valley Harriers did exactly that) was painful to contemplate. The Duke of Beaufort, the *capo di tutti capi* of Masters of Foxhounds, made a decisive gesture. He sent a circular letter to all his fellow MFHs suggesting in gloriously lofty and detached third-person language that 'it is thought desirable that all Masters of Hounds in Great Britain should form an Association, and from their body appoint a Committee to settle any disputes that may arise between Masters or Countries . . .' So they did. The first General Meeting (as the foreword to the MFHA's Constitution, Rules and Recommendations still points out) was held at Tattersalls on June 2, 1881.

In 2003 the MFHA Constitution and Rules dealt with an astonishing range of tricky minutiae, from the provision of appropriate headgear for hunt staff and the etiquette of mobile phone use in hunting (never for the purpose of locating or rediscovering the fox), to what to do if the hunted fox runs into someone's drawing room (hounds must be removed and the fox not hunted again. The owner of the drawing room must then be consulted as to 'how he or she would like the fox dealt with'). At the time of the Ashford Valley's emergence as a fox hunt, however, the MFHA's most frequent preoccupation was with questions of hunt boundaries. The AVH needed a country.

As Harriers, their country extended from Headcorn to Lympne, and from Stone, on the Isle of Oxney, to Chilham, though the accounts of their famous hunts suggest that they quite frequently overran it. As a fox hunt, they could no longer afford to do this without risking a serious falling-out with neighbouring hunts who, moreover, already owned large slices of the country over which the harriers had hunted. The country that was carved out for the AVH, with loans of country from the Tickham to the north and the East Kent to the east, was an irregular rectangle extending from Tonbridge in the west to the Grand Military Canal in the east and from the M20 in the north to the river Rother in the south. Crisscrossed even then by road and rail, heavily settled and intensively cultivated, the country was nevertheless full of foxes (and still is) and offered, if not the glorious long, fast gallops and flying fences of the Shires, an interesting, demanding, thoughtful sort of hunting that attracted love and loyalty in the same unemphatic way as the countryside in which it took place.

John Buckland died in 1926. There was an enormous funeral service at Great Chart and his black hunter, Sambo, followed the hearse. Harry Buckland inherited his hounds and the Mastership of the Ashford Valley. Soon after that, things began to go wrong.

It was money that was the problem. Somehow, even during the agricultural depression of the 1870s John Buckland had contrived to keep his pack going. It wasn't easy. One of his hounds, whelped in 1879, the same year that Harry was born, was given the name 'Poverty'. And it is plain from Siegfried Sassoon's remark about 'Harry Buckman's' father doing without his own dinner rather than stinting his hounds that John

Buckland struggled at times to keep his hounds going, even though the overheads of a private harrier pack were considerably less than those of a fox hunt, with professional hunt servants to dress, mount and keep.

We know that John Buckland often fed his hounds on fallen stock, and financed his pack by buying difficult horses, making hunters of them, and selling them on. Harry's career had taken him in a different direction, riding show horses for Walter Winans, who 'spent money like a gentleman'.

You needed to be able to spend like a gentleman to keep a fox hunt going. Mr Selby Lowndes, who took over the mastership of the Ashford Valley's next-door neighbour, the East Kent, in 1900 and stayed for 30 years, considered mastering a full-time job. It wasn't just the breeding, care and hunting of the hounds that took the time, but all the administration: the endless keeping up of relations with farmers, landlords and shoots, the maintenance of the country, the picking up of fallen stock, the interminable fund-raising. How to do that and earn a living at the same time? Mastership was, in effect, unpaid. Subscriptions were supposed to cover the cost of hunting the country, which they might or might not do, but they almost certainly didn't extend to keeping the Master and his family fed and housed, furnishing his wife with dresses and his children with new boots and an education.

In keeping his harrier pack, John Buckland had combined a multiplicity of roles: the duties of Master, huntsman and kennelman, all of which represented a cost to him in both money and time, with the horse-broking business that actually produced an income. In doing all this he had had Harry to help him. Now Harry was alone in charge of a new fox hunt, with all the extra expense and keeping up of appearances that that entailed. Help would have to come from outside.

This was change at an alarming rate: not the stately, organic progression that had seen the harriers mutate gradually over a

50-year cycle from a convivial band of like-minded farmers in tweeds and gaiters to the formal grandeur of a fox hunt with pink coats and a meet card, but change sudden, catastrophic and uninvited. It was as though John Buckland's death had made a breach in the family structure of the Ashford Valley Hunt, through which the outside world now came bursting, in the person of Alfred Chester Beatty.

Mr Chester Beatty was an American magnate – strange how they kept popping up in Harry Buckland's life – who had made a fortune in mining. He was an Anglophile, a cultivated man with extravagant tastes in books and art, and he kept a country house at Cale Hill, Little Chart, which made him a kind of neighbour of the Bucklands and their 52 couple of hounds. Now, in neighbourly fashion, he offered to help them out of their trouble. He would assist with the hunt finances, but there was – as there always is with miraculous solutions to intractable problems – a condition. The condition was his son, A. Chester Beatty Jr, a recent graduate of Cambridge University, who was to become joint Master with Harry of the Ashford Valley Foxhounds.

Fox-hunting at this time had an uneasy relationship with wealthy Americans. On the one hand, it loved their apparently unlimited quantities of money, so redolent of the open-handed 'good old days' of good sport and good fellowship and never count the cost. On the other, it harboured for them and their money the angry, snobbish resentment for a rich foreigner of an insular culture that was beginning to encounter difficulties in keeping up its own wonderful old traditions. 'Gone are the sport-loving farmers of fifty years ago, gone that charming old country life that made so many great Englishmen. Unless English agriculture is to be run as a trust by an American syndicate, that too will soon be gone, I fear,' mourned the historian of the Brocklesby Hunt in 1902.

Hunting writers love a dying fall. What is more, they are

infinitely susceptible to the seductions of the past. For them, no hunting is ever quite as exciting, no fox as cunning, no hound as clever, no horse as brave, no meet as elegantly convivial and no hunt tea as uproarious as the ones that took place just before their time. They are perhaps the only people who have ever felt able to use the expression 'the good old days' without the faintest trace of irony. One of the enigmas of hunting is that it is so much nicer in retrospect than it is either in prospect or while you are actually doing it, that it is a mystery how anyone manages to summon the morale to get out of bed to go hunting at all, let alone carry on doing it, day after day while the season lasts.

At any rate, the thought of past meets is very much more glamorous than the present one, at which there is no scent, rain is falling with sullen persistence and your horse has refused the first jump of the day, an easy post-and-rails that any Pony Club five-year-old could have sailed over. And infinitely more attractive than the one in three days' time, at which – who knows – you may actually fall and break your neck.

This gap between experience and perception extends to cover not just the actual event of the hunt – the meet and the chase – but all the wispy intangibles of emotion that surround hunting and make it, like love or kinship, so fascinating and hard to relinquish once you are drawn in. Fear, excitement, the complicated nexus of intellectual and physical pleasure, like chess on horseback, that is the business of the pursuit; friendship, jokes, the sense of familiarity and acceptance – and more than that, of existing, of having a place in the world, and not just floating about, invisibly and at random, like an atom – that comes with belonging to a place and a tribe: all these are feelings that lend themselves to mythologizing of the most seductive kind.

In its turn, the mythologizing feeds back into the experience. A deed isn't really done until someone has told a story about it; turned it into part of the extended chronicle by means of which the tribe is simultaneously amused and reminded of its collective identity. The nature of stories is at once to exaggerate and to simplify; to intensify contrast, distil what is dangerous, brave, ridiculous, ignominious into its pure essence and at the same time tidy things up, remove what is awkward, irresolute, inexplicable; an impediment to the free flow of the story.

Until 1927 the story of the Ashford Valley had been a *roman fleuve* of a peculiarly untroubled kind: its characters, its setting, its mishaps and even its villain, in the person of the unlucky Bloggs, were all comfortingly local and familiar, with the element of exotic fantasy essential to fuel the narrative momentum provided by Harry and his extraordinary horsemanship. The essence of such stories is their rippling pace. Misfortunes and dramas arrive with the turn of the seasons, and pass away again at their inexorable rhythm. If a character from beyond the pale erupts suddenly into such a narrative, as though in a puff of green smoke through a trapdoor in the floor, upsetting the arrangements and interrupting the punchline of someone's rambling anecdote, you may be sure that his role in the story will be either comic or sinister, or possibly both.

When Mr Chester Beatty Jr arrived in the Ashford Valley from America, via Cambridge University, he didn't look like anyone's idea of an archetypal MFH. A photograph shows a fat young man with the awkward, straddling stance of someone whose thighs are too plump for them to stand easily with their feet together. Beneath a low-crowned black velvet cap he peers short-sightedly through large round horn-rimmed spectacles. His stock is slightly crumpled, his coat rather short in the skirt and sleeves, his hand, gloved in white knitted string, looks like a bunch of uncooked sausages. Altogether there is a haunting resemblance to Tenniel's illustrations of

Tweedledum and Tweedledee in Lewis Carroll's *Through the Looking-Glass*.

'It is perhaps not surprising,' remarks the Buckland biography, 'that after a time a certain incompatibility should have developed between the two Joint Masters – the one a typical English countryman, born and bred with hounds, the other the son of an American business-man.' The new Joint Master was dissatisfied with the existing AVH pack, with its harrier bloodlines and its Leconfield drafts, and he had his own ideas about kennel management.

In 1930 he introduced a pack of Welsh Foxhounds to kennels. Harry Buckland believed in feeding hounds on flesh at least twice a week, to keep them keen. Chester Beatty's Welsh pack was not allowed flesh. The two packs had to be separately fed and exercised. The cost of feeding rose from £22 a half year to £200 for the same period and the hunt subscription was doubled to cover it. The hunt now had, in effect, two separate packs of hounds: Harry's pack, which he continued to hunt himself, and the Welsh hounds, which were looked after by the whipper-in.

Evidently this fox-hunting version of East and West Berlin couldn't continue. At the end of 1930 Chester Beatty Sr threatened to withdraw his financial support but was persuaded to continue, with extra conditions. Specifically, that the kennels should move from Goldwell Farm, Great Chart, where Harry lived with hounds as his father had done, to share the kennels of the Mid-Kent Staghounds at Smarden. At this point Harry Buckland made an extraordinary decision. From this distance of time it looks like the self-lacerating gesture of a man in an extremity of anger or distress who felt he had nowhere to turn. He resigned his Mastership, sold his hounds to the new sole Master and left to take up a Mastership elsewhere, severing his links with the place where he was born, grew up and raised his own family, and with the hunt that he and his father had made between them. He died in Kent in 1953.

After the turbulence of what sections of the 'old' Ashford Valley evidently regarded as a hostile takeover, Chester Beatty Jr settled into a long Mastership and the narrative of the hunt resumed, though in a form quite different from its beginnings as a family saga. Cleverly, he didn't try to make the hunt's story his own, in imitation of the Buckland era, but instead widened and extended the range of personalities in charge of running the Ashford Valley, drawing in people from outside who were well known in Kent hunting and could be expected to have a soothing influence on the nerves of subscribers alarmed by the brutal amputation of Harry Buckland's departure, a sharp rise in their subscriptions, the introduction of the Welsh pack, and who knew what other precipitate changes to the comfortable regime to which they were accustomed.

In 1934 a retired Royal Artillery officer, Lt-Col. H. C. Hessey, who had his own beagle pack, the Brissenden, became Joint Master with Chester Beatty and the kennels moved to his home near Bethersden. Sandys Dawes, then Master of the Mid-Kent staghounds, hunted the Ashford Valley hounds for a while. He, too, came from a famous local hunting family. His younger sister, Betty McKeever, was given a beagle pack, the Blean, by her father in 1909 when she was eight years old and held the Mastership of them for 80 seasons, having been plucked from the nursery before breakfast and taught to boil a good oatmeal hound pudding by William Selby Lowndes, the Master of the East Kent, when she was nine.

The willingness of such stately ornaments of local hunting *nomenklatura* to work with the new Master, despite his unfortunate lack of Kentish origins, his background in industry, his aesthetic tastes, Welsh hounds and modernizing tendencies, evidently helped consolidate the healing process by which even the most quarrelsome hunts generally contrive to settle their differences in the interests of hunting on. The joint Mastership of Chester Beatty and Col. Hessey lasted for five years, until 1939 when war broke out. John Buckland had somehow contrived to nurse his hounds through the years of the 1914–18 war, but this time it wasn't thought feasible. The whole pack was destroyed (and with it, the last trace of the Bucklands' old Southern Harrier bloodlines).

When peace returned, hunting resumed in the Ashford Valley under the old joint Mastership with new drafts of hounds and a certain bravura manner, not quite usual in a farming pack: the hunt staff were mounted in grand style, on matching greys. Col. Hessey continued as Joint Master until 1949, Chester Beatty until 1953, when he resigned and the Ashford Valley then succumbed to a fairly familiar hunting rhythm of bursts of short, quarrelsome, irresolute Master-ships and financial crisis, interspersed with longer periods of comparative peace and stability, one of which was provided, in an elegant resolution of the narrative strand broken and left dangling on Harry Buckland's departure, by his son, Phil Buckland, a land agent and chartered surveyor who returned to his birthplace in Kent, having lived in Berkshire and hunted with the Garth, and became Joint Master between 1961 and 1974.

I wasn't to know it, but when I stumbled on the Ashford Valley, lurking camouflaged among what I thought were the familiar landscapes of my past, the hunt was going through a fairly good patch. By now, like most hunts, it was run by a Committee which was responsible for appointing the Masters. The Mastership had recently changed, but the outgoing Masters had served a stretch of six years during which they had recruited a huntsman from the south-west, Neil Staines, with a brief to create 'the best pack of hounds in the south-east in three seasons'. Neil was a pragmatist. He told the Masters it would take longer than that to improve the pack he found on his arrival. There is a video documentary of the Ashford Valley, made for the American market in the mid-nineties, soon after he was appointed to the huntsman's job, in which he appears, speaking directly to the camera, kindly but firmly as though to a not very bright hound. 'The Ashford Valley,' he says, smiling slightly, 'is a good third division hunt.' A beat. 'Of four divisions.'

The Mastership consisted now of four people, of whom Mrs Rogers was the most recently appointed. The others were Ian Anderson, a civil engineer with a small farm at Bethersden who spent half his year advising governments on irrigation developments in hazardous parts of the world – Afghanistan, Bosnia, Ethiopia – and the other half hunting; his wife, Lynne, and Matthew Knight, a solicitor who was later succeeded by Brian Fraser, a farmer who had already served as Joint Master from 1982–92. Apart from the twin anxieties of a nagging shortage of money and a superfluity of urban creep that are the baleful outriders of any small hunt in a densely populated area, the most troublesome worm in the AVH's apple was anti-hunt activity. The Valley's splendid rail and motorway links made it a popular day out for hunt saboteurs.

Now, unexpectedly, I might become part of all this – if only I could learn to ride well enough. 'Aim for the end of the season,' Mrs Rogers said when I asked her whether I could come out with her. 'And in the meantime, you can come out on foot.' But a couple of weeks later, when I was still struggling ineffectually with canter transitions, she said I should think of taking two lessons a week. 'Isn't there somewhere in London you could go, if you can't come down here twice a week?' she asked.

Actually, there was. Soon after I had begun lessons at the Rooting Street yard, I was excitedly describing it to an old friend, a civil servant who had been riding since childhood.

'You'll never get anywhere on one lesson a week,' he said crushingly. 'You ought to join the Civil Service Riding Club. Then you can go every day, if you've got time, and ride out in Hyde Park.'

Riding out in Hyde Park was exactly what I thought I didn't want to do: tame excursions on dull horses bored into a state of resentful coma by the spirit-eroding passage of a stream of so-so riders across their backs. Not my idea of interesting riding. On the other hand, the Club was based at the Royal Mews, and there was a definite glamour to the thought that I might arrive at the stout black iron railings on Buckingham Palace Road, where visitors press their noses through the bars and peer longingly in, like mirror images of the animals at the zoo gazing wistfully out, and at a signal from a guard, a wicket gate would magically swing open to admit me.

London, like Paris, is a city of secrets. Very little of its life is visible to the casual passer-by. There is no *passeggiàta*, no comfortable gathering in cafés under the plane trees to gossip and watch the world go by. Almost everything important happens out of sight, in private places where you may enter only if you know the secret code. And how do you find out the code? It's a secret, of course. In Paris, you peer through the wicket gates of closed *portes-cochères* and see a courtyard with a pale stone fountain spitting rainbow curves of droplets, orange and bay trees in pots, a prim child in corduroy rompers pulling a wheeled horse on a length of string, like a picture in a storybook, his mother clip-clopping across cobbles in her spindly heels, eyeless in narrow black sunglasses; nails, hair, lips all lacquered to an impermeable gloss.

In London you walk the pavements in the evenings when the lamps are lit and see between the branches of lilac, magnolia and syringa that grow in the locked garden squares, through the curtains left open to catch the last of the daylight, glimpses of hidden life: high-ceilinged rooms in houses in Chelsea, Belgravia and Notting Hill, poised like stage sets with expectation of the evening to come. Mulberry or library-green walls hung with pictures, each lit with a polished brass half-cylinder lamp on a curved swan's neck; a marble fireplace with tinkling cut-glass sconces; a white bust with a broken nose, curls clustered like hyacinth petals and tender, cold stone ears. And among all this frozen richness, a burst of animation: men in striped shirts with fat silk ties hanging loosened at their throats, women with bare shoulders and tired legs squeezed into glossy tights, holding glasses filled with red and straw-coloured wine, laughing, gesturing, flirting: as fascinating and unreachable as the little laughing figures of a brightly coloured *fête champêtre* painted on a porcelain urn housed in a museum vitrine.

It would be interesting for once, I had thought, to be on the other side of the glass; to be the person for whom the door swung obediently open when the secret code was tapped into the keypad. Six months earlier, soon after the conversation with my friend, I had rung up the Civil Service Riding Club and put my name on a waiting list to become a member of the Club, which at the time kept a dozen or so horses stabled at the Royal Mews, and offered evening lessons there in the indoor school. I filled in innumerable forms, had a police check run on me and my photograph taken by an ironical functionary in a dingy office in the strip-lit melamine hinterlands of Buckingham Palace. After all this I received a credit-card-sized pass with a hideous mug-shot of me laminated into it – a talisman which, if I showed it at the gate, would disarm the guards and unlatch the arrow-headed iron wicket.

Even before the gate was opened, I felt a faint sense of familiarity with the buildings of the Mews. From the vantage-point of the pavement you could see a vanishing series of honey stone quadrangles opening on to other quadrangles. It was an enclosed community, like an Oxford college. Three years of living among quadrangles had given me the illusion of having mastered a kind of fluency in the mores of people who lived in them.

Just inside the gates was a little porter's lodge where guards and policemen drank tea in a cheerful, gossipy fug. Beyond the lodge was a broad arch leading to a vast double quadrangle with a granite mounting-block at the centre and cars parked in rows, lending it the transitory air of an out-of-town shopping centre of unusual architectural distinction. A railed walkway ran round the quad at first-floor level, with a series of identical front doors opening on to it. Small items of domestic trivia cluttered the insistent geometrical sharpness of square, rectangle and straight line: a child's pink bike lying on its side; a doll's pram parked askew outside one of the front doors. These must be the flats of people who worked in the Mews.

That was as much as you could see from outside the gates. Once inside, as you walked under the first broad arch into the double quad you were faced with another arch, much taller and narrower than the first, set slightly out of true on the opposite side of the square. As you passed under the second arch a door opened into an airy, high-ceilinged stable block with half-barred loose boxes and square tiles underfoot: the London quarters of the Queen's carriage horses. Emerging on the far side you passed into a different world: darker, humbler, built without regard for appearance, of blackish brick. To one side, behind the stable block, was a gleaming assortment of vehicles. A couple of sleek black motors were parked near a lone petrol pump, but everything else was horse-drawn, from neat two-seaters perched high on spindly, lightweight yellow wheels picked out in black to heavy, glassed-in carriages painted sombre burgundy and black with gilt curlicues on their panelling.

Past the carriages two walls of sooty brick converged,

honeycombed on either side with cell-like stables whose occupants' heads poked nodding over the half-doors. I went there first on an early Monday evening in midsummer. There was a smell of cut grass, of something sweet – lilac, perhaps, or laburnum – from the Palace gardens, of horses, leather and exhaust fumes. It was very quiet: the only sounds the shuffle and munch of the horses in their stalls, and the distant seashore roar of the traffic beyond the walls.

Almost at the apex of the narrowing angle formed by the two rows of stables, a set of black iron fire-escape stairs led to a white door, behind which were the offices of the Civil Service Riding Club. They were a homely set of rooms, converted from a staff flat. There was seagrass matting on the floor, and when I pushed open the door of the main office, it seemed full of brisk women in jodhpurs and CSRC sweatshirts and ties, their emphatic buttocks comfortably propped against various bits of furniture, drinking tea out of mugs, eating digestive biscuits and talking at the tops of their voices. I hadn't encountered horsey women en masse before. Mrs Rogers, though evidently horsey, seemed rather too complex and formidable a character to fit quite tidily into the mould. A silence fell when I entered the room. The women in jodhpurs all looked at me for a moment over their teacups, then turned back to their chatting and biscuit-crunching.

There was one man in the room, leaning over a desk where a piece of paper lay pinned to a clipboard. He had short silvery-iron hair, a bristly moustache and a kindly eye which he turned on me as he straightened up from the desk. 'I'm Ernie,' he said. 'Who are you down to ride?' I didn't know, but there was my name, written on the piece of paper he had been looking at: a list of the people in the novice class and opposite them, the names of the horses that had been allotted to them: Horlicks, Bunker, Seamus, Montana, Sophie. Sophie's name was written against mine.

'She's already down at the school, someone's riding her in the lesson before ours. So is Bunker – I'm riding him. Come with me,' said Ernie, clattering off down the fire-escape in his black rubber boots. The school was all the way back past the stables and the carriages, under the narrow arch and the broad arch, then left down an alley that I hadn't noticed on the way in, between a high, blank wall on one side and a monumental, sharp-cornered square building in the same sand-coloured stone as the front quadrangle.

Through the glittering plate glass of its sash windows, crammed in their upper reaches with bunchy swags and loops of printed fabric, a mute domestic interior was visible, as self-consciously tidy as though arranged for a magazine shoot of someone's Lovely Home. A spindly throng of polished occasional tables and leggy plant stands bearing china *jardinières* planted with spider plants and gardenia mingled with a dwarf-ish crowd of overstuffed low benches, crouching on fat bow legs beneath a burden of glossy magazines. An affable scattering of sofas, their cushions undented by any sign of wilful sitting, was reflected in a brilliant overmantel glass framed in blobby scrolls of gilt. In one corner a large television set turned its blank, dead-fish gaze on the room.

'We're not supposed to look in there,' said Ernie. 'It's the Crown Equerry's residence.' Chastened, I cut my eyes away. Just past the residence the alley turned a sharp dogleg and came to a dead end: a high wall with a vast pair of arched double doors let into it, painted dark green. A small wicket gate was cut into the right-hand door. Ernie pushed it. It opened and we stepped through into the indoor school.

I had seen nothing quite like it before. It was a mid-eighteenth century building, an airy enclosure of emptiness with an almost shocking combination of space and formality. On one side, light came in through vast square plates of metal-framed glass. The ceiling arched over us in a flattened barrel curve, cream-painted. Flags of the Commonwealth hung from the roof. The whole school was panelled in brown-painted wood to the height of a horse's shoulder and a chest-height wood-panelled partition stood between us and the school. Where we stood the floor was covered in the same small, heavy square tiles as I had seen in the Mews stables. Within the school was a deep layer of sand, heavily trampled with hoofmarks. At intervals around the walls were painted black capital letters, A to M. Above our heads was an immense black clock-face with gold roman numerals and gilded hands. It was telling the right time. Next to it, poised on a cream-painted beam, stood a stuffed owl with brown tufted ears and a glassy yellow stare. Pigeons cooed outside the windows. There was a smell of cold stone and hot horse.

Classes, I gathered from the business-like sheaf of introductory information that had been sent to me on confirmation of my membership, alternated between jumping and flatwork. There were four possible grades: beginners, novice, intermediate and experienced. Riding and stable-management skills were both taken into account when grading a new rider. I had graded myself, rather optimistically, as a novice, on the grounds that I could ride turns and circles in walk, trot and (on a good day) canter, was sometimes able to recognize the correct canter lead (if not always to strike off on it), and was on my way to 'working up to a simple course of fences of 2ft–2ft 6in'. I noted that novice riders were allowed to hack out in Hyde Park. I also noted the list of stable-management targets for the beginners' grade. You had to be able to 'lead a horse, tie up a horse, pick out feet, tack and untack, care for tack when putting it down and returning it to the tack room, hang up a hay net, groom a horse in preparation for riding, rug up a horse, look after and out away a hot sweaty horse'.

With the exception of the bit of grooming (and tack cleaning, of which the list made no mention) that I'd done at

Rooting Street, I hadn't an earthly about any of these, especially not tacking up and untacking. And what might 'out away' be, when you were doing it to a hot, sweaty horse? A misprint, possibly? Still, la la la, how hard could they be to pick up? And my riding skills were surely well up to novice level. In any case, at the moment I was much more interested in the intermediate jumping class that was in progress.

There were just three people in it, jumping a dogleg of crossed poles and a single bar set at about 2ft 3in. What with the echoing acoustic, the damp stone smell and the austere grandeur of the building, the overwhelming impression was of showjumping in a cathedral. They seemed to be making quite heavy weather of it too, I thought. The jumps were titchier than stuff I'd done loads of times in Mrs Rogers's less exalted sand school, to the accompaniment of shrieks of 'Get your leg ON!' No one was shrieking in here, mind you. The cathedral atmosphere was intensified by a reverent silence, broken only by the thudding hooves and labouring breath of the horses, an occasional gasp from the girls riding them, and from time to time a low, soothing mutter from a youngish chap in pale breeches and green gumboots smoking a stubby small cigar in the centre of the school, who was evidently the instructor ('Russell,' whispered Ernie).

There were two horses in the class – big, leggy bays – and a bright pink pony, the luscious colour of home-made strawberry ice cream. He was a gelding – Sophie must be one of the big bays – and clearly a terrible handful: as naughty as a wayward toddler, jumping when he felt like it and when he didn't stopping short, veering sharply away from the poles and then cantering uncontrollably around the school while the other two-thirds of the class waited patiently for him to stop. The two bay horses were far more obedient. There was a gelding with a Roman nose and knobbly knees who made a sharp, air-expelling grunt as he cantered, like someone jumping repeatedly on a half-inflated football. That must be Bunker. Which meant that the other horse, a mare with a pretty head, carried high, a deep chest and an improbably long back, like a mahogany dining table with an extra leaf set into it, must be Sophie, who seemed kind, willing and exceptionally keen on jumping. A bit of luck, to start on her, I thought. 'She'll look after you,' whispered Ernie, thought-reading.

The atmosphere here seemed a lot easier on the nerves than the one at Rooting Street. There the lessons were like armed skirmishes between me and my incompetence, punctuated by grunts of effort and tears of frustration from me, and piercing cries of dismay and wrath from Mrs Rogers ('If you're going to cry, I'm going indoors NOW,' she used to bark). Here the lesson was conducted in a scholarly, almost reverent, near-silence. The wayward antics of Seamus, the naughty pony, and the idleness of Bunker ('ex-racehorse,' said Ernie) who was flopping contemptuously any old how over the low jumps drew no public reproaches from the instructor, just an inaudible murmur of advice to the riders. I imagined for a moment what Mrs Rogers would have said about them and felt a twinge of alarm even at 50 miles' distance.

Watching two of this class of three scrambling untidily over their jumps, I felt a sudden puffing sense of my own competence. I had no idea how I was getting on at Rooting Street. I'd tried asking Mrs Rogers whether I was progressing at an average rate, or better, or worse, and she'd simply ignored the question. Would I like half a dozen nice brown eggs from her Rhode Island hens? For some reason they had started laying again. That would be £1, then. See you next week. I was haunted continually by a hollow sense that what I did wasn't really good enough; always slightly short of her expectations; always disappointing. I thought it must make me unrewarding to teach and wondered why she bothered.

Years before, when I'd got the results of my ludicrous

mixed bag of 13 O-levels, all passes, mostly at mediocre grades, I carried the slip of paper into my parents' bedroom, where they were drinking early morning tea. 'Is that OK?' I said, as they looked at it. 'Not really,' said one of them, and they went on sipping their tea. Most weeks at Rooting Street I had the same sense of being an object of exasperation by not doing quite as well as I ought; not that I was ignominiously bad, just plodding dully about in the featureless plains of the lower average. Unlike my schoolteachers, most of whom it had been a positive pleasure to disappoint, Mrs Rogers had a quality that made you long to please her and a mysterious ability to make you feel that with just a little more effort you might actually manage it, if not today, then one day quite soon.

At the Rooting Street yard, I had had to get used to being described, to onlookers and the occasional sharer of my lessons, as 'a very novice lady', a turn of phrase that made me grind my teeth. Still, looking at these so-called intermediates galumphing ungracefully about the place, I thought I must have been doing all right, for a novice. 'I can do that,' I said vaingloriously to Ernie, who widened his eyes and chewed his moustache in a vigorous pantomime of being impressed.

It was the end of the lesson. The jumping girls formed up in a neat row along the centre line of the school and waited as the instructor spoke to each of them in turn. As he finished speaking each rider dismounted and stood at her horse's shoulder holding the reins, ready to hand on the baton to the next person. 'You go on,' said Ernie. 'I'll catch up with you in a minute.'

I trudged across the sand, sinking a little at every step, like walking through deep snow, to where Sophie stood. 'Hold on to her, and I'll get you a mounting block,' said her rider, jogging over to where Ernie and Russell were dismantling the jumps and returning with one of the plastic blocks on which the poles were propped. I lodged it in the sand, teetered on top of it for a moment, and then was sitting in the saddle, which felt strangely broad and loose beneath me, like someone else's too-big shoe. Hesitantly – was this the right thing to do? – I turned Sophie away and began to walk her on a long rein around the perimeter of the school.

Other people began to arrive with their horses. Soon a crocodile of us was ambling round the hoof-marked outer track: Ernie on the Roman-nosed Bunker (who must be ancient: there were great sunken hollows above his eye sockets); Seamus had swapped his intermediate rider for a tiny gnome of a woman in a blue handknitted jumper. The fight seemed to have gone out of him now the jumping was over. At any rate, he was walking around the school as placidly as a cow coming in for milking. Behind him were two horses which hadn't been in the jumping lesson. One was a wheat-coloured mare with a creamy mane and tail ridden by a slender, dark-haired girl in a neat quilted waistcoat. They were an arrestingly elegant pair, circling under the swaying flags. I wished my horror of looking too bandbox hadn't led me to turn up for this lesson in an elderly navy jumper sprinkled with horsehairs. The last to arrive was a solid, cheerful girl on a stocky piebald with one brown eye and one a terrible pale blue with a piercing horizontal black pupil, and a neck of solid muscle, arched like a Babylonian warhorse.

I was feeling my way on Sophie, settling into the slack armchair of a saddle; getting used to the distance from the ground – she must be 16 hands. I hadn't been this high up before; feeling the reins, and trying to remember the techniques recommended by the author of a book Mrs Rogers had encouraged me to read, called *Centred Riding*. The centred rider had, above all, a vivid imagination. She could think herself into a proper balance by imagining herself to be a doll weighted at the bottom, or visualizing her body as a set of building blocks poised one above the other.

For various other purposes, she imagined a spring pulling her centre forward to the sky, the tops of her legs as mobile flippers extending from the pelvis, her head as balancing like a billiard ball on the end of a cue, her lower legs as weights dangling from the end of a string, and the reins as little birds, one in each hand, which must on no account be squeezed too hard. Prone as I was to gripping the reins as though they were handrails at the edge of an abyss, the fate of those fragile little birds troubled me. The book was full of eloquent line-drawings of unhappy horses with knotted, ill-balanced, tense riders, all of whom I knew, even without having seen myself on horseback, looked exactly like me. 'For extra energy in lateral work, put a grand piano in your pelvis and play great rolling chords,' advised the book. I hadn't done much yet in the way of lateral work and the pelvic grand piano was defi-nitely beyond me at the moment, but I kept the book by my bed and read it at nights like a novel, to the extent of looking ahead sometimes, to see how it would end.

Building blocks, flippers, little birds, said I to myself, wrig-gling about in the saddle, trying to drop my heels, straighten (but not tense) my back and loosen my grip on the reins. Sophie politely ignored the squirming going on above and continued to walk quite smartly along at the head of the crocodile. In the centre of the school Russell dropped the stub of his cigar into the sand, crushed it out with his boot and spoke. 'You,' he said, 'on Sophie. What's your name?' I told him. The small woman on Seamus was Catherine, a regular, like Ernie. The other two, whose murmured names I didn't catch, were both newcomers. 'All right then, Sophie,' said Russell, 'do you want to be leading file?' Whatever leading file was, it sounded responsible and I didn't want to be it.

'No? Take the lead, then, Ernie,' said Russell. 'Whole ride, walk on. Leading file and in succession, pick up working trot, then circle left at the A end of the school.' I was still deciphering this when Bunker ahead of me shambled into a trot followed by Sophie, who evidently required no instructions from me. Round the school we went, to the left, to the right, in circles at one end and the other. Then we got ambitious and worked our way from the A end of the school all the way to the F end in a dizzying series of successive circles. We stitched our way in great trotting loops from letter to letter across the width of the school and ended with a series of attempts at something called leg yield, which turned out to mean getting the horse to move sideways on a diagonal and swiftly established a hierarchy of those whose inner grand pianos were at concert pitch (Catherine and the girl on the Palomino mare, whom someone had thought it a good idea to name Horlicks) and the rest of us.

There was a dreamy, hypnotic quality to this lesson which was the reverse of what I was used to. The vaulted formality of the school, its monumental plainness – a fusion of grandeur and utility – the unfamiliar argot of 'files' and 'dressing'; the flags waving above our heads, the ancient clock and its attendant stuffed owl made the place seem full of shadows: an insubstantial throng of other riders, other horses, long-dead now, who had trotted and cantered their exercises inside these panelled walls.

I found an unexpected comfort in being part of a herd. At Rooting Street, alone in my lessons, I was permanently in the position of the solitary antelope on whom the advancing lioness has fixed its eye. Nothing escaped the terrible scrutiny of Mrs Rogers. Probably nothing escaped the scrutiny of Russell, either. But there were five of us, all at subtly different levels of ability and with different problems, so the intense consciousness of being watched was nothing like as great. For the first time ever I found myself riding on autopilot, following the horse ahead as though driving a route so familiar that one draws up at a destination with no memory of having travelled to it.

Lulled into half-trance by the steady up-and-down of four other people rising to the trot in the same rhythm as my own, the flexing and extending of four other sets of legs, the muffled beats of five sets of hooves in the sand, the swooping serpentines and wheeling circles, round and round like the wooden horses with gilded manes and flaring scarlet nostrils on the funfair merry-go-round, I felt as though I'd become safely invisible, and was horribly flustered when Russell suddenly began picking us off, one by one, to circle away from the ride and canter around the school. Montana, the wall-eyed piebald, seized the opportunity to charge, ricocheting off the panelling while his rider squeaked unhappily and heaved on the reins, entirely without effect.

The hubris with which I had begun this lesson was definitely leaking away. I might be able to get over a jump or two, on a willing horse, but I didn't really know how to ask for a canter and get it, and I'd no idea how to strike off on the right leg, or even how to tell, once cantering, whether I was on the right leg or not. It was hard to be certain, because of my inexperience, but I had a feeling that my riding was turning out to be rather like my piano playing: showy at odd moments, but entirely without technique. Anyway, it was my turn now. As always, at moments of stress, the gentle visualizations of *Centred Riding* – the little birds, the flippers, the dangling weights – vanished. I could only concentrate on them when I hadn't got anything else to do. Present me with a problem and the wicked counter-intuitive Left Brain, so seductive, so much disapproved of by the properly Centred Rider, seized the controls at once.

'Off you go then, Sophie,' said Russell. Sit up, look up, tap tap tap on the girth. And off we went. A steady canter, a circle at the far end of the school, a downward transition to trot before rejoining the back of the ride. 'Good,' said Russell. 'Good,' I said to Sophie, and thought, nothing to do with me. She knew what she had to do, from watching the others, and like the sensible mare she was, she had done it. It was the first time I'd felt a horse looking after me.

The lesson ended. We stood in a row along the centre line, waiting for Russell to come and make his final remarks. 'You need to relax more,' he said to me. 'But that was quite a nice canter. Well done.' One side of the great double doors at the end of the school was pushed aside to let us lead the horses back to their stalls, but before we left the school we had to pick out their hooves and brush the sand off them, so that no trail of sandy hoof-prints should disfigure the immaculate surface of the Mews tarmac.

It was only mid-evening now – 9.30 or so – but I felt as though I'd been there all day. Something about the physical structure of the place, the orderly succession of one large geometrical space after another; the tidiness of everything, the idiosyncratic routines, made it feel very easy to learn. I was still looking at it with an outsider's eye, but already it felt familiar, with the complacent protectiveness of a well-organized institution. I walked to the gate with Ernie and Catherine. The light was fading crimson to violet overhead. The iron gate gave a sharp electronic trill and swung open to let us out.

'Good night, ladies,' said Ernie. 'See you next week.' The evening was lurid with yellow taxi lights and the red neon sign, in giant loopy freehand script, of the Rubens Hotel on the opposite side of the road. As I walked towards the Tube I thought people were looking at me strangely, which seemed odd in London where all kinds of extremity goes unremarked. Then I got it. The breeches, boots and whip that made me invisible within the mews were both conspicuous and inexplicable outside its gates. 'Where's your horse?' yelled a man from the opposite platform of the District Line and I realized that I must have the bereft, earthbound look of the unseated rider.

I shifted my whip out of sight and concentrated hard on my book, as though reading would restore my lost invisibility. But inside I was hugging to myself a voluptuous sense of excitement, like that of a new love affair. Right in the middle of London was this secret enclave, a little walled village populated by horses and surrounded by cars and I, along with a couple of hundred other people among all the masses that teemed daily along the pavements outside the mews, knew the combination that would unlock the gates and let me in.

Inside the Mews, the dress code of the Civil Service Riding Club was no more exigent than that of any other riding school. You had to dress safely, with proper boots and a crash hat, but that was all. Otherwise you could wear what you wanted. But if you wanted to ride beyond the gates, you had to follow the rules laid down by the Mews. What's more, the Seeing Finger, as practised by Mrs Rogers, seemed busily in operation here, too.

'Members have been seen leaving the Mews in polo shirts with ties, muckers and half-chaps,' read a reproving item in my first ever copy of the CSRC newsletter, *Mews News*. 'The correct dress is: A correctly fitted riding hat in black or navy. A white shirt and tie or stock. A hacking jacket (a dark show jacket is also acceptable). Long boots or jodhpur boots in black or dark brown (half-chaps may not be worn). Beige or plain colour jodhpurs or breeches.' On summer evenings, classes were held in the manège at Hyde Park. You could volunteer to ride a horse back and forth on the rota between the Mews and the Park, but only if you had the proper kit. It was time I got myself a hacking jacket.

Buying a hacking jacket and a pair of long boots felt like an important moment. It was the end of the ironical, I'm-not-really-doing-this approach to my riding with which I'd been keeping myself at a safe distance from minding too much about doing it badly. You couldn't be ironical and ride about in a hacking jacket. It was an unambiguous statement of something-or-another, if only a basic competence. Having made it, you had to live up to it.

I found that I minded very much what my jacket was to look like. The uniform for riding out of the Mews was precisely the garb, unattractively known as 'ratcatcher', that everyone wore for Autumn hunting, and novices like me continued to wear throughout the season. This hacking jacket would be my first hunting coat. It felt like a rite of passage – much more interesting than that other sartorial highlight, my first bra, the purchase of which had involved an exquisitely humiliating expedition to Hulbards of Sittingbourne's lingerie department, where my mother, the saleswoman and I all somehow silently contrived to ignore the fact that, aged 15, I had a chest as flat as a five-year-old's.

I didn't know where you began looking for a perfect hacking jacket. Hovering in my mind was an unformed idea of what I wanted. The details were vague, like the shadowy vision of the perfect boyfriend that prowls the periphery of the mind when you are unsatisfactorily attached to an imperfect one. On the whole, I thought the right one would probably appear in its own time. And it did.

I was trolling down Bond Street in my lunch-hour, idly window-shopping during a walk to flex the library stiffness from my shoulders, when I took an unaccustomed turning on the way back to the reading-room. And there was the jacket, all alone in the window of a little shop sandwiched between an Oriental art gallery and a place selling designer furniture. It was buttoned around a headless dressmaker's dummy and dominated the space as arrogantly as the Chanel and Versace jackets in the glittery vitrines a hundred yards away on the main Bond Street drag.

It was made of tweed; not hairy, but finely woven and dense-looking, as though it would be very warm. Its colour was indescribable: a greenish, brownish, lichenous sludge whose surface was misted with deep sea-blue and an ochreish yellow. If you wore it to play hide-and-seek in the forest, no one would ever find you. It was at once very striking and almost invisible: the colour of ancient woodland. It looked pinch-waisted on the dressmaker's dummy, with an elegant curve from the waist into a slight fullness over the hips. It had two flapped pockets, set on at an angle and a couple of dandyish details: a lining of primrose silk and bronze buttons stamped with a tiny beribboned hunting horn. It was my coat: so beautiful that I'd have wanted it even if I'd never sat on a horse.

Inside, the little shop was an interesting mixture of richness and plainness. The walls were lined with glass-fronted wooden display cabinets, thickly stuffed with stout woollen garments: rows of stiff black and navy jackets with full skirts and checked linings; waistcoats in matching check with little brass buttons down the front, a showy clutch of red hunt coats; in the body of the shop were heaps of saddles on saddle-horses, swags of reins, another glass-topped display case with bits, bootjacks and spurs artistically arranged inside; a bucket full of whips in plaited leather; sheepskin numnahs and at the back of the shop, quantities of shiny black and mahogany-topped boots, arranged with military neatness. Something about the place – the shiny wooden cabinets and drawers, and the profusion of goods heaped up in orderly chaos – reminded me of the cosy pictures of the shop in Beatrix Potter's *Tale of Ginger and Pickles*.

Behind the imposing brass and wooden counter two ladies were standing. They seemed delighted to see me. I wondered if they got much passing trade. You might have thought not, but the shop had the sleek, prosperous look of a place whose stock is moving along at a brisk rate. There was none of the Miss Havisham air of certain places in Jermyn Street and the Burlington Arcade, where nothing ever seemed to change in the window displays and you felt certain that if you actually went in and touched anything, crowds of indignant mice and spiders would scurry out, furious at having their comfortable lodgings disturbed.

I explained what I wanted. The saleswomen opened cabinets, sorted through rails of breeches in a spectrum of beige from milk through putty and old ivory to fawn, slid out wooden drawers filled with sugary heaps of folded white shirts, climbed up little wooden stepladders to reach the racks of boots, showed me to an upstairs corner of the shop, drew a curtain in front of me, and hovered on the other side, calling encouragement.

They were quite a struggle to get into, these clothes; or at any rate the lower half of them was. An alarming amount of tugging and wriggling was involved. Halfway into the breeches I took fright and said I thought they were too small, even though they were a size larger than I usually took. Keep going, urged the voices from beyond the curtain. They're not supposed to be loose. I grappled on. After a bit, the breeches succumbed and did up quite docilely around my waist, though they maintained a ferocious grip on both legs.

The boots were worse. Halfway up my calf, the first one stuck. I hauled on the boot-hooks so hard, I was afraid the tape loops stitched to the lining might give way. Images of tightness jangled in my brain: Winnie the Pooh stuck fast in Rabbit's front door; Molly Keane's hunting heroines sprinkling face powder inside their boots to ease the passage of their calves. If any of my ordinary clothes had put up this much of a fight, I should have given up forcing them long before, for fear the seams would crack. Wriggling my ankle, I gave one more pull on the boot-hooks and the left boot suddenly slid on. Panting a little, but feeling that I'd got the upper hand, I got into the right one and stood up.

Between them, the breeches and the boots were like a sartorial metaphor for getting a grip. Much later, I met a man who said that his hunting nerves only began to settle once he'd got his boots on. I grew to love my own boots dearly, but they never quite had the power to cure my nerves on their own. I always had to be up on my horse with everything in place – boots, waistcoat and coat securely buttoned, hairnet, gloves, whip, hat, riding money and roll of peppermints – before I ever felt at all convinced that I was really going hunting.

Still, there was definitely something about these breeches and boots that made it clear that they were unlike other clothes. The sensation of them didn't disappear from the skin as soon as you got them on, like everyday garments. Reaching for the jacket that hung by the mirror, I felt a hyperaesthetic awareness of the clutch of stout cotton-Lycra twill around my thighs, the ovals of moleskin strapping on the inside knees; the bracing tubes of leather around my calves, which gave way to a strange, hollow looseness around the ankle and toes, where the boots were cut to allow room for the joints to flex. I put the jacket on and looked in the mirror.

I was unaccustomed to the transforming effects of a uniform worn without irony and my reflection gave me a shock. It looked sleek and competent; somehow rather grand and aloof. Not like me at all, in fact. Or rather, like an idealized version of me, with all the faults of proportion neatly corrected by good tailoring, or simply obscured by the magnificence of cream stretch twill, cotton voile, shiny black leather and fine tweed. An enticing vision of myself riding out of the Mews in this get-up (on one of the prettier horses, to be sure: Sophie or Horlicks, not the pink pony or the wall-eyed piebald cob) came to mind. Flat-footed in the heavy-soled boots (there was a horseshoe of silver nails around the curve of each heel), I stumped out from behind the curtain and twirled about while the saleswomen twitched at the jacket and made me stretch out my arms to be sure it wouldn't be too tight across the back if I found myself on a pulling horse.

Then we all stood and admired the effect for a reverent moment, before I went back behind the curtain to change into my ordinary clothes, already rehearsing the adroit evasions with which I would justify spending more than a month's mortgage on clothes in which to pursue a hobby. Cost per wear is a crucial element in the construction of such evasions. All this kit (I told myself) would last for ever. By the time I'd hunted a couple of seasons and ridden out from the Mews a dozen times, the cost per wear would be down to pennies. Reasoning thus, I added a nice little whip in black plaited leather to the heap in my arms and stepped out briskly towards the till.

Saturday 9 March – Owley Farm, Wittersham

It is the second half of my first season. I have been hunting perhaps a dozen times altogether. Not so many that I've stopped throwing up convulsively beforehand, but enough for the panicky sense of chaos and dread by which my first meets were marked – What's going on? Will I get lost, run away with, or left behind? What if I stop at a jump that everyone else goes over? – to have begun to reveal the blurred outlines of a pattern. We meet, we move off towards the first covert, where we check, chat and eventually move on. The pace, which at first appeared so terrifyingly fast over unknown country, now seems quite steady and comfortable, partly because I have grown used to it, but it also helps that I have at length mastered a hunting canter, which I could never get the hang of during lessons in the school – rising from the horse's back as though at the trot, but in the canter's three-time beat, rather than the up-and-down two-time of the trot.

It is a fine day. Bird's-egg sky, muted late winter colours in a spectrum of different shades of brown: earth and briar, dead leaf, twig and stone. It has rained in the night, so the branches and pine needles are beaded with drops, shooting rainbow points of light where the pale sun catches them and scattering as the horses brush by. The ground feels soft, almost luscious, underfoot. The mare is going effortlessly. We have cleared a couple of little jumps in the woods and now she is brisk but not pulling, ears pricked forward, happy to be out at the start of a day's hunting, which is what she likes doing best. A thread of vitality seems to rise from the springy earth, up through the mare's muscles and into mine. I feel wonderful, filled with energy, capable of anything as we canter along the margin of a meadow where a line of old chestnut and oak trees marks the boundary, their twigs tipped with buds that are fat and almost ready to burst into leaf.

'Headlands, please,' warns Mrs Rogers, meaning, stick to the field margin, don't stray onto the pasture. I tuck myself more closely into the edge and as we near the corner, where the woods thicken, I feel a resistance: just a tug to begin with, then a sharp pull that makes me think I'm about to fall. I grab for the mare's breastplate and as I look down, I see my three bronze buttons with their little hunting horns fly off the front of my jacket and vanish into the turf at the mare's hooves. She is moving blithely on, but I'm still held back by something – the sharp end of an old broken branch, I think it is. 'Molly, Molly, stop!' I squeak, but there are people coming up fast behind us. I wrench free and we are cantering on again.

At the corner we stop. The huntsman is inside the covert,

at whose margins hounds momentarily appear, heads down, trotting busily, snuffling the ground, before plunging again into the thorny, crackling dark. My jacket is flapping open over my shirt. I feel unaccountably naked, though I am wearing two thermal vests, a cashmere camisole and a fleece sweatshirt underneath my shirt. 'I've lost my buttons,' I say. But then I look down again and see it is worse than that. The branch has become somehow lodged in the corner of my pocket, and in pulling free, I have torn two long slashes in the fabric of the jacket, one vertical and one horizontal, so that the whole pocket is laid open in a great triangular wound against my flank, the tweed and primrose silk ripped and shredded to show the white interlining, like bone gleaming through gashed flesh.

'You are in a state,' says somebody, and people start to gather round and peer interestedly, offering advice, as though at the scene of some horrible accident. 'Perhaps I can pin it,' I say, taking the stock pin out of my tie, and trying to draw together the edges of my jacket. But when I run the point of the pin into the tweed, the soft gold snaps and the pin falls into two useless pieces. For a moment, I have the ominous sensation that anything I touch will lose its shape and crumble away to nothingness. Then, 'Baler twine,' says Boyd. 'You can tie it up with baler twine. It'll be safer than leaving it to flap about.' We are standing in a group by a metal gate around which orange twine is knotted in several places. Boyd dismounts, unpicks a strand of twine, passes it to me and gets back on his horse while I loop it around my waist and tie the ends together where my middle button used to be.

The transformation is remarkable. The insistent glamour of this jacket, which even Mrs Rogers described as 'very tidy' (a term of high praise) when she first saw it, has completely vanished, leaving something maimed and squalid in its place. I look like one of the loosely tied bundles of dirty sheets that my mother used to leave on the doorstep for the laundry van to collect. One of the older, yellow-collared hunting ladies, rather distant until now, comes over to commiserate. She has lost her buttons over a jump, and like me is ignominiously parcelled up with orange twine about her middle. They were old-style hunt buttons, she says, and she is mourning them as I am my bronze hunting horns with their flourishing knots of ribbon. We hunt on, feeling diminished.

Back in London the following day, I laid the jacket out on the floor and, patching as I went with snippets of silk and tweed from the sewing box, I tried to stitch the different layers of ripped cloth back into place, drawing the torn edges together as painstakingly as a surgeon suturing wounded sheets of muscle. The result was better than I had feared. Inside, where the fragile pale yellow silk pulled away from the mends in threadbare puffs of floss, the seams lay puckered and imperfect. On the outside, though, all that was visible were two neat, flat scars.

There was no time to replace the bronze buttons before the next meet, and nothing in the button boxes of John Lewis's haberdashery department with anything like their fantastical charm. The choice was between the sort of leather knot button generally seen hanging by a thread from the aged tweed jackets of decrepit old dons, or vaguely Bavarian slices of rough-edged deer horn. Reluctantly, I took the deer horn, thinking that I'd go back to the shop off Bond Street when the season was over, and ask if they could find me another set of bronze buttons.

But the next time I went, the soothing brace of motherly saleswomen had gone, replaced by a stout, bustling person to whom, for some reason, I felt unable to explain my pressing need for bronze-coloured buttons with beribboned hunting horns. There was nothing really wrong with the jacket. It was still perfectly wearable; its scars were honourable, and in any case, hardly visible unless you knew they were there. Nevertheless, something was gone that could not be mended. The flicker of muted elegance that caught my eye in the shop window had fallen away with the tumbling buttons and now lay lost with them in the springy winter grass, leaving just an ordinary greenish tweed jacket behind.

It was high summer when I first wore the jacket. Hardly the weather for tweed, but I didn't care, as I strode with elaborate unselfconsciousness up the alley beside Knightsbridge barracks towards the Hyde Park manège, striking flat, metallic chimes from the hot pavement with the crescent moons of nails in my boot heels. The manège was just behind the barracks – a large sandy oval with a low fence of wooden palings. Some sly quirk of landscape design semiotics had sited it just next to the children's playground, and the scene as I arrived was of a busy urban *fête champêtre*.

As far as you could see, grass and trees, still in the fresh green leaf of high summer, not yet parched to rusty August tinder, stretched away to the distance, where the silvery high-rise of Park Lane and the Bayswater Road formed a jagged, ethereal boundary, like a wall of glaciers. A little way off, a football match was in progress. A bit further on was a mass picnic – blankets, beer and coke bottles, open packets of biscuits, plastic tubs of dip and salad, leggy youths and girls leaping for a frisbee. In the playground, scrambling children in bright clothes swarmed and swung on complicated geo-metrical structures of log, rope and painted metal tubing, while their mothers sat watching around the perimeter wall, dark-robed dowagers with sharp black or gold beaks scrutiniz-ing an excitable debutante dance. The noise, a high-pitched, cicada shrilling, was astonishing.

Some of the children had migrated towards the horses. Several hung longingly over the fence, and one father had swung his toddler up to perch on top of it, her short legs in lacy ankle socks and white sandals dangling from a bunchy frill of pink skirts into the arena. 'Don't do that, it's very dangerous,' called one of the riders reprovingly. The father nodded and smiled courteously, misunderstanding or ignoring her bossy tone, while his little girl waved shyly, then lowered her eyelashes.

There was something about having a lesson in front of an audience of interested children that made it feel as though we were taking part in a slow, very dull circus act. It was flatwork again this evening, and as we trotted our dutiful circles to the right and left (amazing how much worse I was at riding from right to left than from left to right) and made our turns down the centre line, I wished we had something a bit showier in our repertoire with which to astonish them.

But the evening was drawing on in any case; the light fading from gold to mauve, a coolness dropping through the air. The shadows we cast across the school lengthened until we resembled a class of attenuated Don Quixotes astride spindly Rosinantes. The frisbee players gathered up their blankets and bottles and vanished; the footballers packed it in and set off for the pub; the black-robed mothers sailed towards home, trailing children like moorhens with a string of chicks. The playground fell silent. It was time for us to go home too. We formed up into two files, confident riders on the outside, nervous ones on the inside, strapped red lights to our outside legs and reflective yellow Sam Browne belts over our hacking jackets, and set off at a stately pace down the Carriage Drive towards Apsley House.

I hadn't done any riding on main roads before, which was probably a good thing. It meant that, too ignorant to be scared, I didn't dwell on all the things that might go wrong when you tried to take a crocodile of a dozen horses with mostly novice riders around Hyde Park Corner, up Constitution Hill, past the front of Buckingham Palace and back down Birdcage Walk and Buckingham Gate to the Mews. With a placid lack of imagination, I failed to feel anxious about traffic lights, tricky junctions with three lanes of impatient motorists revving for the off, or chance encounters between nervous horses and enthusiastic tourists with flash cameras.

Thinking back on that journey now, I am not sure that I'd fancy it doing it again, even riding one of the resolutely urban Mews horses, who lived among traffic and took no more notice of it than the Rooting Street horses did of hounds. Then, however, serenely unaware of danger, it struck me as pure excitement. These were the bits of London where I never went: the exclusive preserve of tourists and traffic, to be avoided with scorn by the people for whom London was a habitat, rather than a theme park. But here we were in our long boots and hacking jackets, momentarily reclaiming the great formal boulevards at the city's heart for horse traffic and in the process, seeing the world from the generous, exhilarating angle that is the height of a human sitting on a horse.

Once, in the days when everyone rode, that little shock of elevation was a commonplace of human experience, and so were the other small enrichments of horse travel, from being out in the weather, whatever it might be, to the slightly base satisfaction of being able to see over people's walls into their gardens. The effect is the exact opposite of travelling in a car, where you are screened from the sun, the wind and the rain and couched in your seat as though sitting on a sofa. Your line of vision lowered to human waist height and bounded by the rectangular frame of the windscreen, you look out on the world as disconnectedly as though watching it on the telly.

Actually, there was a certain stagey glamour about the progress of our little cavalcade back to the Mews. For a start, the timing of the lights at Hyde Park meant that the traffic there never quite came to a halt in every direction, so the leading rider had to hold back a stream of snorting vehicles as the red lights changed to green, in order to give the rest of us time to scurry across to the comparative safety of Constitution Hill, where the visitors drifting back through the park to their hotels smiled and waved and let off an electric storm of flashes from their dinky little cameras. Kicking on (but not too vigorously – on no account must there be cantering on the tarmac) past her lonely figure as, with a single imperious gesture of her upraised hand, she interrupted the homeward journeys and dinner appointments and hot dates of goodness knew how many impatient people in shiny, low-slung BMWs and taxicabs and thunderous red London buses, I felt a sudden spark of gratitude for the self-assured horsey bossiness that had seemed so insufferable when directed at a small girl in a frilly pink frock.

It was almost dusk. Over Buckingham Palace the sky was streaked and fish-scaled in crimson and fiery orange; pink candyfloss clouds floated showily against a darkening blue sky in which the first stars were beginning to glitter. It was an outrageous colour scheme and by the time we reached Birdcage Walk it was gone. We trotted past the barracks, shrouded in gloom like the five and twenty smugglers' ponies, trotting through the dark, in the Rudyard Kipling poem that my son liked me to read to him before he went to sleep at night.

Back at the Mews, the police from the lodge threw open the big gates. Another imperious gesture, and the column of horses turned right across the flow of traffic and was swallowed up in the darkness beyond the first arch. The gates closed on us with a snap, like the mountain doorway shutting behind the beguiled children of Hamelin. Only the sound of horseshoes ringing on asphalt to show that we had ever been there.

131

I got home from the Mews to find an invitation among the post on the doormat. The Joint Masters of the Ashford Valley Foxhounds requested the pleasure of my company at the Puppy Show at the Kennels, Hothfield, on Sunday July 30, 2000 at 3 p. m. The judges would be Captain R. E. Wallace MFH and Miss S. L. Whitehead.

'What do I wear?' I asked Mrs Rogers, who was trying to improve my jumping skills by lending me her beautiful old hunter, Sam. 'A hat,' said Mrs Rogers. 'And a dress,' she added firmly, envisaging perhaps some fanciful London combination of hat plus low-slung combats which would frighten hounds and appal the judges and her Joint Masters. A hat, I repeated, aiming Sam at a triangular cul-de-sac made of brightly coloured giant plastic building blocks at which he stopped quite gently, with a sort of tolerant contempt.

The puppy show day was a creamy, high summer scorcher, with a faint tinge of bruise-mauve to one edge of the sky and a bronze glint to the sunshine. In London, 3 p. m. would have meant 3.40 for 4 p. m. In Ashford Valley-speak I guessed it probably meant 2.30 sharp. I was right. I arrived at the kennels a fraction after half-past two, to find the field beyond the tea tent banked deep with rows of parked cars and people already installed with a comfortable, territorial air on the orange plastic chairs ranged in rows on a couple of low-loaders parked at right angles on two sides of a fenced square of grass with a small flagged area at its centre. The third side of the square opened onto a barn in which bales of straw had been piled to make a steeply raked bank of seating. In the fourth was a gate opening onto a narrow alley of whitewashed brick secured with high metal railings, on the other side of which was the kennels. An ingenious system of interconnecting gates, like a rustic version of the airlocks in *Star Wars* space stations, kept the dog hounds from the bitches.

Standing in the alley between the showing square and the

kennels I could see Mrs Rogers as I had never seen her before, in a full-skirted dress of bright yellow with a pattern of large blue flowers, a straw hat and lipstick. She was talking energetically to two men dressed, with heroic disregard for the weather, in grey suits and black bowler hats. One was tall and urbane with a proprietorial air, as though he were in charge of proceedings, the other shorter, stouter and older, with a firmly buttoned waistcoat and beetroot jowls. The heat was tremendous. I had dressed, after considerable thought, as though for a summer wedding in a white piqué shift and high heels. Fanning myself with my programme, I wondered what the conditions were like inside a grey flannel suit and a black bowler hat.

It looked shady in the barn and the straw bales, though prickly, would certainly be less clammy to sit on than an orange plastic chair. Still I hesitated, wondering if that was an enclosure for the elect of the Ashford Valley. There seemed to be no one here from the yard other than Mrs Rogers; no one I knew at all, apart from her. Knots of people stood about on the rough grass chatting: elderly ladies with symmetrical rows of grey curls like the Queen's; a girl in a tight dress of sea-green Chinese silk and a mass of pale red-gold hair; a mother with a fretful toddler demanding ice cream and a drink.

The knots began to break up and move towards the trailers and the barn. I was climbing onto a trailer behind the restive toddler and his mother when I suddenly saw someone I recognized; a face from a vanished world of 20 years before: the girl from whom, as an undergraduate, I'd inherited my room in college. MGA1, the room was called – the first of a honeycomb series of cells in a rebarbative 1930s accommodation block named after some defunct benefactor of St Hugh's called Mary Grey Allen. Men's college rooms, when I was at Oxford, had charm but no sanitation (generally the quickest route to the distant lav involved climbing out of the window and edging along the guttering to the staircase on the other side of the quadrangle that harboured a freezing privy). Women's rooms had neither. MGA1 was a forbidding rectangular box of dark wood, dingy white Artex, toffee-coloured linoleum reeking aseptically of floorpolish, and a central patch of worn crimson carpet.

My predecessor in this angular cross between an office and a nunnery had contrived to lend it a certain boudoir allure by hanging her evening dresses (of which she had a great many, because she was something important at the Oxford Union, where the undergraduate officers wore elaborate evening dress as a mark of their authority) from the picture rail, so the grimy Artex was obscured by trailing breadths of Annabelinda velvet and crêpe de Chine with contrast satin bindings to the bodice and sleeves. I lacked both her wardrobe and her sense of style, and made do with blu-tacked posters of Millais's waterlogged Ophelia and various wispy Burne-Jones maidens from the Athena shop on the High Street.

'Alicia?' I said, reversing down the trailer steps into a crowd of flowered hats and Tattersall-check shirts. 'Do you remember me?' She seemed not to have changed at all since I had last seen her, but she had been in the year above me, reading a different subject and we had been acquaintances, rather than friends. 'Of course,' said Alicia, tidy in a navy sailor suit with a faint sheen, flashing the affable, slightly guarded smile that you bestow on people you once knew vaguely, on meeting them again after an interval of decades. She introduced me to her daughters; I mentioned my son. Who had I married? No one, actually. Ah. We delivered self-effacing thumbnail sketches of our respective professional activities. There was a tiny pause. And do you hunt with the Ashford Valley? I asked. At university, Alicia had not, as far as I knew, been part of the closed coterie of beagling and point-to-pointing girls with straight mouse hair, high complexions, green quilted jackets, penetrating voices and nursery nicknames. Then again, nor had I.

'No, no,' said Alicia, laughing a little uncomfortably, as though the idea of her hunting was quite out of the question. 'Damian is the local MP.' She glanced towards the barn and there was her husband, the former President of the Union, a tall, mild-looking man with a navy blazer and an indoors complexion, stooping with an expression of unwavering interest towards the shorter, monumental figure of Captain Wallace in his sweltering flannels and bowler. Behind them, a throng of hounds stood on their hind legs, the ones at the back clambering over the front ones, whose paws and noses were pressed beseechingly as far as they could reach through the kennels bars.

'We'd better go,' said Alicia. 'I think it's beginning. See you at tea.' She and her girls made for the barn. I teetered crabwise back up the trailer steps in my high heels and inconveniently tight skirt, and perched on a hot, hard chair next to the small child, who was still mournfully calling for refreshments.

Captain Wallace had taken up a position in the corner of the showing square, where he was joined by a lady in a hat. They looked very still and intent. It was summer fête weather, and in the adjoining field I could see steam rising from the tea tent, but this part of the afternoon was evidently a serious business. The programme, now I came to look at it, signalled as much. For a single sheet of A4 paper, it contained an astonishing amount of information. On one side was a list of entered hounds (hounds, that is, who had hunted for a season or more); 33 couple in all, classified chronologically, alphabetically and by sex, names set left for dog hounds and right for bitches. Stallion hounds were marked with an asterisk, brood bitches with a superscript B, and to each hound was attached a lineage: the hunt it came from, if it hadn't been bred at Kennels, and details of its sire and dam.

Crimson, a brood bitch, one of three hounds surviving from 1994, the oldest in the pack, was the daughter of Duke of Beaufort Rambler '90 and East Sussex and Romney Marsh Crumpet '87. One of her two contemporaries was also Rambler – Roffe-Silvester's Rambler, son of Exmoor Escort '90 and Exmoor Rainfall '90. The names were extraordinary: an anarchic mixture of concrete and abstract whose cumulative effect was both comic and haunting: Patience, Pastry, Packet, Pardon; Maybe and Madam; Hostile and Naughty; Playful, Doubtful, Crafty and Crocus; Carefree, Callow, Careless and Caution.

'It is indeed of little consequence what huntsmen call their hounds,' wrote Peter Beckford, the great eighteenth-century authority on fox-hunting, who then proceeded to confound his own statement by writing pages on the subject. His *Thoughts Upon Hunting* contains his views on what not to call your hounds (Tippler or Tapster – too vulgar; Titus or Trajan – too fancy); and on the misnaming of hounds ('However extraordinary you may think it, I can assure you that I have myself seen a white Gypsey, a grey Ruby, a dark Snowball and a Blueman, of any colour but blue').

On names without meaning he turns philosophical ('The huntsman of a friend of mine being asked the name of a young hound said "it was Lyman." "Lyman!" said his master, "why, James, what does Lyman mean?" "Lord, Sir!" replied James, "what does any thing mean?"'). And on the habit of naming hounds Madam he makes a little eighteenth-century joke: 'Madam, a usual name among hounds, is often, I believe, very disrespectfully treated: I had an instance of it the other day in my own huntsman, who, after having rated Madam a great deal to no purpose . . . flew into a violent passion, and hallooed out as loud as he could, "Madam, you d★★★★d bitch!"'

The Ashford Valley's pack contained a Madam, I noticed. A couple of weeks later, out on hound exercise with Mrs Rogers, I was pleased to find Beckford's creaky jest still thriving, some 200 years after he recorded it (and I bet it was ancient, even then), its teeth slightly sharpened by the fact that Madam is also what you call a lady Master of Foxhounds.

Anyway, having said that what you call your hound is of little consequence, Beckford proceeds to give a list of 825 possible names, from Able to Wreakful, via Crusty, Grumbler, Saucebox, Strumpet and Volatile, noting that 'it is usual to name all the whelps of one litter with the same letter which (to be systematically done)' – Beckford loved a system – 'should also be the initial letter of the dog that got them, or the bitch that bred them.'

Beckford's system was evidently followed by whoever did the naming of the Ashford Valley hounds. The forbidding duo of 1999 dog hounds, Landlord and Lawyer, and their enchanting quintet of sisters, Laughter, Lavish, Lattice, Lavender and Ladybird, were the progeny of Exmoor Marvel '96 and the homebred Lottery '97.

In the wealth of genealogical information provided by the programme, there was evidence of a thrifty recycling of names across the generations, rather in the manner of the Victorian Hinges and Shillings in the back of my family bible, who went on doggedly naming their sickly children William, Florence or Louisa until one of the batch eventually survived beyond infancy. In the hounds' case, it was Mistletoe '91, dam of Exmoor Marvel '96, who had passed her name on to her granddaughter: a new Mistletoe, sired by Marvel in 1999 out of Crinkle '97, was one of this year's young entry, along with her sisters Midnight, Mischief, Milkmaid and Miracle and her brothers Minstrel and Miller.

On the other side of the programme sheet was a shorter list of names: the young entry on show today: 11 and a half couple, with their names and their dates of birth (there were four litters, one born in March, the others in April 1999), their parents' names and those of their walkers (the same names – Palmer, Thomson, Ridley, Sillars – repeated in batches of two and three puppies each). These were people who had taken hounds from kennels as 12-week-old puppies, kept them for half a year or so, taught them to answer to their names and walk on a leash, given them an idea of what they might and might not hunt, and had now returned them to kennels to see them judged before they began their working lives by the formidable Captain Wallace, whose reputation as an MFH and houndsman was so richly encrusted with myth that I had heard of him before I ever had anything to do with the Ashford Valley.

They brought the dog hounds in first: a delicate manoeuvre involving four men in white dustcoats and black bowler hats. Inside the square were the huntsman, Neil Staines, his elder son, Joe, a handsome boy in his early 20s with his father's flashing vulpine smile, and a lean, spare man with pale blue eyes set in the slightly wizened face that some types of men acquire who spend their lives around horses: you see it on jockeys, less often on owners. Harry Buckland had it. Chester Beatty didn't. This turned out to be Rick Thomson, a whipper-in and puppy walker to Minstrel, Miller and Milkmaid.

In the alley just outside the square, operating the airlock system that separated the hounds that were needed for showing from the rest of the pack, was Neil Staines's younger son, William: a solid, shortish youth with red cheeks and spikey black hair whose white coat was a trifle too large for him, fluttering about his fingertips and ankles, making him look like a small, stout medical student. He swung open the gate and in rushed Drummer, Drayman, Dragon, Glancer, Glazier, Glider, Damper, Danger, Dapper, Minstrel and Miller, who surged about the square with the anarchic Brownian motion of small boys playing bombers in the playground, leaping like dolphins at the sides of the fence from pure high spirits and swirling around Neil's knees as though imitating the tigers in the children's story who chase each other in circles around a tree until they turn to melted butter.

From time to time Neil called to a hound by name, tossing crumbs of biscuit to make it stand on the small flagged square in the centre of the enclosure, holding its head and stern high to show it to best advantage. Captain Wallace and Miss Whitehead gazed from all angles, conferred inaudibly, scratched black marks on bits of paper clamped in the jaws of their clipboards, then spoke. One after another, the rejected hounds were sent out of the ring. Some of them went willingly enough; others resisted and had to be chased by Joe and Rick, picked up and bundled ignominiously out of the gate in William's arms, their paws and sterns pathetically tucked up beneath them. At length only five were left, posing in turn on the flags, heads cocked and eyes melting like supermodels vamping the cameras.

Mutter, mutter, scratch, scratch, went the judges. What on earth were they looking for? I could scarcely tell one hound from another, never mind which was a good hound and which was not. In the end, Danger, Damper and Dapper were first, second and third. I conscientiously wrote down their names in the little boxes provided for the purpose on the programme, feeling – just as I always did on the rare occasions when I went to the ballet in London with my friend Sarah, who liked that sort of thing – a baffled frustration at finding myself a spectator at a ritual of palpable finesse and subtlety, every nuance of which – beyond the fact that I could tell something very clever and complicated was going on – was utterly lost on me.

When the bitch hounds came in – smaller, finer, prettier than the dogs – I had had enough of being a passive spectator.

At least, I thought, I could test my own ignorant eye against the judges' omniscience. While Dreamer, Drama, Glitter, Glamour, Glimmer, Dazzle, Daring, Midnight, Mischief, Milkmaid, Mistletoe and Miracle loped and curvetted gracefully around the square, I made my own shortlist. I was tempted to pick Drama, because she was easy to recognize, marked with a *Phantom of the Opera*-style dark half-mask across one side of her face (I suspected that hounds probably didn't have faces, in the same way that they didn't have tails, but no one had told me the technical term for the front end). Eventually I decided that ease of recognition was an insufficient reason for putting her on the shortlist and chose instead her sister, Dreamer, because she seemed endearingly vague, and an elegant pair of sisters from a different litter, Milkmaid and Mistletoe, with creamy coats and liquorice-drop eyes.

Milkmaid was the first to be discarded by the judges, swiftly followed by Dreamer. But Mistletoe and Drama made the cut – respectively first and third with another of Mistletoe's sisters, Mischief, in second place. I was still none the wiser – why was Milkmaid the worst and Mistletoe the best when they looked more or less identical? I had to wait a year for an answer, but when Captain Wallace returned to judge the class of 2001, he remarked at the end of the show that Milkmaid, discarded from the previous year's class for being timid and lacking confidence, had proved after a season's hunting to be one of the best of her year's entry.

Crikey, it was hot. By the time the stately business of judging the couples class began its unhurried progress I had started to fidget almost as badly as the poor thirsty child sitting next to me. 'Oh, when is the drinking going to start?' he demanded of his mother. Like him, I could hear the siren call of the tea urns. Looking at my programme, I see that I didn't even write down the winners of that class, so insistently was my mind running on cucumber sandwiches and fairy cakes.

At last they finished and we were free to get down. The mass standing up was accompanied by a volley of knee joints crackling like dry kindling as we shuffled stiffly towards the edge of the trailer.

The tea tent was magnificent: as familiar and comforting as the judging had been mysterious. Actually, there were two of them, pitched in the corner of a field: not smart, pale wedding marquees with pretend glazed windows, but khaki dinosaurs with sharp ridges that looked as though they had probably seen service in the Second World War, or at the very least were veterans of many decades of vigorous scout camps. Lashed to the ground with stakes and great loops of rope, as though on the slightest pretext they might try to give us the slip and drift away across the fields of ripening corn, they were covered all over like elderly rhinoceroses with excrescences – scars and patches of material in a different shade of khaki, and mysterious vents and flaps, each held open with its own special little rope and peg.

One was filled with empty plastic chairs and small square picnic tables, covered with skittish paper tablecloths anchored with clothespegs. There was a vivid green smell of crushed grass, hot canvas and, faintly, of mildew: the scent of childhood outings to school fêtes and agricultural shows. In the other tent a band of tea ladies, pink and perspiring in their pinnies among the sauna clouds of steam from the simmering urns, were formed up behind a barricade of trestles heavy with food. This wasn't a mere cup of tea and a biscuit, but an elaborate meal of ritual celebration between the serious business of judging and the equally serious business of the speeches, which would come a bit later.

At the near end of the trestle ramparts a queue had begun to form, each person in turn picking up a paper plate with a coloured napkin folded into a neat triangle, then moving steadily along the great bank of food towards the tea urn at the far end. Egg and cress sandwiches, cheese sandwiches, tuna sandwiches, bridge rolls with meat paste, sausage rolls, squares of quiche, cheese scones, fruit scones, plain shortbread, strawberry shortbread, chocolate cake, coffee cake, fruitcake, custard tarts, iced buns, chocolate digestives, Rich Tea biscuits, orange squash or tea. Oh my, oh my, as the Mole in *The Wind in the Willows* said in similar circumstances. I carried off an egg sandwich, a piece of fruitcake and a warning from the lady with the tea urn that I'd fade away to nothing if I didn't do better than that.

Alicia was waving from a table in the sunshine where she and her children were already settled. They were sitting opposite Captain Wallace, who was putting away fruitcake with great purpose, talking intently between mouthfuls to a military-looking person in a pale summer jacket. I hadn't known that children would be welcome and had left Alexander with his grandparents. Now, with the astonishing quantities of cake, the other children and the hounds, which surely he would have liked, I felt a stab of regret for not having brought him and a simultaneous twinge of relief and pleasure at the sight of a known face – at this improbable reunion of old St Hugh's girls around a teatable in the exotic setting of the Kennels, Hothfield, under a sky of purple and bronze.

'Well,' began Alicia, as I settled into the empty seat beside her. 'So what brings you here?' I was a bit taken aback by that. I opened my mouth to say that nothing had brought me here, it was where I came from. And then thought that technically, that wasn't quite true and in any case, we'd both been transplanted here from the atmosphere of plain living and vigorous intellectual calisthenics that was North Oxford and MGA1. So instead I explained about finding the yard and Mrs Rogers, about learning to ride, about thinking I might start to hunt in this part of Kent where I both did and didn't belong. 'And now they might ban it just as you're getting started,' sympathized Alicia.

I was just about to ask what her husband thought of Lord Burns, whose report on hunting with dogs had been published only a month before, and whether he really thought a ban was likely, when the speeches began. The former President of the Union rose from the remains of his tea and moved towards yet another rickety trestle table, this one covered in silver-plate spoons wreathed in polythene bags, and small white cardboard boxes. (He hadn't changed, I thought, not a bit, since I had last seen him, grandly seated in his white tie and tails on the great, gnarled Gothic throne that was the President's seat in the union debating chamber. But then I remembered the bit in *Love in a Cold Climate* where the grown-ups say admiringly of each other that they haven't changed at all, and the children think, how strange and horrible they must have looked in youth, then, all wrinkled and faded and streaks of grey in their hair . . .)

The spoons, suitably engraved, were for the puppy walkers, each of whom came up in turn to shake the MP's hand and turn towards the flash of the camera recording the moment for posterity and the local papers. Damian was good at this, angling himself, the handshake and the handshakee expertly towards the shot like a professional dance-partner whisking a hopeless toe-treader smoothly through the steps of a tricky cha-cha. The puppy walkers blinked in the bright light, looked pleased and shy and vanished back into the anonymity of their tea-slops and scone-crumbs. The Percy Amos Hickman Challenge Cup for Best Working Hound of Last Season's Entry was won by Cannon, walked by Mr C. Willett & Family. Mr C. Willett was another of the whippers-in, with an expression at once soulful and roguish, like one of Trollope's heavy swells.

The trophies bestowed, the MP delivered a short speech

in which a sombre vista of the political future of hunting was lightened with shafts of encouragement and praise for the splendid role of what he referred to as 'country sports' in bringing together rural communities, and the continuity of tradition that they represented. The senior Master, Ian Anderson, exhorted us all to spare no effort to defend hunting against the threat of a ban, which was one of five possible alternatives under the Government Bill to regulate hunting with dogs introduced by Jack Straw at the beginning of July.

Captain Wallace acknowledged the uncertain times for hunting with an expression of disgust, as though forcing down a mouthful of something nasty, then settled more happily to discuss the hounds. He was pleased with this year's entry. They were a credit to our huntsman and the breeding programme Neil had devised with our Hound Trustee, Colonel Parkes. Over the years in which he had been judging the Ashford Valley's puppy show, it had been a pleasure to see the quality of our hounds improving steadily and he wished us all in the Ashford Valley many more years of hunting in this beautiful part of Kent.

I thought while he was speaking that he seemed less like a person than a subtle and complicated artefact: an ancient building, or the portrait of someone from another age, freighted with wisdom and influence – one of Queen Elizabeth I's politic and ingenious advisers, say, with their immobile features and bright, knowing eyes. Even though his manner was quite direct and unadorned – weighty with authority, but not consciously grand – there was a feeling of monumental distance about him, as though he were so encrusted with the knowledge and experience of 70 seasons' hunting, 58 of them as a Master of Foxhounds, that he had become unknowable, unless you already knew him.

When, two years later, he died in a motor accident, aged 82, there were obituaries with photographs of him as a child, as a schoolboy Master of the Eton College beagles, as a young man, which mapped his progress from a Kentish nine-year-old with a bobbery pack of beagles, terriers and a golden retriever to a living monument 'known simply' – said one of the obits – 'as God', without quite decoding the process.

The newfound splendour of the Ashford Valley hounds was a confection partly of bloodlines from hounds given or lent us by Captain Wallace himself, in particular the stallion hound Exmoor Greycoat '94. He became the foundation of the remade Ashford Valley pack, which during the 1990s had been bred back to bloodlines established by Captain Wallace during his 25-year Mastership of the Heythrop. Those lines in turn can be traced back for centuries, to the formation of the breed. 'You will find,' wrote Colonel Parkes, the Hound Trustee, in a letter describing the breeding of the Ashford Valley pack as I first saw it, 'if you look at pictures of the hounds of 200 years ago, the better ones look surprisingly similar to those of today.'

It was odd and disturbing to be sitting here surrounded by all this past, wondering if its time was all behind, and almost none ahead. The arching trees – beech, oak and chestnut, losing their sticky early summer freshness now, with prickly, pale-green miniature conkers forming on the spent chestnut candles; the straggling foam of faded meadow-sweet at the field margin; the tents, the tea urns, the smell of crushed grass, the flowered hats and bowler hats worn in honour of the year-old bearers of those 200-year-old bloodlines, springing now around Captain Wallace in their final parade, caramel and cream whirling and leaping against the mown kennels turf . . . All this freight of instinct and lore distilled into an afternoon vignette of that most English paradox: a game of deadly seriousness. Had I really arrived on the scene just in time to see it all vanish in a ragged unravelling of destroyed hounds, redundant kennelmen and shot foxes, the coverts abandoned, the countryside picturesque but empty, the people dispersed, the tradition effaced, the story finished?

The two possibilities – hunting or not-hunting – seemed to dissolve back and forth into one another, like an image that reads both positively and negatively: the yellow and black Batman logo, or Wittgenstein's primitive doodle of something that changes bewilderingly from a duck to a rabbit and back again as you look at it. It was late; the afternoon cooling to evening, the lurid mauve darkening ominously over the chestnut trees. There was a flicker across the sky and after an interval a faint rumble, as of distant demolition. A storm was moving towards us. It was time to go home.

I first saw the hounds as a pack a couple of weeks later, when Mrs Rogers asked if I wanted to go out with her on hound exercise. We were to leave from the kennels on a Wednesday morning promptly at 8 a.m. The hounds would travel on foot. We would be on bicycles. 'You can ride a bicycle, I suppose?' said Mrs Rogers, sharply.

She was right to be suspicious. Wobbling along behind her on a rickety kennels' boneshaker held together by dog leads ('Couples!' said Mrs Rogers), I wondered which would be worse, to run over a hound, or fall off. Mrs Rogers took a dim view of fallers, as I'd already discovered. 'Don't fall off!' she'd once bellowed, as I began to slide earthwards after completing a clear round of microscopic jumps on the fat cob Herbie. Such was the force of her personality that for a second or two, before I hit the ground with an ignominious slither and thud, it seemed almost possible that I might defy gravity and achieve a cartoon scramble up through the empty air and back into the saddle.

The huntsman in his brown kennels overall rode at the head of his pack of 60 or so hounds ('Thirty couple. We count them in twos'), while we pedalled at the rear, behind a sea of waving black and tan and lemon tails ('Sterns!'). 'When my young hounds are taken out to air,' wrote Peter Beckford, 'my huntsman takes them into that country which they are designed to hunt. It is attended with this advantage, they acquire a knowledge of the country and, when left behind at any time, cannot fail to find their way home more easily.'

This was the purpose of our morning constitutional. The hounds were there to learn, as well as exercise. Some inexperienced hounds — the new season's entry — were coupled to older, wiser animals and the pack moved along the road as a kind of flowing entity: jostling, brawling and yelping, disintegrating at the edges as the younger hounds, entranced by scents of rabbit and pheasant, left the pack to hunt the verges before being recalled by Neil's whoops and growls of reprimand.

The morning was pristine; brilliant blue and gold. The day would be hot, but the sun had not yet burned the dew off the hedges, from which sparrows and goldfinches sprang into the air as we passed. How extraordinary, I thought, that as a teenager I had lain in my bed on perfect early summer mornings such as this, absorbed in a volume of Trollope or Molly Keane, oblivious to the presence of the huntsman and his hounds trotting along the road, not five miles from my bedroom.

'That's Crimson,' said Mrs Rogers, pointing out a heavy-boned black and tan bitch hound in the middle of the pack. 'She's one of the older hounds. She's already done five seasons. And that's Coral. She's very loving. You'll see when we stop at the top of the hill. The one who keeps getting left behind is Dreamer, and that's Drama, from the same litter, with the patch over half her face. Those two are Milkmaid and Mistletoe. And over there in the hedge are Glitter and Glamour. You saw all those at the puppy show.' Like the young hounds, I realized, I hadn't been invited out just for the exercise and fresh air.

Standing at the top of the hill, looking down over the familiar fields on a sunny morning in the first summer of the new millennium, surrounded by a pack of hounds with eighteenth-century names, yelping and whining excitedly in response to a huntsman crooning admonition and encouragement – 'Leu in, eleu in there. Huic, huic to Crimson . . .' – in the courtly language of Norman French venery which would have been recognizable to Neil Staines's fourteenth-century predecessor, the royal huntsman, William Twiti, I felt confusedly that I was becoming a microscopic detail in a vast, intricate, living pattern; a tapestry of fox and hounds, huntsmen and riders, all performing their complicated dance of pursuit and evasion across a landscape changed, cultivated, scarred, built over, but still patchworked as it had been for a thousand years with fields and pasture, spinneys and streams.

Fox-hunting and I must have missed each other by a matter of a few miles quite regularly throughout my childhood. My grandparents' bungalow was so close to the Hothfield kennels that it seems perverse to think how nearly we must have met the pack when they were out on morning exercise, or trotting towards the first covert on a winter morning and we were trundling about the countryside on one of Grandpa's erratic errands, in search of two-by-four, or fish glue, or getting hopelessly lost on the trail of some old shipmate who was supposed recently to have retired to the district.

Even our house in Bell Road, with its twin front drives, one for people, one for cars, was poised on the fault-line between the suburbs and what lay beyond. If you turned right out of the front gate you came to Sittingbourne high street, where Celia Fiennes, passing through in 1697, noticed St Michael's church, 'all built with flints headed so curiously that it looks like glass and shines with the sun's reflection'. But

I, who went to St Michael's every other Sunday, saw no such strangeness. Just a dreary old blackish church, surrounded by dreary old blackish yew trees, in which at about the half-way point of the interminable service of Matins a priest in a dreary old black cassock climbed into the pulpit and intoned, in a nasal chant that would have been soporific if it hadn't been so irritating, a sermon on some such uplifting text as 'The fathers have eaten sour grapes, and the children's teeth are set on edge.'

On alternate Sundays we went to a different church, St John the Baptist at Tunstall. Tunstall was a village set among apple orchards which hadn't yet been grubbed up and replanted with houses. To get to it you turned left out of our gate and struck away from the town, following a network of roads with lime or flowering cherry trees planted at intervals along the pavement and big, square houses set back from the road behind rose beds and mown front lawns. Woodstock Road, Park Avenue, Park Road and then suddenly the pavement ran round in a big loop and there was no more road, only a chicken alley with an orchard on one side and a flock of brown fowl with floppy red wattles scratching behind a wire mesh fence on the other.

The other end of the alley opened onto a curve of road. There was a large house in crumbling rosy brick with pointed arched windows and tall thin chimneys, a stable block and a sort of turret with a white diamond-shaped clock face on the front of it, the hours marked in Roman numerals. The road swept past the house, between a paddock with a big black horse and an orchard with a cross white pony and disappeared into a gloomy tunnel of trees. The church was on the right, perched above the road at the top of a steep bank with a footpath that used to turn to a sheet ice slide in the winter. Like St Michael's it was built mainly of flint, but the flints here were grey rather than black, and mixed up with odd bits of brickwork here and there which made the effect somehow friendlier, or at any rate less awful.

The churchyard was filled with thin, flat, leaning tombstones, carved with blurred skulls or winged cherubs' heads and incised with a half-effaced tracery of spidery script with 'f's for 's's, commemorating the virtues of defunct Josiahs and Suzannahs. On Sundays this was as far as we went, but on schooldays we walked on, past a second large house of rose brick, half-hidden behind a high wall self-sown with orange-brown wallflowers and purple clumps of toadflax and aubretia, to a building made of yet more knapped flint, with pointed gables edged in white wooden lacework, like the gingerbread house in Hansel and Gretel. This was my primary school, where time moved at a different pace from Sittingbourne time.

It was a church school, on the edge of farmland, and the rhythm of our lives there followed those of the church and the land: neatly separated into seasons, punctuated by the changing colours of the vestments and altar frontals – purple for Lent, white for Christmas and Easter, red for Whitsun and the festivals of martyrs, green for the endless summer Sundays After Trinity – and by more-or-less pagan rituals.

Between Ascension Day, when the whole school went to church (which we did in any case with great frequency) and sang 'The Head That Once Was Crowned With Thorns', and Harvest Festival, when we sang 'We Plough the Fields and Scatter' and the entire church was filled with Archimboldo arrangements of fruit and veg (every horizontal surface lined with polished apples, feathery bunches of carrots, tough-skinned brown onions with plaited tails, bursting green marrows and, propped against the altar, a shiny brown loaf of bread in the shape of a sheaf of corn), the summer months were punctuated by a series of picturesque amusements that might have served to illustrate a modern Book of Hours.

At shearing time we were taken to see the sheep, struggling naked and pink-white from their dingy, matted fleeces as the shearers clipped the last strands of wool and released them. They looked confused, awkward and newborn, rising from their cloddish winter coverings like the newly animated bodies in the Stanley Spencer painting of the Resurrection in Cookham Churchyard. There was a sharp, ammoniac smell in the sheep-pen, which I thought might be like the smell of the graves cracked open at the sound of the Last Trump and a shrill cacophony of panicky bleating and whirring clippers. Occasionally a sheep wriggled so much that it got nicked by the clippers, and a bright strip of blood soaked the pink-white skin. It didn't seem to bother the sheep unduly and it didn't worry us much, either – we were all perfectly at ease with the Blood of the Lamb, having heard so much about it at church.

At the end of the summer term we had a big outing, with a packed lunch and a coach trip with singing on the way home, to the Kent Show at the Detling showground a dozen or so miles from the school. The show seemed enormous: a monstrously oversized world within a world. At school our surroundings were constructed to our own scale. Our teachers stalked like giants through classrooms filled with tiny desks and little bentwood chairs with spindle backs.

Within this diminutive world a miniature hierarchy of relative size prospered. To the infants, the 11-year-old Big Ones seemed both physically overwhelming – huge, strong, noisy, oppressively skilful at football and conkers, marbles, jacks and complicated skipping steps – and unreachably sophisticated, with their haughty expressions and their 11-plus passes to the Big School, where you wore uniform and did homework.

But at the Kent Show, even the Big Ones seemed diminished, shrunk to the size of Borrowers by the freakish vastness of combine harvesters as big as our classroom, soaring canvas cathedrals packed with mesh cages containing hissing geese as big as the Infants in class 1, straw-strewn enclosures barely encompassing the great flesh-mountains within: slack pink sacks of recumbent pig with bristly backs and long white eyelashes, lumbering bullocks whose living state seemed incongruously temporary (I knew what they looked like under the skin; I had seen whole beasts hanging headless, hoofless and skinless from hooks in the back of our butcher's shop. He had a picture of a jointed animal hanging over the counter and I knew to the inch which of those muscles shifting under the curly chestnut or black-and-white hide was the sirloin, the brisket and the skirt).

The heart of the Show was the show ring, a carousel of expressionless stockmen in white coats and flat caps leading choleric bulls by the nose before the assessing gaze of a judge in tweeds and a black bowler. They had horses there, too. Sometimes we saw them in the distance: teams of heavy horses with coloured quills knotted into their manes; fat-bottomed cobs the colour of filberts; the bobbing velvet cap of a show-jumper rising and falling above the heads of the watching crowd. But somehow we never made it to the ringside. There was too much to see on the way there: writhing ferrets in a glass tank; beady-eyed hens with feathers like white lace over black satin; champion onions, big as babies' heads; prize-winning jamjars of wild flowers; a woman with a spinning-wheel turning a sheep-coloured fluff of raw wool into a fine, twisted thread.

And so I missed the Ashford Valley again, by a few yards' distance. They paraded hounds in that show ring, and did team jumping too and I never once saw them. Not until 30 years later, when it was my own grey mare that I was watching in the ring, arching tidily over the hunt jumps with her forelegs neatly tucked up and the economic figure of Rick the whipper-in riding her with his scarlet coat-tails flying.

Roaming the Detling showground, 30 years after my first visit (less sternly agricultural now, I thought it, and much keener to ingratiate itself with the non-farming public. Fewer massive combines and a great many more bouncy castles and ride-on mowers) it was impossible not to flirt with alternative versions of the story. What if my ghostly 11-year-old self had read *National Velvet* instead of *Charlotte's Web*, and consequently not lingered by the pigpens, on the lookout for literate spiders, but made straight for the show ring and seen there Phil Buckland, his huntsman and his hounds parading? Might I have felt then the inexplicable sense of certainty, the clicking into place of mental tumblers that I heard in my mind's ear when Mrs Rogers said she had become an MFH? And if I had, how differently might that other story have turned out?

I might have insisted on being taken to a meet – one of the big, convivial set-pieces that draw the crowds on Boxing Day or New Year's day. And what then? Perhaps I might have learned to ride while I was still a light and reckless child, rather than taking to horses as a mother, made stiff and cautious by the constant shimmering spectre of the awkward fall, the broken neck, the child orphaned by his parent's idiotic caprice. I might have learned to mind failure less, or at any rate, I might have got my weeping over misbuckled straps and misjudged jumps done with at an age when weeping over failure is less painful and incongruous than it becomes in middle age. I might have been, if not good, at any rate better than I would ever be now.

'What does it matter when you started?' said my new acquaintance, the hunting lawyer from the office on the corner, whom I'd met while jaywalking across the Trafalgar Road. 'You're hunting now.' He meant to be kind. Better hunting than not hunting, for sure. But the burden of everything that I would never know sat on my heart like a stone. I would never be able to say to anyone, as someone proudly said to me on my first evening's autumn hunting, that I was about to begin my 50th season with the Ashford Valley.

In fact the political rumblings whose real significance I felt ill equipped to interpret seemed to threaten a fair chance that my first season might also be my last. Better hunting than not. But still – to have encountered it at such a moment felt as enchanting and as sad as finding true love in middle age, when you are starting to curl up a bit at the edges: infinitely better than never finding it at all. But hard not to feel gripped at moments by a sense of regret like a sharp squeeze to the heart for all that time lost in the looking.

The meet card was a folded piece of bright yellow pasteboard bearing the logo of the AVH, a hound's head in profile above two crossed hunting whips with thongs looped and twining into a sinuous love knot. Mrs Rogers handed it to me at the end of a lesson, balanced on top of a box of half a dozen brown eggs. At the bottom of the card she had written in her upright, curly script, 'Autumn hunting starts late Aug early Sept – Opening Meet is late Oct or 1st Sat in Nov.' Inside was a slip of paper in the same eggy yellow and the same hound's-mask logo: a list of Autumn Hunting meets punctuated by hunting get-togethers: Countryside Alliance summer barbecue; Countryside Alliance Dinner Dance at the Great Danes, Hollingbourne, with guest speaker; Weald of Kent Ploughing match at Sheephurst Lane, Marden. Hounds parade at 11.30 hrs; AVH Hunt Ball at the Ramada Hotel.

There was, I noticed, with the little clutch of fear that had begun to accompany the thought of hunting, now it grew close to being a reality rather than a picturesque idea, an entry for cross-country schooling at Rooting Street Farm on 31 August, just before the first Autumn hunting meet, on 2 September at Potters Farm, Bethersden (Breakfast provided).

Ought I to sign up for cross-country schooling? It seemed a bit ambitious, given that I'd not so far gone into the paddock containing the cross-country course. I knew where it was, though, because we passed it when we went hacking, and I'd taken a hard look at the post-and-rails that led from the paddock directly onto a narrow track bordering a wheatfield, the solid black wall of tyres, the coffin, a sort of longitudinal ditch into which you had to jump and directly out again, a couple of horrifyingly solid-looking wide wooden jumps, a brushwood hunt jump that looked inviting enough, if you liked that sort of thing, and a thumping great telegraph pole balanced over a shallow ditch, which provided a second exit point at the far end of the paddock, onto another narrow track with a choice of a sharp right turn down the track or an electric fence straight ahead.

In my braver moments, I could imagine tackling some of the less challenging obstacles in the cross-country field (the small, narrow ones that didn't require a right-angled turn immediately on landing). In my more frequent moments of cowardice I thought the whole lot was simply ridiculous for someone of my ability. Then I noticed the small print on the meet card. 'Autumn hunting will be mounted on Wednesdays & Saturdays (time: 07.00 hours) and unmounted on Mondays (time: 17.00 hrs) unless otherwise stated,' it said. I was saved, for the time being.

I said with elaborate casualness to Mrs Rogers that as she'd originally suggested, I'd go to a couple of the foot meets first of all, just to see what was involved. And then perhaps we could discuss mounted hunting a bit later on. Fine, said Mrs Rogers. The meet near Great Chart in early September was a good one. She would give me directions and when I got there, introduce me to someone knowledgeable who would look after me and tell me what was what.

I set off from London on a beautiful September mid-afternoon. It felt odd to be stopping work at 3.30 on a Monday, and odder still to have to ask Alexander's nanny if she'd mind babysitting, because I was going fox-hunting. I was afraid she might disapprove and was conscious of asking with a sort of underlying defiance, in case she did. But she simply smiled her habitual Mona Lisa smile and said no problem, have a nice time, see you later.

The first part of the drive was automaton stuff: the same route that I now drove twice a week for lessons at Rooting Street: the London suburbs shading to fields and in turn to familiar landmarks. I knew now precisely the point at which the square tower of Charing church would appear in the distance, had begun to anticipate the shallow, insistent lean of the chalk escarpment above the point-to-point field, the startling suddenness with which the tidy ribbon development on either side of the A20 turned to haphazard, secretive village and hamlet as soon as you turned away from the main road. Villages I had never been to: Egerton, Pluckley, Shadoxhurst, Marden Thorn and Smarden, Mundy Bois, Bethersden and Boughton Malherbe, had begun to seem familiar from the repeated litany of their names on the road signs. The same pattern of names now wove its away across the meet card. By the end of the season this realm of the imagination would have become a solid geography of the Ashford Valley's country.

Trundling at a sluggish 20 m.p.h. down the main street of the village marked on the directions Mrs Rogers had scribbled for me on a bit of paper, I wondered where, among all these tidy cottages with their gardens full of regimented Michaelmas daisies, there could possibly be space in which to hunt. Fifties' council houses clad in a peculiar Utility pebble-dash and concrete version of Kentish vernacular weatherboarding fringed the outskirts; then came the heart of the village: crouched brick cottages clad in white-painted wooden weatherboarding and the clustered indispensables of village life: the church, the pub, the sub-post office with faded postcards and boxes of tourist fudge in the window; a small branch of Spar, a junk shop selling sad bits of china ('A Present From Southend') and expensive brass coal scuttles, and an estate agent's office.

'Turn right at the pub,' said the directions given me by Mrs Rogers. 'Follow the track past the cricket pitch, over the bridge, through the metal gate.' I made a couple of passes in front of the cricket pitch without spotting the track, then saw it on the third go: a rutted grass path leading directly past the little pavilion. It didn't look like the sort of thing you were allowed to drive down, but I turned onto it, expecting at any moment that an angry groundsman would pop out from behind one of the sight screens and tell me to clear off.

At the end of the track, a clump of trees. Beyond the trees, a hump-backed bridge. Across the bridge, an expanse of open parkland and stubble fields. To the right, a five-barred metal farm gate hanging open at the entrance to a tussocky paddock with knots of men in gaiters and green waistcoats talking and smoking among a ragged group of parked cars. The only face I recognised was that of Neil, who was standing in waistcoat and breeches by the hound van – a white vehicle with slatted sides through which a row of disembodied muzzles discon-certingly protruded. Mine was the only car without a set of dog bars in the back and a Countryside Alliance sticker in the rear window.

Now I was here I felt a cowardly reluctance to get out of the comforting squalor of the car, walk over to all those green-clad men, explain who I was and then go off with them to do whatever it was they were going to do. I wasn't sure about my clothes, either. I had on a pair of tweed trousers, especially chosen for their tree-bark invisibility, but I thought now they looked a bit new and sharply creased, and also rather stagey, like something an actress might wear to signal that she was Doing Rustic. As I got out of the car and started to walk towards the hound van, I saw Mrs Rogers come in at the gate wearing pale canvas jeans with paddock boots, a coral polo shirt, a panama hat and sunglasses – a much better look for a warm evening than my grizzled tweed. 'Hello Jane. Aren't you rather hot in those?' said she. 'Now, come and meet Peter Deacon.'

Glancing at the green men when I drove in at the gate, I had thought they all seemed quite old. But as we walked towards them, I realized that most of them were probably a good deal younger than me. They had a hard look of assurance about them, and the high colour of people who work out-doors. Most of them held thumb sticks; several had dogs on leads. One man, dressed with unexpected formality in a Tattersall-check shirt and tie, had a spade with a sharp, leaf-shaped blade – the sort of thing the gravediggers in *Hamlet* might carry. It was thrust into the ground beside him: attached to it was a double leash with a couple of eager terriers straining at the end of it, front legs off the ground, paddling the air with excitement.

Peter Deacon was a slight, elderly man with cropped silvery hair like fur, and very blue eyes. Like everyone else he carried a stick – longer than a walking-stick, about armpit height, with a notch in the top to rest your thumb in. Behind us, the yipping from the hound van reached a crescendo as hounds streamed down the lowered ramp and formed an excited circle around Neil, muzzles tipped upwards, sterns thrashing, eyes fixed on him in an ecstasy of anticipation. He took his hunting horn from between the buttons of his waistcoat, blew a sharp couple of notes. It was the first time I had ever heard that wild and stirring sound – eloquent as a church bell in its ability to conjure exultation, dismay, hope or disappointment from a single note. Then he set off up the dusty track with the pack around him and the rest of us following.

We were making for the little stand of woodland 100 yards or so away. There was a cattle grid and a narrow field gate in the way – an elegant design of a latchless gate pivoting on its hinge within a semi-circular metal framework, designed to allow humans to pass, but keep stock in. Most of the hounds were just too long in the back to take the human route around this barrier and there was a tremendous pile-up as they tried to negotiate it: the slenderest ones managing to sidle around the gate, the rest squirming sideways under the low crossbar, one or two jumping the top rail and the rest, desperate not to be left behind, shoving blindly forward in a solid wedge of hound.

At last they made it through to the other side. The whipper-in picked up the final dithering straggler ('Dreamer,' said someone exasperatedly) and heaved her over, and the pack closed up again, tight behind Neil. We walked across grass to the corner of the field where the spinney began and then paused. Mrs Rogers, more formidable than ever in her new incarnation as Master, was barking orders like Napoleon in a coral-pink polo shirt.

'You, you, you and you two,' she said, waving at Peter and me, 'Go to that side of the field and spread out along the edge of the wood, right to the top.' We went, plodding ungainly over the cracked ground and scratchy stubble. Stumbling behind Peter, I envied him his knotty stick, which I had thought of as a sort of picturesque prop deployed by rustic style victims (Prince Charles is often photographed glumly resting his chin on top of one), but which had now metamorphosed from a decorative chin-rest into a thoroughly useful bit of kit, propelling its owner over the hard-baked broken clay at a steady pace while I trailed behind, turning my ankles and panting in my hot tweed.

'Don't go too close in to the wood,' advised Peter. 'It's a mistake people make, holding up. They go in too close, and then the fox pops out and he doesn't even see them. He just runs straight past them and away. You stand off from it a bit, and then if Charlie comes out, you'll be able to turn him back.' To either side of us a row of people stood at intervals of about 20 yards from one another, and about 25 yards back from the edge of the wood.

Holding up, which is what we were doing, is the standard occupation of the field during what was once called cubbing – the preliminary months of hunting between the end of harvest and the start of the full hunting season in early November. 'The object of cub-hunting,' wrote the Duke of Beaufort in his book *Fox-Hunting*, 'is to educate both young hounds and fox-cubs . . . The young hounds and foxes are not the only ones, believe me, who derive benefit from the lesson they get during those early mornings in August, September and October. They are invaluable times for everyone . . . to learn. I myself never cease to find out something new, and I am a fairly old hand at the job!'

By the time I came to it, the educational process of teaching young foxes how to flee and young hounds how to pursue them had officially changed its name from cubbing to the more neutrally pastoral 'Autumn Hunting' – though I noticed that most people had difficulty remembering the neologism except on official occasions.

Autumn hunting differs from full hunting in several important ways. If hunting is a performance, autumn hunting is the rehearsal for that performance: the moulding of the actors from a disparate gaggle of shy or headstrong individuals into a troupe capable of working as an ensemble. As with most rehearsals, the audience isn't generally invited to watch. Before the official beginning of the season, hunting is by invitation of the Master (whose role, to extend this metaphor until it screams for mercy, is approximately that of producer, while the huntsman directs). You may attend, but you don't dress

160

up or expect to be entertained: no fast runs, no jumping, no excitement for ambitious riders but something intent, concentrated, almost invisible: the imperceptible building of technique, confidence and skill that comes from patient repetition. If you are on a horse, you turn out in ratcatcher, which means a tweed jacket and an ordinary tie, with the horse's mane unplaited.

And then you stand about quietly outside the covert and wait while the huntsman and hounds get on with it. Most of the time, you have no idea what is going on, because whatever is happening, happens inside a covert which is still in full leaf and you can't see anything, only hear. What you hear is the crackling of trampled undergrowth, a lot of confused squeaking and yelping; a good deal of the eerie, eldritch sound, part scream, part hoot, part yodel, which is the huntsman encouraging his hounds: 'Eleu, leu in, leu leu little bitches. PUSH him up, PUSH him up. Hark [pronounced 'hike'] to Crimson.' And the occasional toot on the horn, which makes the field start suddenly awake from the trance of cosmic boredom into which it has fallen and say to its neighbour, with a great show of animation: 'What was that? Has he gone to ground? Well, I think he might have been blowing for the terrier man. It wasn't a kill, was it? Is he leaving the covert? No, I think the note for that is a bit longer?' And wish it had spent the summer studying horn calls, so that it could now have some idea of the narrative unfolding so tantalizingly out of sight within the wood.

Even on cubbing mornings early in the season, when you had got up at 4 a.m. while the stars were still out to get to a 6 a.m. meet, you daredn't fall into a comfortable doze in the saddle. As well as standing quite still and silent, you were supposed to watch intently for any sign of a fox leaving the covert. In full hunting, that sight would be the preliminary to some kind of excitement: hounds streaming away on the scent followed, after a decent interval, by the cavalry charge of a field more-or-less in control of its horses. But in the early part of the season, when the young hounds were still learning the rudiments of hunting as a pàck, that sort of pursuit across country was deliberately avoided. If a fox appeared at the edge of the covert, you were supposed to turn him back, by tapping your whip against your saddle flap if you were on horseback and if not, by shouting 'Aye, Aye, Charlie' at the top of your voice. I found it hard to imagine myself shouting 'Aye, Aye, Charlie' at a fox, and hoped it would not be necessary.

The reason we were holding up this particular covert was that fifty yards to the back of us ran the Eurostar line to Paris. Neither foxes nor hounds could be allowed to run that way; if it looked like happening, we must turn them back into the wood. The difficulty of remaining both perfectly still and absolutely focused is familiar to people who make a habit of meditative prayer. However you try to master your thoughts they slither about like beads of mercury. The early evening sun was warm on my back and poured, viscous and syrupy gold, over the stubble, the fissured clay beneath, the parched foliage, green on the cusp of crisping to infinite paintbox gradations of ochre and umber, cadmium, gamboge and lake. The harder I fixed my gaze on the wood, the more everything blurred in the sun dazzle into abstract patches of intense colour and lengthening slatey-violet shadow.

Did I hear the woodpecker? asked Peter. I hadn't until he mentioned it, but now I noticed a rapid, insistent knocking that I had taken for something to do with the hunt, confusing it with the deathwatch tap, tap, tap, of beaters driving birds over guns at a shoot. And look at that old heron over there. What old heron over where? I could see nothing but a greyish fence post which, as Peter pointed with his stick and I said, Where? Where?, raised a snakey head, unfurled battleship-grey wings and flapped unhurriedly away, legs trailing, languid as a broken-spoked umbrella bowling down a gusty street. The jay, added Peter, which was flying away just above the tree-tops at the far end of the covert, had certainly been disturbed by a fox. If I kept watching, I'd probably see him in a moment or two.

Behind us in the twilight the Eurostar whooshed past on its way from London to Paris. Beyond the lit windows, the travellers' faces were turned towards us. What did they think we were doing, a line of people standing in a stubble field, staring intently into an apparently empty wood? The final carriages curved away into blue-orange dusk over Ashford. I looked back from the train to the trees and there was a fox: small, darkish red-brown, barrelling along the field margin, apparently with nothing in pursuit. 'Aye-aye-aye, Charlie,' roared Peter. At the corner of the wood the fox paused for a moment, then nipped back into the undergrowth and was gone.

I had wondered what might happen at this moment – the first time I set eyes on a hunted fox. Might I, like Siegfried Sassoon's fictional hero, George Sherston, squeak 'Don't do that! They might catch him!' And if I did, might not that be the proper reaction? I'd never seen anything hunted before, except for the bald nestlings with which our cat used to play a grim game of catch when he found them fallen from the eaves but still alive. In that case, my mother would generally rush up with a dustpan and brush and intervene to save the nestling. Not that it did any good in the long run, since the birds invariably died anyway, from shock or starvation or injury. I found it hard to decide which was worse: a cruelly playful death at the claws of the cat, or the kindlier but still more lingering demise that we offered, with our rescuing dustpans, our field hospital nests of straw and pointless little saucers of water and raw mince or chopped-up worm.

That evening in the field beside the Eurostar track I found

myself in an uneasy, Alice-in-Wonderland frame of mind, suspended in the force field of two powerful and mutually contradictory feelings. I was enchanted to see that fox, as I had been to see the heron and the jay and hear the woodpecker. And I wanted him to get away, just as much as I wanted the hounds – those hounds whom now I knew by name – to do what they were in that wood to accomplish and catch him.

'Come forward, please,' came the clarion voice of Mrs Rogers, floating over the tree-tops from the other side of the covert, and we began to trudge towards it, uphill towards the next covert. 'Did they catch him?' I asked. 'Marked to ground,' said Peter, meaning that a fox – not necessarily the one we had seen – had gone to ground and, if the landowner had requested it, been dug out and shot by the terrier man in his grimly respectable collar and tie.

Gnawing away at the conundrum of whose side I was on, fox or hounds, I thought less of myself for not being able to define what I felt with greater precision. Several meets later I was still poised on an uneasy fulcrum of sympathy with both fox and hounds when it occurred to me that this wasn't necessarily a starting position: a moral conundrum that had to be resolved before I could Pass Go – so that if I came down on the side of the hounds, I could carry on hunting; if on the side of the fox, I would have to stop. There might, I thought, be other ways of looking at it.

If you have never hunted anything, even a fish or a rabbit, the idea of respecting – even loving – your quarry for its own animal nature (something that was axiomatic in the time of William Twiti, the fourteenth-century Royal Huntsman who wrote a grave and thoughtful treatise on *The Art of Hunting*, full of curiosity and affection for the quirks of his quarry) may seem eccentric to the point of waywardness. And if you encounter animals rarely, as pets or two-dimensional images, showing their best side in TV wildlife documentaries, it becomes quite easy to think of all creatures, both wild and domesticated, as possessing miniature human sensibilities attractively veiled in fur or feather: all hedgehogs are Mrs Tiggywinkle, all foxes Mr Tod. If these are your feelings about animals, then the notion of hunting anything – or at any rate, anything with legs – becomes instantly and irrefutably as appalling as hunting children. And then by extension, there develops a sort of unease about exposing an animal to any other experience that you yourself might find inimical.

But if you allow that even the pet chihauhau trotting along a Knightsbridge pavement in a Burberry overcoat and Gucci collar doesn't experience love, or dread, or anticipation in quite the same way as the child for which it is a less demanding substitute, at once an ambiguity is engaged about what it does feel; what sort of things it might fear, or dislike (and whether, in its chihuahua heart, it would really rather its little coat came from Dolce than Burberry). It is this ambiguity that enables animals to be all sorts of things other than proto-humans: companions, food, objects of curiosity, admiration, pride and aesthetic pleasure, bearers of the burden of our wishes (what is a racehorse, if not an animated wish?) and quarry.

Ambiguity is one of those bad-fairy gifts, like free will or contraception. It makes the world at once more interesting and more difficult. Above all it makes people disagree (which is of course the purpose of bad-fairy gifts) by making it possible for people to hold violently opposing views, each of which appears unassailably armoured with justification based on morality or science (or both). When touched by ambiguity, bulwarks of certainty suddenly reveal themselves as clever exercises in *trompe l'oeil*: their solidity an ingenious illusion, the edifice they appeared to be supporting no more than a stage flat: an exercise not in moral or scientific proof, but in aesthetics.

Aesthetics, or you could call it style, is a notion both

insubstantial and essential. It extends a Tom Tiddler's ground of ambiguity between the pure precepts of morality and the way they are interpreted in real life. The policies of governments and the legislation that those governments enact is partly a matter of morality but pre-eminently a matter of style: the Government's own, and what it judges to be that of its electorate.

I was slow to make the connection between morals, politics and style where hunting was concerned. I was in the early stages of a flirtation with fox-hunting when the Burns report on hunting with dogs appeared in June 2000, but already sufficiently engaged to feel glad of the report's conclusion that fox-hunting, while (in the report's deadpan turn of phrase) prejudicial to the welfare of the fox, was on the whole less objectionable as a means of pest control than the alternatives of gassing, poisoning, snaring and so on, although more cruel than lamping.

Lamping, a sideline to his knackering business that kept Boyd busy during nights when the moon was full, meant dazzling a fox with a strong light and shooting it with a rifle. It is fairly efficient from the fox's point of view – a quick death or a miss more likely than the chance of injury and suffering; less so from the human. You couldn't always get a clear shot, and you had to be very sure indeed before squeezing the trigger that the eyes gleaming in the lamplight were those of a fox and not some dear old family pet, prowling the darkness on private business.

When the Burns report appeared, its observations about fox-hunting – not just the conclusions about cruelty, but other remarks, about what was called 'utility', and the function of hunting as a social adhesive in the countryside – seemed to offer grounds for cautious optimism about hunting's future. Fox-hunting, when properly practised, seemed to me quite clearly not cruel in the way that bullfighting, for example, was cruel. That seemed to be a spectacle whose sole purpose was the ingenious and artistic infliction of pain, with only one possible outcome for the bull: quite unlike the fluid and chancy narratives of fox-hunting. But it was evident that a great many people, in particular a majority of MPs, thought hunting cruel in precisely the same way as bullfighting, and I felt relieved that Burns seemed to advise that this view be questioned. I thought that whatever legislation followed would be bound to take his advice into account. I had not then understood about the importance of style in politics.

Without ever having been politically engaged, I was inclined to believe that political convictions, though evidently formed by reasons that were impure as well as pure, probably had their foundation in something nobler and more considered than the private preference that inclines one person to like mountain holidays, couscous and Beethoven, while another prefers the seaside, roast chicken and Norah Jones. But the longer the arguments about the future of hunting continued, the plainer it seemed that the differences of opinion were very much more about style than about an earnest effort to arrive at objective truth about the cruelty, utility and so on of hunting.

Three years after Burns, while the argument about hunting – to ban, or not to ban – still rumbled crossly on, there appeared an issue of *Hunting* magazine, an imposing glossy monthly crammed with advertisements for the field sports equivalents of Gucci and Prada – Purdey, Patey, Schnieder, Gidden – which contained a perfect illustration of the way in which facts and style skirted each other in the hunting debate, without ever quite making contact.

'Science explodes Hunting Bill' roared the magazine coverline, introducing research commissioned by the Middle Way group of parliamentarians, a cross-party group in favour of a welfare-based compromise on hunting. The research appeared to show that foxes when shot with a shotgun or rifle were as likely, or more likely, to be wounded than killed outright. The less skilled the marksman, the less likely the chance of a clean kill. 'All this,' wrote the study's authors, 'begs the question – why wound the fox in the first place? Why not just use hounds and thus ensure that wounding is zero.'

Well, why not? The same magazine contained a hint why not, in the opening paragraphs of an article by the newly-appointed Chief Executive of the Countryside Alliance, Simon Hart. 'Earlier this year,' he wrote, 'a Labour MP took me to one side and said, "The countryside represents everything that we despise – wealth, exclusiveness, feudalism and cruelty – and we don't really care if that offends you."' Simon Hart's response to this was interesting: not the gusty huff of moral indignation that was the distinctive prevailing note of the Countryside Alliance's discourse, but a rueful admission that 'it brought home how bad we country people have allowed things to become when our own elected representatives see us in this way . . . This attitude of hostility and disdain is as much our fault as it is theirs.'

It was an interesting acknowledgement that the arguments – about hunting in particular, but many other aspects of the town/country divide besides – are not really concerned with objective notions of what might be right or wrong, cruel or not cruel, but, in effect, about whether Beethoven is preferable to Norah Jones. And the country side of the argument was losing, because its PR and communications skills were worse and its image less attractive than that of the opposition.

The crucial difference was that, even if Norah Jones is universally acknowledged to be a sexier piece all round than Beethoven; even though he is a minority interest, so loathed by some sections of the population that enterprising local councils and education authorities have been known to use his music in public places as a form of vandal deterrent, or to punish naughty schoolchildren, the most fervent Jones-ite would not suggest legislating to ban Beethoven's work, destroy his manuscripts, smash the instruments on which it was played, force the musicians who played it to retrain as shop assistants or computer operators and criminalize the audience who wanted to hear it.

I became more and more interested in this question of style and presentation, because it was style that had drawn me to hunting – though not to riding – in the first place. When I booked my first riding lesson, it was for the very simplest of reasons – as a way of filling dead time. I hadn't even thought of it as a serious hobby. I thought an interest in horses was something you might take up, like the piano, or ballroom dancing (in fact, I booked some dance lessons at the same time as I booked my first riding lessons at Rooting Street, not understanding – how could I? – the extent to which horses, if you let them, suck all the air out of your life until there is no room left to care for anything else).

Learning to ride was like mastering a new language. Every advance was made over unfamiliar terrain and the sheer diffi-culty of making progress was so absorbing that I never looked further than the next step. I was too busy thinking about how to approach a jump to consider that riding might be something more complicated than the mere act of doing it: a pursuit with a hinterland; an accumulation of custom and convention; with its own culture, in fact.

Hunting I approached from quite the opposite direction, having wandered about in the hinterland for decades before emerging by accident into a place full of noise and activity and animation where it was actually going on. Since I was a reader, rather than a doer, it was the narratives of hunting that attracted me. Over years I accumulated a sort of cabinet of curiosities:

oddments of writing about foxes and hounds and horses and huntsmen, accumulated with no particular system or purpose in mind, beyond the mere fact of their having some quirk that caught my fancy. I hoarded stories about hunting because I was intrigued by its contradictions: strange, eloquent contrasts of plain and fancy, secrecy and display, spontaneity and ritual, love and death.

I began very early, as soon as I could read, with scraps from the white-painted bookshelf that hung on the wall above my bed at Bell Road. From here came *The Oxford Book of Nursery Rhymes*, an austere, navy-bound volume illustrated with severe black-and-white woodcuts of small animals – a rat, a bat, a whimsical cat – in the style of Thomas Bewick. Among a quantity of mysterious dialect skipping rhymes and spiteful Anglo-Saxon riddles – the sort lent by Tolkien to Bilbo Baggins and Gollum for their riddling underground duel – it contained a selection of bracingly heartless ballads, of which I liked best the one about the fox who went out one winter's night, praying to the moon to give him light. It was very grim and very funny and I liked the fox's insolent, dandified conversational tone, like a gentleman highwayman.

Creeping up on the poultry-yard, he announces his intentions with the ruthless charm of Don Juan on the pull: 'He seized the grey goose by the sleeve/Says he, "Madam Goose, and by your leave, I'll carry you off without reprieve/And take you home to my den-oh!"' There follows a scene of intensely active tragi-comedy: a battle between the fox on the one hand, and the owner of the poultry-yard, Old Mother Slipper-Slopper, and her man, John, on the other, for the life of the grey goose versus the lives of the fox's hungry family of 'little ones, eight, nine, ten'. 'John, John,' cries Old Mother S, flinging up the sash and sticking her head out of the window, 'the grey goose is gone/And the fox is away to his den-oh!' Whereupon John loads his gun, takes aim – and shoots the grey goose through the head. Off goes the fox, laughing and promising to 'come again in a day or so!'.

Underlying the jubilant feast of goose and duck with which the poem ends, though, is a vein of pathos pronounced enough for a small child to be vividly aware of it, even if lacking the vocabulary to give it a name: the reason the fox will 'come again in a day or so' is that although he has won his skirmish in fine style, he hasn't gained any ground. Like Don Juan, he cannot pause for more than a single night to enjoy his triumph. The next night, he must again make the long, dark, wearisome journey to the farmer's yard – and one day the fine balance of risk will tip the other way. The fox will grow old and stiff, John's wavering aim with the shotgun will improve. Eventually the moonlit night will come when the laughter and triumph will all be in the poultry pen, when the fox's raffish banter will be silenced for ever and his family go hungry.

The same cloudy, ambiguous appeal to a reader's divided sympathies shimmers just below the surface of another of my early favourites: Beatrix Potter's *Tale of Jemima Puddle-Duck*. Here the fox – again, an immensely personable and attractive figure, the possessor of a winning manner in his dealings with female poultry – persuades the idiot duck, Jemima, not merely to lay her eggs in his unpleasant outhouse, crammed full of feathers, but furthermore to wander about the farmyard kitchen garden, nibbling off sprigs of the herbs used for stuffing roast duck. While she is thus employed, the fox, who has undertaken to look after her nest, adding that 'he loved eggs and ducklings; he should be proud to see a fine nestful in his wood-shed,' furtively unlatches the door of the woodshed and goes in to inspect the nine large, greeny-white eggs that Jemima has laid in her downy boudoir.

During the early passages of what can only be described as his flirtation with Jemima, both animals are shown in the exquisite accompanying watercolour illustrations dressed in versions of human clothing: Jemima in a beribboned blue satin poke bonnet and a trailing paisley shawl, vividly expressive of a kind of feather-brained coquetry; the fox, slyly, in an elegant version of a gamekeeper's thornproof tweed plus-fours and Norfolk jacket. But in the picture showing him turning over the eggs while Jemima is gone, the clothes have vanished. Relieved of the necessity for artifice, the fox has reverted to his natural self and turns on the eggs a shining topaz gaze of naked greed, while clad in nothing more than his own beautiful fur.

Meanwhile, the object of his cunning is traipsing around the kitchen garden, gathering ingredients for a celebration ('I intend to give you a treat. Let us have a dinner-party all to ourselves!') in which she herself is to provide the centrepiece. While thus employed, she runs into Kep, the collie-dog and tells him the whole story: 'he grinned when she described the polite gentleman with sandy whiskers.' Off goes Jemima to her date with the sandy-whiskered gentleman, 'rather burdened with bunches of herbs and two onions in a bag', followed at a discreet distance by Kep and a couple of friends: 'two fox-hound puppies who were out at walk with the butcher'.

Suddenly the languorous pace of the narrative puts on a terrifying turn of speed. Someone locks Jemima in her shed. 'A moment afterwards, there were most awful noises – barking, baying, growls and howls, squalling and groans. And nothing more was ever seen of that foxy-whiskered gentleman.' The accompanying picture shows the white tip of a tawny tail, and a pair of fleeing hind legs. The lead hound is closing fast. The fate of the sandy-whiskered gentleman is not in doubt. Now they have chopped their first fox, the puppies' blood is up. When Kep opens the door of the shed to release Jemima, they rush in and gobble up every one of her eggs. She is escorted home in tears ('on account of those eggs,' says the story,

172

though we may think that it isn't just the eggs she is mourning).

Is this a happy ending? If so, it is a happy ending in much the same way that the endings of *A Midsummer Night's Dream* or *Così Fan Tutte* are happy. Much of the story's charm resides in the austere, almost mythic, contours of its structure. Potter's wayward heroine defies convention by leaving the farmyard and striking out on her own. Order is upset, innocence almost corrupted by cunning before a counter-stroke of matching disorder – Kep and the foxhounds – averts the threatened disaster. The crisis is stilled, the natural order of things restored to its previous state.

Except, of course, that it isn't the same as before. Eggs have been broken, lives lost; moreover, the villain of the story, the murderous dandy whom we first meet sitting on his tail on a tree stump (in order to keep his elegant suiting dry), leisurely scanning a newspaper in a pretty thicket of foxgloves, is undoubtedly its most attractive character. Certainly more attractive than the nitwit Jemima, her officious saviour, the collie Kep, or his loutish foxhound henchmen. The result is that the tension of the narrative, rather than being a straightforward tug-of-war between the Good and the Bad, becomes a sophisticated cats' cradle of emotion in which admiration for the fox's qualities and a recognition that it is part of his predator's nature to chase and be chased tremble in an uneasy balance.

The history of fox-hunting is steeped in this ambiguity. The fox is personalized, given names: Chaucer and Somerville & Ross call him Dan Russel or Russell, more commonly he is known as Charlie, after Charles James Fox. With the rise of hunting as a mass pursuit in the mid-nineteenth century, the preservation of the fox becomes a kind of fetish and vulpicide – or the killing of a fox by any means other than hunting with hounds – a taboo of extraordinary power. You get the distinct impression, on reading accounts of certain nineteenth-century huntsmen and Masters, that they would be far less disturbed by the idea of a baby being shot than a fox.

In Anthony Trollope's novel *The American Senator*, two narrative strands entwine, both uneasily concerned with social order and change. In the first, a young woman, Arabella Trefoil, devotes herself to the pursuit of a good catch, Lord Rufford, whom she hopes to ensnare on the hunting field. In the second, the institution of hunting itself is observed through the eyes of the American Senator of the title, Mr Elias Gotobed, who takes up the case of one of Lord Rufford's vulpicidal tenants. Lord Rufford wishes to preserve the foxes on his land, so that he can hunt them. The tenant, Mr Goarly, lays poison for foxes, to prevent the damage they do to his livestock.

Mr Gotobed, attending a hunt which begins with the melancholy discovery of a fox poisoned by Mr Goarly ('It was as though some special friend of the [hunt] had died that morning, and the spirits of the sportsmen were too dejected for their sport'), is mystified by what he observes: 'I should say that it is one of the most incomprehensible things that I have ever seen in the course of a rather long and varied life . . . You get a fox to begin with, and are all broken-hearted. Then you come across another, after riding about all day, and the chances are you can't catch him.'

Trollope, for his own satirical purposes, is allowing Mr Gotobed to believe that the purpose of the hunt is straightforward fox-killing. (His uncomprehending position was later adopted by the twenty-first century politicians debating the future of hunting.) For huntsmen and for the landowners who allow the hunt onto their land in order to be rid of a troublesome pest, the death of the fox has always been an animating principle; for the field rather less so.

They are pleased if they hear a kill blown, because they tend to feel, with Surtees' greengrocer MFH, Jorrocks, that

'It ar'n't that I loves the fox less, but that I loves the 'ound more.' But really it is the journey, rather than its destination, that is for them the point of hunting. They turn out for the ride, the company, for the exercise, for the feeling of being out in the weather, whatever it may be, or the hours spent crossing and recrossing a particular piece of country, so that eventually it becomes mapped in your head – a part, almost, of the person that you are. They come because they like to see hounds work, or possibly because they fancy the whipper-in and hope to make him love them.

Or perhaps – and this is why I began and, having begun, continued – because they are gripped by the *Arabian Nights* aspect of hunting: the narrative that always begins with the same formula: 'Once upon a time,' and then goes on to weave a pattern that is strange and different and captivating with every repetition.

On my first evening's autumn hunting what I thought, as the edge of the sky turned from blue to violet to indigo to black and we trudged back down the hill towards the field where the hound van was parked, was that we, the foot followers, were like the chorus in a drama: observing the action, commenting and sometimes speculating on its progress, engaged in the outcome, but only marginally involved in influencing it. We were a part of the story – small, but not quite insignificant.

When I was asked if I wanted to come to some of the other events listed on the meet card: the Countryside Alliance Host-A-Roast, the Dinner Dance, the Hunt Ball, I was absurdly pleased. I thought it meant that I was becoming absorbed into the life of the Ashford Valley and said yes to everything.

The Host-A-Roast was a dinner party to which everyone had to contribute a course. I was to bring a starter and after a good deal of thought prepared three: a salad with rocket and pear, Parma ham and parmesan, two dishes of chicken liver pâté and a great Italian earthenware platter of Elizabeth David's Piedmontese peppers, roasted with tomato, garlic and anchovy. When I had made these things and they were laid out on my table in London, ready to be taken to Kent, I thought they looked beautiful: the tangle of dull green jagged-edged rocket leaves, the curved slices of creamy pear and grainy pale yellow flakes of Parmesan and silky translucent slices of rosy pink and white marbled ham; the white-glazed dishes of pâté, sealed with ovals of semi-translucent butter in which a single bay leaf lay suspended; the brilliant red, orange and yellow peppers lying like sunflower petals on their shallow terracotta dish.

But on the motorway a mysterious transformation came over them. They emerged from the journey in some disarray – the moulded wreath of fruit and flowers around the edge of the earthenware platter smeared with anchovy-tinged olive oil, the salad rather limp and curling on its old willow-patterned ashet, the two dishes of pâté pale and greasy beneath their coatings of butter. A thick smell of roasting meat billowed from the front door as I went in (and what about my clothes? A combination of slate-blue velvet shift and ruby velvet slippers had looked restrained-but-original when I checked the looking-glass in Greenwich before setting off. But a panicky glance round a room full of little black dresses and dressy two-pieces with important bits of costume jewellery pinned to the lapels made it clear that I was suitably got up only for a role as the evening's token Boheem. Which, I supposed, was fair enough).

'Now, Jane,' said our hostess kindly, marshalling us to the table. 'Suppose you tell us what these lovely things are.' I told. There was a brief, bleak silence (this was before Jamie and Nigella had really got revved up on the Mediterranean front), then people began to help themselves to teeny tiny portions. In the candlelight, the Parmesan looked like toenail gratings and the rocket like weeds. The chicken liver was too salty. It was all wrong. But what on earth would have been right? (The answer, it turned out, was mackerel pâté. The next time I was invited to one of these dinners, they didn't just say what to bring, but thoughtfully provided a recipe – mackerel, Philadelphia cheese, lemon juice, horseradish; whizz together, chill – as well.)

The first course was tactfully cleared and replaced with huge plates of lamb and roast potatoes, carrots and peas and gravy. The wine went round, and the ladies grew hilarious. The conversation turned to Men Behaving Feebly. One of the men present – my right-hand neighbour, it turned out – had stepped from his commuter train onto the station platform at Pluckley one winter's night to be met, as a surprise treat, by his girlfriend dressed only in a fur coat and suspenders. Seeking the perfect place to take advantage of this opportunity, he had driven into a field and there stuck fast, the wheels of his car spinning hopelessly, the winter chill striking cruelly around the edges of the fur coat. In the end he had been obliged to get out and trudge over the soggy plough until he found a farmer willing to get a tractor out of the barn and haul him back on to the highway. A surprising number of other people had had similar experiences which they were prepared to share. The wine went round, and the ladies cackled, and the men talked about work, and shooting, and refilled each other's glasses.

There was a pause in the conversation and both my neighbours turned to me simultaneously. 'So,' they said,

'Where do you live?'

'What do you do?'

'London,' I said to my right. And 'I'm a journalist,' to my left.

'So you're a townie/reptile, are you?' said either side, with astonishing animus. Too slow to realize that it was women in general they were cross with, not me in particular, and too awkward to charm them into good tempers, I began an indignant defence of my rural (well, semi-rural) credentials and my occupation, contriving to make them even crosser than before. Then all three of us lapsed into a thundery silence which slowly rolled, like fog, the entire length of the table. 'Well, what about coffee and some liqueurs?' cried our hostess, rallying bravely at the far end.

Not for me. I gathered up my half-eaten dishes – I would be living on the leftovers for the rest of the week – and stumped off into the night, tripping over the irregular ground in my velvet slippers (I hadn't realized about the dense, impenetrable dark of late nights in the country, with stars, but no streetlights), saying furiously to myself that I would never go to a dinner like it, not ever again.

I did, though. The very next month I went to the Countryside Alliance Dinner Dance at the Ramada Hotel, Hollingbourne. The Ramada Hotel was a squat collection of buildings next to the A20, rather dishevelled and impromptu-looking, as though they had their back view turned to the road, and their best side facing the other direction. A minibus-load of us was going from the Rooting Street yard. We met beforehand for drinks at Mrs Rogers's farmhouse and stood about making desultory conversation, crunching crisps deafeningly in the nervous silences that kept falling and trying to get used to the sight of each other in long dresses and make-up, instead of our sweaty yard uniform of saggy breeches and half-chaps.

By the time the minibus arrived the glasses of fizzy and our elegant frocks had combined to produce a giggly, festive atmosphere which survived our ferociously early arrival at the feast (Mrs Rogers had a horror of being late for anything). We found our table, bought some wine and settled down to be amused. The Ramada Hotel did a solid line in mass catering:

slabs of roast meat on warm plates, with mixed vegetables and ladles of gravy disconcertingly served over the left shoulder by nervous youths in black bow ties, preceded by the sort of soup that doesn't move about much, and followed by profiteroles with extra cream and coffee with an After Eight Mint in the saucer.

Then it was time for the speeches. The first was from Michael Howard, another local MP (it was a source of chagrin in the Ashford Valley that while two of our MPs, Damian Green and Michael Howard, were thoroughly good sorts and utterly sound on hunting, a third was Anne Widdecombe, who was said to have curtains featuring hunting scenes in her house, but couldn't be doing with the real thing. Despite our efforts to convert her with trips to the kennels, to see how sweet the foxhounds were, she had a lamentable tendency to vote in the House for hunting to be banned).

Then came the main guest speaker, who was not a hunting man, but a fairly well-known professional countryman. He had a big round face, like the Man in the Moon, only crimson, and a cummerbund that spanned his front with difficulty: John Bull in black tie. And he gave a distinctly John Bullish sort of speech, excoriating the Government, which was full – he said – of shirt-lifters (this was the time of Peter Mandelson's ascendancy), for its effete favouring of the rights of immigrants, single mothers (Mrs Rogers rolled her eyes at me) and disabled lesbians over those of the honest sporting man.

This was not a line likely to play well at our table, the female occupants of which were mostly quite a bit younger than John Bull and already jockeying fiercely for the right to sit next to Mrs Rogers's gay hunting hairdresser at the Hunt Ball, on the grounds that he was extremely good looking, full of gossip and absolutely guaranteed not to be sick into one's handbag before the disco even got going. Which was not (I gathered) invariably the case with AVH men. In fact, the speech didn't go down awfully well at all and the applause at the end was distinctly muted. 'Misjudged his audience. And a drop too much beforehand,' said Mrs Rogers tartly, into the subdued darkness of the charabanc on the way home.

Rather in the teeth of experience, I was looking forward to the hunt ball. Single motherhood, invariably coupled by people like John Bull with the adjective 'feckless', had turned out, during the ten years I'd been doing it, to be an education in Victorian standards of virtue and duty. I never went out in the evenings, and when I moved house a friend who was helping me gave all the old evening dresses I'd kept since university to the Oxfam shop, on the grounds that I wouldn't be needing them any more because they 'didn't fit in with my lifestyle'.

Overcome with excitement at the prospect of an evening spent dancing in a long frock until late ('carriages at 2 a.m.', it said grandly on the ball invitation), I had bought a new ball gown at Monsoon in Canterbury. It was black velvet, with a cyclamen silk flounce around the bottom and a bodice held up with the slenderest of cyclamen silk straps, draped at the bosom and lined in the same colour silk. I thought it looked like the scandalous black velvet ball dress painted by John Singer Sargent and was enchanted with it. Even the girls in Monsoon went 'Oooh!' when I came out of the dressing room.

We met for drinks beforehand in someone's converted barn (open fire, milling labradors, soaring glass roof through which the stars shone coldly, the Ashford Valley men looking constrained in their black ties), then set off for Hollingbourne in a hired people carrier with a world-weary driver who seemed already to be anticipating the state of joviality or collapse in which he'd have to take us all home again.

They were still hoovering the swirly carpet in the entrance

lobby of the Ramada Hotel when we arrived, a good twenty minutes ahead of the official start time. Heavy metal grilles were pulled down over the bars, the door to the cloakroom was uncompromisingly shut and the girl with the key nowhere to be found. We stood in our coats making conversation at the tops of our voices while the Hoover roared around us. Eventually a harassed-looking manager came with a great bunch of keys like a prison warder and opened up the cloakroom and the shuttered bars.

By the time we got back from fussing with our hair and trying to check our back views in the cloakroom glass, horribly lit with a fluorescent glare like a supermarket fish counter, the men had a row of drinks lined up along the bar and the place had begun to fill up. I was growing more used to the sight of the Ashford Valley *en fête*, but was still struck by the extraordinary mermaid silhouette of the women, emphasized this year by a fashion for evening gowns crocheted from skeins of gold or silver thread with fish-scale sequins, which stretched like fishing nets over arms and torsos rippling with bodybuilders' muscle from years of grappling with pulling horses, then dwindled from the waist down into ordinary human proportions.

To my dismay I found when we went into dinner that I was not, as I had hoped, sitting with Jamie the hunting hairdresser and his partner, or Mrs Rogers's gentle, dressage-rider friend Amanda, down from Oxfordshire with her husband, but with another pair of visitors, who were in property and were house-hunting locally. We had barely sat down before the husband's hand attached itself to my knee with the insistent grope of a clematis tendril blindly searching for solid support and he began, between spoons of the Ramada's distinctive glutinous soup (tomato and basil, it said on the menu), to tell me what a lovely girl I would be, if only I would take the trouble to Make Something of Myself.

I felt distinctly miffed about this, having spent most of the afternoon trying to do exactly that, with the aid of curlers and Firm Control hair gel and eyeliner and little puffs of glitter powder to the cheekbones and décolletage. I was wondering, as the blood-warm platesful of beef and individual Yorkshire puddings came round, whether to stick him sharply in the wrist with my fork when there was a disturbance on the other side of the table. Mrs Househunter had thought this a good moment to take off her knickers. Now she'd decided to put them back on again and Mrs Rogers's husband had gallantly interposed his person between her and the rest of us. He was quite a slight man and Mrs Househunter was a substantial figure of a woman. The effect was unmistakably that of a saucy seaside postcard in which the disrobing bathers were unaccountably wearing evening dress.

At the sight of the individual Yorkshires, Mr and Mrs Househunter concluded that this perhaps wasn't their sort of evening after all, and left to find excitement elsewhere, leaving the rest of us to eat up our lemon meringue pie with rosettes of squirty cream in something of the atmosphere of frisson that you get in a girls'-school dining room when someone is known to have done something Really Awful.

Fortunately, just as the rattling of the coffee pots and the cheerful tinkle of liqueur glasses of Tia Maria and Baileys began, attention was deflected from our table by a fearful crash at the opposite end of the room. Someone had toppled over on to a table, demolishing the centrepiece and several people's half-eaten puddings, and was now reeling about like a wounded elephant looking very poorly, his lovely brocade waistcoat all covered with crumbs and dabs of cream, streams of party popper tissue and the multi-coloured confetti of glittery stars with which the tables had been strewn.

As he lurched for the exit, trailing streamers, Mrs Rogers seized the microphone set up for the speeches and the band

and took a grip on the evening. First we all had to play a game where you put a £5 note with your name on it in a box and then held your arms in the air or left them by your sides and the table with the most arms in the right place won (or something like that. I couldn't get the hang). Then there were speeches and a presentation to an outgoing Master and then the band struck up and we all rushed on to the tiny dance floor and jumped up and down to a deafening set of hits from the seventies.

'At the Old Surrey ball, they have a marching band. And a vodka luge,' screamed one of my partners, but he was drowned out by 'Hi Ho, Silver Lining', and I never discovered what other refinements the Old Surrey went in for. On my way to the cloakroom I saw the wounded elephant in the brocade waistcoat laid out on the chill hard paving outside the Ramada foyer and heard the distant wail of sirens.

Having gone to bed very late, I woke early, feeling un-accountably fresh and energetic, and went down to the yard, where I found Mrs Rogers vigorously mucking out a stable by way of a hangover cure. 'What a lovely evening,' I said. 'It was fun, wasn't it?' said Mrs Rogers, heaving a clod of horse dung towards the wheelbarrow. 'Though at the Tally Ho club dances,' she added, almost wistfully, I thought (the Tally Ho club were the Ashford Valley's foot followers), 'they never feel the evening's complete until there's been a knife fight.'

I continued to go out on foot on Monday evenings, slowly becoming accustomed to finding a meet in a remote field up an unmarked track with the help of a set of instructions scribbled on the back of an old dressage test. Getting there while it was still light was usually a puzzle, but leaving again in the dark could be terrifying. Often I found myself driving, completely lost, in circles along narrow black tree-hung tunnels, unmarked by signposts (my guess was that they'd all been taken away during the Second World War to confuse the invading Germans, and never replaced), unlit except by the car headlights, twigs whipping the windscreen and small creatures of the night fleeing across the road ahead of me – badgers, rats, rabbits, foxes and once a fast-moving weasel.

But by degrees the contrast between a London life of deadlines and appointments and 400 words by this afternoon, always talking or thinking, always on the run, always slightly late, and the Ashford Valley opposites of earliness and stillness interrupted by flurries of contained activity became less strange. Then one day when I was at the yard for a lesson, a girl called Claire, who had a couple of ponies in livery and hunted regularly, offered to lend me one of them so that I could join the mounted field on a Saturday morning.

Star was a snappy little beast, against whose diminutive sides my legs trailed like Don Quixote's. If I'd tried, I could probably have locked my ankles under his belly. He had a busy, twinkletoed gait, very different from Mrs Rogers's old hunter, Sam, on whom I was now having most of my lessons. 'You'd better have a lesson on Star before you go out,' said Mrs R. 'Ponies are very different from horses.' She took me out into a paddock and made me canter the pony all the way round the edge of it, singing 'D'You Ken John Peel' at the top of my voice (to keep me from tensing up, she said) while she and her friend Bridget hung over the fence and cackled.

She was right about the difference between the pony and what I had been used to. I couldn't get used to him at all: the jiggling action, the nearness to the ground which felt, for some reason, more alarming than sitting high above it on 16-hand Sam, the narrowness of the bulk between my knees. It was like sitting on a merry-go-round horse, but less predictable.

I don't remember working myself into a state of terror about going hunting on Star. It is probably because I had no idea of what was involved in the build-up to the moment that I had read about, the meet, with everyone up on their horses, looking tidy and composed and chatting convivially with a glass of port in one hand and a sausage roll in the other while hounds stood obediently in the corner of someone's yard or pub car park, eager as a class of children waiting to be let out of school. As soon as I had my own horse to get ready, I was sick beforehand for an entire season with nerves and terror. But for that first morning out on Star, Claire did everything. She got both ponies ready, rugged and loaded, hers and mine, for a 7 a.m. meet, while I stood about and dabbed ineffectually at unfamiliar buckles and knots.

The morning was sullen: cloudy, damp and cold. Perched uncomfortably on Star's tiny saddle, which was growing slippery with the drizzle, and in any case was designed for a bottom narrower than mine, I sat in a row of horses and riders, ranged at intervals along the edge of a bare-twigged apple orchard, ready to head the fox if he came our way. We sat and sat. We listened to the sounds of whooping and crashing from the wood beyond the orchard. Nothing happened. We sat some more. After half an hour of sitting damply still, I was almost grateful for the sight of a file of black-masked figures moving down the hill towards us.

They came on in silence, not acknowledging us at all. We might have been invisible, if it hadn't been for an extraordinary sensation of menace in the air. With their black clothes and their hidden faces, they reminded me of the silent, deadly Sand People from *Star Wars*. The semiotics of uniform work in both directions, I thought, trying to slow my breathing, so as not to let my sense of dread leak down my spine and communicate itself to the fidgety pony. We, in our tweed coats and velvet caps, with our shiny black boots and horn-handled whips, must seem as loathsome and menacing to the black-shrouded army with its narrow, pillar-box eye-slits, as they did to us. More so, in fact, because we were perched so high above them – arrogantly high, it must look – on these mountainous creatures of metal-shod bone and muscle whose jittery fragility, of which we were so poignantly aware, must appear like pure provocation to these people who considered us their enemies.

The antis filed past, close enough to grab a stirrup iron or drag a rider out of the saddle. They stared hard at us through their eye-slits, but said nothing. The only sound was the cry of hounds in the thicket and the penetrating note of Mrs Rogers's voice from far up the line, calling the police on her mobile phone.

Within the covert, a commotion broke out. Hounds were hunting, the huntsman urging them, branches snapping. The antis moved swiftly towards the noise, which had spread to the end of our line. Someone had seen the fox. Suddenly I remembered what I was doing here, wet and cold and cramped on my child's saddle. 'Ayayayay, Charlie,' I yelled with everyone else. The moment of animation passed. Two of the horses began to dance, anticipating action, but no one gave the order to move. The sounds from the covert seemed different now: not the formal yelps and cries of venery; more a sort of brawling noise, punctuated by infuriated bellows. Then the antis began to stream past us, moving swiftly back towards the brow of the hill.

Now they were no longer silent and frightening, but angry and upset. They looked smaller; diminished, deflated from iconic Sand People to pale teenagers in rusty combats. 'Whore!' they said, in low, intent voices as they passed us. 'Cunt!' 'Murderer!' One of them was holding up something heavy and slippery inside a plastic supermarket bag. 'How would you like a face full of this, you ugly cow?' she yelled, as we turned and began to walk the horses around the margins of the sodden orchard.

At the far end, there was a hunt jump into the neighbouring field: very small, just a telegraph pole, really. 'Are you going to do that?' asked Claire. 'Might as well, just to finish.' 'Oh no,' I said. 'No, no, no I couldn't possibly.' 'Yes you could,' said Claire. 'You don't have to do anything. He'll do it for you. Just sit down and kick. Shall I go first and give you a lead?' 'No, no don't,' I said in a panic. What if she jumped and I couldn't and I got left behind? It was one of my main hunting nightmares, next only to over-riding the Master, for which I had heard that you got sent home. 'Don't do it if you really don't want to,' said Claire, 'but I'm going to go for it.' Ahead of us a pale little girl on a pony as round as a ball cleared the little pole neatly. 'OK,' I said, and I turned the pony round and pointed him at the jump and gave him a kick and over he went before I'd even realized it. And that was it. I'd been hunting, I'd jumped my first hunt jump. I'd begun.

At breakfast in someone's warm farmhouse kitchen I found out what had happened in the covert with the antis. 'They got the fox. Went in among hounds and grabbed what was left of it. The Master was furious. Didn't you hear him shouting, "Give me back my fox"?' 'But why did they want the fox? What will they do with it?' 'Oh, they'll take a photograph of him and stick it on a poster, I expect. You look out for it at the Boxing Day Meet.'

It was 10 a.m. Four hours ago, we had been driving to the meet, our ties neatly knotted and fixed with gold pins, our jackets brushed, our hair impeccably sleeked and netted, our boots polished to a parade gloss. Now our boots were piled outside the back door, our mud-spattered jackets were heaped anyhow inside the horse lorry. In our sweatshirts and thick socks, the ankle cuffs of our breeches flapping open, our faces flushed every shade from rose pink to broken-veined beefsteak crimson, we looked as though we'd changed back into our pyjamas, an infantile version of our earlier intent, focused selves. I ate my plate of bacon and baked beans and drank my mug of sweet tea and a delicious fatigue crept over me, as though I'd successfully completed some enormously difficult and worthwhile task. It was like nothing I had ever felt before.

The borrowed pony was better than no pony at all, but I felt silly, sitting on top of him with my long legs dangling, dwarfed by the others on their big-boned hunters. I didn't exactly decide to buy a horse. Like so many other things about my hunting career, it overtook me, slightly before I was ready for it. Executing an effortful series of crooked leg yields in the rubber school one day, I opened my mouth without thinking. 'Perhaps I should get a horse,' I said idly. Mrs Rogers and I used words in different ways. She was not much given to verbal experiment, to trying on concepts like Miss Selfridge T-shirts, constructing fantasies and holding them up against herself to see whether or not they suited her. She used words for a purpose, like the implements around the yard. So she took me seriously. 'Say when you're ready, and we'll do something about it,' she said. 'I guess I'm ready now,' I heard myself reply.

It wasn't true. I knew it wasn't, as soon as I'd clambered off Flossie, the skittish mare on whom I'd been riding my ungainly leg yields, and followed Mrs Rogers into her kitchen. It was lunchtime and her husband was hovering by the microwave in a green boilersuit. When he saw us, he scuttled away. Under the table Buster, the long-legged chocolate terrier, was gnawing a battered toy swan that had seen better days.

'Can't do this weekend,' said Mrs Rogers, flicking at speed through an enormous diary. 'Not next weekend. Walking country the following Friday, but the Friday after that is free. OK? We'll go to Ireland. You pay for my flight and hotel bill. I'll call Michael, he's a dealer, I've known him since I was at school, and get him to line us up a few horses. Nothing too strong. We'll tell him to find you something brain-dead for your first horse. And it doesn't have to be pretty.' 'I'd like it if it could be a little bit pretty,' I said, feebly. Mrs Rogers ignored me. 'Good,' she said, getting up. 'Stansted to Dublin. Here's the number. Let me know when you've booked the tickets.'

Everything about this excursion felt wrong to me. Who was going to look after my boy while I went jaunting off to Ireland in search of an ugly, brain-dead horse for which, Mrs Rogers had said, I should budget about £3,500, plus another £1,000 or so for tack. Why was I even considering buying a horse when there were damp patches all around the chimney in my bedroom, where the roof was clearly letting in water?

Perhaps, I thought as I drove back to London, I could call Mrs Rogers in the morning and say I'd made a mistake, that I couldn't afford it, that I'd decided to wait until my riding improved, or until next season. I could do this, of course I could. But there would be a cost. She was a woman who used words carefully, as though they had a worth. If I took back what I had said, I would be devaluing my own currency. Would it really make any difference if she thought me silly and vacillating? Why should her opinion of my character matter when our lives intersected only in this obscure corner of my life?

It mattered, I discovered, worrying as I drove at the knot of feelings that felt tight and hard in my chest, because I wanted her to think well of me. These feelings took about 50 miles of motorway to identify. They were not sensations to which I was accustomed. Having spent so many years failing to please my parents or my teachers, I had lost the habit of allowing myself to respect anyone else's opinion. Still, here I was, wanting for the first time ever to join in, rather than simply observe. I wanted to be a good horsewoman; I wanted to pop tidily over a hunt jump; I wanted to earn the right to wear a black jacket with yellow facings and hunt buttons.

None of this could happen if I didn't have a horse. Arriving home, I hurried indoors and booked the flights before I could change my mind.

The horse-finding expedition was to be a brisk affair, lasting 24 hours precisely. We would fly to Dublin in the evening, then pick up a hire car and drive to Naas. There we would stay overnight in what Mrs Rogers called 'a nice little B&B' before driving on to Cashel in the morning to meet Michael, the horse dealer, who would take us to inspect however many horses he'd managed to assemble. Then I was to catch the 7.30 flight back to Stansted. Mrs Rogers was staying on in Ireland to do something horsey.

By the time the plane had left the ground and we had poured ourselves plastic goblets of inky screw-top airplane Cabernet Sauvignon, something of my uncertainty seemed to have communicated itself to Mrs Rogers (or Jillie, as I must now try to think of her – we were, after all, about to share a bedroom in the nice little B&B).

Gaze firmly fixed on the grey plastic back of the seat in front, she embarked on a cautionary tale about some tire-some, indecisive woman who thought she wanted a horse and had put Michael to a great deal of trouble before concluding that, after all, she wasn't really keen. I made dutiful noises of disapproval at such feeble behaviour, and tried hard to look like someone absolutely committed to buying whatever Michael had been good enough to select for me.

It was raining when we landed at Dublin. We drove in the dark to Naas and dragged our bags into the glaring tiled entrance lobby of the B&B. A stuffed fox peered glassily through a thicket of dusty silk flowers stuffed into a window alcove. We looked in at the empty dining room, a riot of bright orange varnished pine barley-sugar balustrading and little vases of dried grasses, and retreated for our supper to a raucous steak house full of convivial farmers. We drank Guinness and Jameson's. Several times, Jillie disappeared to make a call on her mobile. I felt I was being insufficiently entertaining.

Outside, it was still raining. We ran up the streaming high street to the B&B and got ready for bed. Jillie changed into a pink satin nightie and set the alarm clock for 5.45. I lay awake in the black night and listened to lorries swooshing through riverine puddles, shouts and sounds of crashing metal barrels from the hotel car park, the ringing of bells and bawled conversations of passers-by. If I slept before the alarm clock rang, I was not aware of it. In the lightless pre-dawn, I wished I had not come.

The rain was worse when we got up. At breakfast in the orange dining room it fell past the window like dirty bathwater. The road was a twin ochre stream, with a slick spine of tarmac separating two fast-flowing rivulets. 'I'll drive,' said Jillie.

Outside Naas, we took a wrong turning and found ourselves off the main route to Cashel, on a winding road through villages with high streets like those of my childhood – butchers, bakers, grocers, ironmongers, all with their names painted in curly fairground letters picked out in scarlet and gold on boards above shiny plate-glass windows. The rain stopped. The sky cleared. In the bright autumn sunshine everything seemed freshly laundered. The horror of the sleepless night subsided into a pleasant, fuzzy vagueness. To the surprise of both of us, I map-read us off the B-road to our rendezvous with Michael, only a few minutes late.

When we picked up Michael, the atmosphere changed again. Now the adventure was really beginning. Affected by Michael's whiff of horses and testosterone, we became animated and cheerful. He was a tall man with a loud, bleating voice, a handsome sheep's face and longish grey hair, plastered against his head, but springing up into a fringe of little curls at the back of his neck above the collar of his elderly Barbour. He got into the passenger seat, next to Jillie. I sat behind him in the back.

First, we were going to Lismore, to see a man called John, who had one or possibly more horses for us to see, and might or might not be there in person. 'I hope he is,' said Michael, craning over his shoulder to speak to me. 'You'd like him. He's a psychology graduate.'

We bounced at a terrific lick along winding roads, through forests, past castles and lakes, up and down mountainsides. Michael, who had seemed rather bad-tempered when we picked him up, became convivial, conducting one busy conversation of horsey gossip with Jillie in the front and another, about books and hunting, with me in the back, breaking off at intervals to point out the sights whizzing past the car window.

The sky darkened, was split by shafts of lightning, then cleared again to reveal a rainbow arching from mountain to lake. I had not been to Ireland before. Scraps of Yeats floated disconnectedly into my head. I felt as though I were on the verge of understanding something remarkable. 'Isn't it pretty?' I said aloud, then hoped they hadn't heard me.

Up into the hills we drove, past a farm with a barking dog on a chain and a solitary child practising skids on his bike, then off the metalled road onto a rutted mud track, through a broken gate into a yard such as I had never seen in England. Hulks of rusting farm machinery like dead dinosaurs, heaps of bald tractor tyres, old doors and rolls of wire and coils of rope lay about in a confusion that seemed so wilful as to be almost artificial. Over it all kittens swarmed. Jillie opened the car boot to get out her cap and half-chaps and at once a couple of the bolder kittens shinned up the side of the car and settled comfortably on a corner of her suitcase.

From a wooden shed, through whose cobwebby window-panes a huge collection of empty bottles could be seen ranged along the window-sill, there emerged a handsome young woman in jeans and gumboots. She had cheeks the emphatic pink of a wild rose and coarse, glossy black hair like a horse's mane. 'Gina,' whispered Jillie. 'John must be away.' He was. We followed Gina into the dark barn, a corner of which had been partitioned into stalls over whose half-doors poked a row of long, inquisitive heads. The whole place was so strange, so fairy-like, that I half-expected one of the heads to speak a greeting.

'This is the mare,' said Gina, buckling a stiff, mud-caked head collar around the throat of a gawky, blue-grey animal with gangling, hairy legs and a startled expression. 'Will you ride her now, so?' she added, trotting the mare up and down under Jillie's inscrutable gaze, then leading her down the mud track towards a field pocked with rabbit holes, bristly with thistles and already occupied by a couple of loose horses who came cantering interestedly up as we entered. 'Whoosh,' said Gina, flapping them away like a couple of wasps at a picnic.

I had been trying hard not to think about this bit of the trip. I knew that sooner or later I'd have to sit on a horse, and Jillie had explained that I was unlikely to be riding in a nice, tidy arena equipped with a mounting block, which was all I was used to. I'd only attempted a leg-up once before. It had not been a success.

'Weighs eight stone and legs-up as 12,' said Jillie warningly to Michael, as he heaved me in the direction of the saddle. With a lurch and a scramble I found myself uncertainly lodged on top of the horse, whose back seemed an improbably long way from the prickly, uneven ground. 'Walk on,' said Jillie. 'Tk tk,' chirruped Gina to the mare, and, 'Away with you, now,' to the loose horses, who bucked and flounced to the side of the field.

Head in the air like a debutante at a Lucie Clayton deportment class, the mare stepped ahead then, gauging the uncertainty of her rider, moved up into a rapid, bouncing trot. 'Stiff on the left rein; pokes her nose,' said Jillie. 'Nice little lady's hunter,' said Michael. 'Too sharp for you,' said Jillie, to me. 'Get off now. She's not for you.'

'But,' I said, 'But . . .' Jillie was already on her way back to the car. I dropped down over the mare's side and followed her down the track, dragging my feet like a sulky child. Back in the yard, kittens were scattering in all directions from the boot and back seat of the car. I took off my cap and looked back at the mare.

She had stopped in the lane and seemed to be watching us. She looked beautiful and comic, with her fine, dark eyes, gawky legs and unclipped, mud-spattered grey-blue coat. 'I know she's the first one I've sat on, and I know I don't know anything about horses,' I said doggedly as we drove away, 'but I liked her. I could feel us getting on, through my bottom.' 'Don't worry,' said Michael kindly. 'We'll find you something better than that. Now I've seen you ride, I know just what you want.'

Three weeks later, the telephone rang. 'Hello, it's Jillie here,' said Jillie, unnecessarily (no one else I know speaks in quite that tone of penetrating command). 'Well, are you coming to see her, or not?' I was. Out through the suburbs I drove, past the cow-headed scrubland ponies, over the muddy Medway, past the earthworks, the orchards and the oast houses, in at the yard gate – and there she was, standing uncertainly at the back of the quarantine pen. Agnes, or Dorothy, or whatever Gina had said her name was. Stiff on the left rein. Pokes her nose. A nice little lady's hunter. My long-legged, dark-eyed, hairy mare. Crikey. Whatever had I done?

PART THREE

The mysterious thread of connection I thought I had felt between me and the grey mare did not manifest itself in an immediate improvement in my riding. In the gap between buying her and seeing her again, poking disdainfully at a bran mash in the quarantine pen, I had undergone a brief relapse into my pre-riding fantasies of competent horsewomanship. We had looked at a couple of other horses after her. By chance they were all mares, and all quite pretty – none of them the ugly brain-dead gelding that Jillie had prescribed as my ideal first horse. One, a kindly 12-year-old schoolmistress – gentle, accomplished, beginning to wind down after a modestly successful career – had seemed an obvious choice.

After seeing her I had spent a long evening on the telephone to my son's godmother, Pip, an artist who had hunted as a child with Meynell & South Staffordshire. She was the only person I knew, outside the Rooting Street yard, who had a clue about horses. We had a peculiar, foggy conversation, handicapped on either side by the fact that she, who was knowledgeable, had seen neither of the alternatives while I, who had ridden the gentle, 12-year-old schoolmistress and the sharp, stiff, hairy, nose-poking but enchanting Irish mare and now must decide between them, knew nothing at all, beyond an inexplicable instinct that the difficult mare was the one I wanted. Round and round we went, arguing the virtues of safety and gentleness against those of a mare who, as Jillie put it, had done nothing but 'hunt all over Ireland with her head in the air'.

All rational argument was on the side of the schoolmistress.

But in the morning, with a lurching, parachute-jump sensation of vertigo, I told my brain to shut up, listened to my heart and ordered a bank draft for the grey mare's purchase price of £3,200 (to include vetting and shipping from Ireland). I had had that vertiginous feeling before. Once on the top of a number 36 bus when, having been for a grim preliminary appointment with a bearded lady at an abortion clinic, I happened to catch sight of the sunlight dappling the Thames as the bus trundled south over the Vauxhall bridge and felt a sudden, light-hearted certainty that I wouldn't be keeping the appointment she'd given me. And a second time, after the baby arrived and living with him in a one-bedroomed flat had become impossible, when I bought, on instinct and against reason, a house that was more than I could afford and quite unsuitable for a baby.

Pip had been in on those two pieces of rashness, too. She was the only person who, when I told her that I was unexpectedly, inconveniently, untidily pregnant, said, 'How marvellous,' instead of 'Oh dear', or 'Have you thought of getting rid of it?' And she'd found the house in Greenwich and egged me on to buy it. 'It's got stone floors and no bath,' I said, in tears, after looking at it. There was another house, much more sensible, better decorated, more child-friendly, that reason said I should buy. But it was in a place where I had been bitterly unhappy for five years and I couldn't make up my mind to it.

'You like the Greenwich house,' said Pip, inexorably. And I did. So after a brief internal struggle I abandoned the elegantly upholstered window seats, the upstairs bathroom and plentiful dwarf cupboards of its better equipped rival and bought it. Then I bought a tin bath with handles at either end ('Most people use them for bathing dogs in,' said the man at the ironmonger's, when I told him what I needed it for) and bathed the baby in that until he was old enough to stand up in the shower, and neither that nor the stone floors seemed to bother him unduly.

In theory the mare was a less alarming commitment than those two pieces of life-changing folly. I could, after all, get rid of her easily enough if I found I had made a mistake, which was not the case with the baby or even the house. She was a pretty, brave, nine-year-old, 15h 3in, Connemara/thorough-bred cross who knew everything about hunting, if not much about anything else (she was, as we swiftly discovered once she arrived at Rooting Street, a stranger to the dressage ring, and had never heard of refinements such as an outline or a bend to the inside. Mind you, nor had I, so we were evenly matched in that respect). Raw as she was, she would make an admirable horse for a (lightweight) hunt servant. I would certainly make my money back on her if I wanted to sell.

But I told myself that I wouldn't be selling. I'd felt she was my mare when I sat on her. Barring some misfortune to one or other of us, I reckoned we would be together for years to come. Plenty of time for her to turn my life upside down.

In the end I bought her frivolously, as you might buy a dress, or a pair of earrings, because there was something about her. In fact, I often bought both dresses and earrings in just this way. Walking down a street, window-shopping idly, suddenly there would be destiny, in the form of an electric blue mohair dress, or a couple of tear-drop pearls, the size of cherry stones, trembling from a pair of diamond chip studs. They came quite rarely, these overwhelming impulses to ownership, which was just as well. But on the whole they turned out all right in the end, in the sense that I had not yet regretted spending wildly on something that had called insistently to be bought. Regret came when I turned prudent and resisted the impulse. I carried around with me a dismal mental catalogue of things that I'd known were right, but had been too cowardly to buy. In a muddled, penny-pinching way, I had the instincts of a collector.

It was a while, though, since I'd collected anything with feelings. Some years before I got pregnant, I bought a Siamese kitten and found when I went to pick him up that his mother, who was nervous, young and silly, and had had to be spayed because of her temperamental inadequacies (she suffered from a feline version of Jemima Puddleduck's maternal ditziness), was coming too – a sort of buy one, get one free, special offer. It was an unexpected arrangement, but it seemed to work quite well. The cats kept each other amused while I was out at work and seemed pleased, on the whole, to see me when I got back.

Then I went and, as my (female) GP oddly put it, got myself pregnant, at which the cats cheerfully and generously became my family. They slept – compact, comforting and I suppose unhygienic weights of shifting bone and muscle – on the end of the bed. They jumped on to the sofa when I crouched drearily in a corner of it, wondering what was to become of me. They allowed themselves to be wept on with only faint moues of dismay at the wet teardrops falling on their nice dry fur. They were beautiful, high-spirited and amusing, and they reminded me that these virtues existed at a time when I was in danger of forgetting them.

The baby was born in bitter weather at the beginning of Advent. The heating in the flat had to be turned up to torrid hospital levels when I brought him home, and for the first time since I'd lived with the cats, a great plague of fleas broke out. My mother came up to London and took control, sprinkling the floor with hoar-frost drifts of some powdery white flea toxin with a macho, Vietnam War sort of name: Dawn Raid, it was called, or Rug Patrol. The cats hated the pungent indoor frosting as much as they disliked the hard frozen ground and sharp burning edge of ice crystals on every blade of grass outside. They picked their way from the garden to the flat and back again with expressions of disgust and sat on the edges of the furniture looking stony and put out.

Somehow it seemed to have been agreed that I couldn't possibly look after two cats and a baby all on my own, so the cats went away, howling dismally, slender mink-brown paws clawing at the grille of their travelling basket, to a better life in the country with the new grandparents, who now lived in Greenways, the raw brick bungalow that my grandfather had built.

They were bold hunting cats. We lived at the point where Camberwell, Peckham and East Dulwich met and when I first got them I worried that their exotic looks and confiding natures would get them stolen directly if they went out. On the other hand, it seemed horrible to keep them prisoner for their own safety in a small flat when outside the back door was a huge garden (with a noisy encampment of urban foxes at the bottom of it). So I turned them loose, with misgiving at first, then more confidently as they survived their night-time adventures with foxes, traffic and pedigree cat-rustlers, returning at intervals to leave delicate black pawmarks over the white bedlinen and the pale sofa.

They survived like that for several years before they migrated from the urban excitements of SE5 to a peaceful retirement in the country. And there, in a matter of months, they were killed on the road, one after the other; first the son, then the mother. 'He was a good friend to you,' said my father, looking at the limp dead body of the younger cat, stretched out in the driveway at what had been the peak of his strength and beauty. And I thought that I must take care not to let an animal into my heart ever again because the sadness when it left was simply intolerable.

My son and I lived for a long time – almost nine years – without any animals at all: not so much as a newt or a stick insect in a jar. And then we got two in the space of a couple of weeks: the grey mare and a black kitten whom I'd found on a card in the window of the Charing newsagent's, saying Kittens, Free to Good Homes. Alexander had been talking for some time about wanting a pet. A cat had even made it on to his birthday list, along with a Man U kit with his name on the back and a pop-up goal, whatever one of those was. I visited the kitten's owners, persuaded them with a little difficulty that ours would be a good home, even though SE10 wasn't quite the rural idyll they'd had in mind, and brought him home, sitting very calm and decorous on a wadded blanket in the bottom of the wicker cat basket which was wedged across the passenger seat of the car.

I stopped the car outside our house, and in the cold dark street where the tinsel and Christmas lights were beginning to go up in the windows I loosened the fastening of the cat basket. Then I put my key in the front door, opened it a little way and gently tipped the kitten out on to the floor of the front room where Alexander was sitting at the table, eating his tea. He advanced quite boldly a few steps into the room. He was all fuzzy, like black thistledown, with huge round eyes not quite turned from kitten blue to green and a little pointed candle of a tail. Alexander looked down at the kitten, and what he said after a moment was, 'Where are we going to bury him when he dies? There isn't room in our garden.'

What? What? This wasn't the scene as I'd been playing it in my head all the way back from Kent. Where were the cries of 'Isn't he sweet!' and 'Is he really mine?' and 'What shall we call him?' Where was the excitement and the pleasure? And actually, wasn't there something quite monstrous about a child whose thoughts on first clapping eyes on a new kitten turned at once to mortality and grave-digging?

'He's a kitten. He's not going to die for years and years,' I said furiously. 'Now, he's had a long journey and this is the first time he's ever left his mummy, so why don't you try and make him feel at home here?'

It was plain that this kitten, longed-for in theory, was felt at first by Alexander to be something of an oppression in the living fur. For his size, he was a curiously dominant presence in the house. He couldn't be put aside and forgotten about like a book or a toy. He had needs – for food, warmth, attention, to be let in, then straight afterwards to be let out again. There was always something. Even when he was absent, we were worrying about where he'd got to. He was constantly about the place, a breathing, scratching, capering responsibility. Even I, who had spent as much time sharing a household with an animal as not, began to feel a frisson of Alexander's unease at the strangeness and the burden of taking a dependent fellow creature into our lives.

After two weeks we were just becoming accustomed to the idea of being a household with a kitten when the mare arrived from Ireland. The first time I went to see her I felt absolutely no sense that she was mine. Her arrival caused a stir of curiosity and interest in the yard. The livery clients who happened to be around all found reasons to come up to the quarantine pen and look her over. 'Isn't she lovely,' they said, and I agreed, but with none of the twinge of proprietorship or gratifying sense of my own cleverness in securing something pretty and desirable that I was accustomed to feel when people admired something that belonged to me. We might have been talking about a new horse that Jillie had bought for herself.

The other thing they all said was, 'What are you going to call her?' She needed two names, a show name for best, and a stable name for everyday. The show name was no trouble at all. She was going to be called Lismore Silver Fox: Lismore, because that was where she came from, Silver because of her colour, and Fox because of the hunting. I hadn't at the time read the remarkable, eerie novel – one of their best – by

Somerville and Ross called *The Silver Fox*. I discovered it later and felt doubly pleased that I had called the mare after it, even if inadvertently. It was the stable name that was the problem.

I had set my heart on calling her Molly, after Molly Keane, but Jillie was having none of it. There was already a Molly on the yard, Mrs Watson the Hunt Secretary's big bay mare, and another one would cause all sorts of confusion. I'd have to find another name. It wasn't as though there was any shortage of pretty Irish names. What about Grainne? Sinead? Siobhan? All perfectly splendid names. Only the mare didn't really look like a Grainne or a Sinead.

Well then, if I couldn't call her after Molly Keane, perhaps I would call her after one of Keane's heroines. I spent an evening leafing through the novels: Cynthia, Susan, Prudence, Lalage, Nicandra, Tossie? Perhaps not. The mare went up on the feed board, the vet's list and the farrier's list as Shilling Mare while I continued to think. The kitten, meanwhile, had been named Caspar with a minimum of deliberation.

I'd had this trouble with naming before, when my son was born. While he was gestating I had come up with all sorts of beautiful and significant names, not all of which sat quite comfortably with Shilling: Florian, Octavian, Fabrice, Sergei, Xavier. I was particularly wedded to Xavier. But then when he came out, he didn't look anything like a Fabrice or a Xavier. He looked like a sort of small, yellowish frog. A little elemental scrap of flesh, almost unformed-looking, particularly around the head and face – a squashed ovoid with the features of a sat-on marmoset – and certainly too new and strange to bear the weight of any of the fancy monikers I had been lining up for him.

Baby Shilling (which was what was written on the opaque plastic bracelets with which they seemed to have tagged him, lamb-like, around his skinny, mottled wrists and ankles straight after birth while I was still catching my breath) seemed like a pretty good name to be going on with while I got used to him (and he, presumably, to me). In any case, I felt in no particular hurry to attach a lifelong label to this funny little jaundiced object. It seemed both singularly unimportant and too important to be hurried.

The health visitor – or rather a succession of different health visitors, each of whom, erupting into my flat on a daily basis at whatever time suited her best for ten days after I had brought the infant home, required tea, biscuits and a full briefing as to who I might be and what my situation was – thought otherwise. 'Has baby got a name yet?' became their constant refrain. It seemed to be the only thing they were interested in. On the ninth day, feeling rather chipper because the lowering pain in my behind from the stitches, like wearing knickers with a barbed-wire gusset, had begun to improve and with it my spirits, I committed the egregious error of making a little joke. 'Nope,' I said pertly. 'He's still called Mrs Antrobus' (which had been his name *in utero*).

Health visitor no. 9 didn't think this funny at all, and communicated her anxieties to health visitor no. 10 who turned up rather early for her tea and biscuits, while I was still feeding the baby, and spoke in a low, sympathetic voice, making herself heard with difficulty above his howls of rage at having his feed interrupted.

'My colleague expressed some concern,' she said gently, 'that you are failing to bond with baby. I understand he hasn't got a name yet.' Some good fairy restrained me from replying that he'd got a couple of perfectly adequate working names, Baby Shilling and Mrs Antrobus, that I'd choose a Christian name for him when he looked a bit more like a human child and a bit less like a hitherto undiscovered trans-species cross between a frog and a monkey. And in the meantime, why didn't she go away and bother someone else, who was having trouble breast-feeding or something?

Instead I said meekly that his name was Alexander, a lie at the time, but one that became true in the telling, though I continued for almost a year, until his face unsquashed itself and he grew some hair, to think of him as Mrs Antrobus. When he went to school, it turned out that half the boys in his year were also called Alexander and I wondered if a whole generation of South London mummies had been chivvied into calling them that by a posse of health visitors with bees in their bonnets about the importance of sticking a label on your newborn infant to show that you were bonding with him.

Anyway, ten years on, and here we were again. 'Time you started bonding with that mare,' said Mrs Rogers firmly when I turned up for a lesson. 'Has she got a name yet?' Mmm, not really, said I. Still thinking. Dymphna, Francie, Nancy, Stella . . . 'You can't call a horse after a beer!' shrieked Mrs Rogers. Not Stella Artois, I began to explain, but Stella, the object of Jonathan Swift's difficult passion, he having been Irish . . . But I'd lost her. 'If you really can't come up with anything else, you'd better call her Molly,' she said. 'Your mare can be Little Molly and Rosemary Watson's will have to be Big Molly. Now get out into that paddock, catch her up, groom her, rug her up and put her back in her pen.'

That settled, she whisked off to do something more important, leaving me standing in the barn, a stream of questions fermenting in my brain. How did you catch up a horse? Wasn't there more to grooming than just brushing it, which was all I knew about so far? Which rugs? And shouldn't there be someone to supervise me while I was doing all this? Slowly, in the raw grey light of the barn, the full awfulness of what I had done in buying this mare began at last to register. I hadn't just bought a horse, I'd bought a great, heavy, slowing-down mechanism; a drain on my energy, a thief of my time. No wonder all the liveries referred to themselves as their horses' 'mummies'.

When the baby was born, I had marvelled at the dreamy, underwater slowness that overspread my hitherto irritable superfluity of nervous energy. The day he came, fed up with waiting around for him to emerge (he was two weeks late), I had whisked up to Harvey Nichols for a brisk shopping trip, figuring that it was probably my last chance for some time and, after amusing myself for a while by making the salesgirls' flesh creep – ('When's the baby due?' 'Two weeks ago, actually.' 'Oh my God! Don't have it here, will you?') – I bought, from a gnomic Japanese assistant, a Mannerist *haute couture* rendition of a biker's zipped black leather jacket in what had once been my size, and would be again, once I'd finished being pregnant.

'Good for pushing the pram in,' she said gravely, as we looked together at my reflection in the changing-room mirror: the double-breasted sides of the jacket failing to meet over the goose-egg hillock of my gravid front, within which the shape of the baby could be seen grappling tetchily back and forth, trying to find a comfortable position. Then I skipped back home with my shopping bags, and out came the baby, and the nervous energy lasted for 48 hours after the birth, just long enough for me to finish the volume of Chekhov short stories I had been reading. And then quite suddenly I turned into a kind of female manatee, drifting placidly about the sheltered inlet of my flat in a seaweedy dream of muslin squares and baby lotion, and little clutching hands emerging from the sleeves of improbably small lacy cardigans knitted by my next-door neighbour in wool of bright egg yellow, to match the baby's complexion, and swimming-pool turquoise.

I absorbed without difficulty the shrinking of my world to a couple of hundred yards in either direction from my front door: the shops lay one way, the park another. It was winter;

dark and cold outside and the most trivial outing – to the corner shop for a newspaper and a pint of milk – could no longer be accomplished in a matter of seconds, but was now a full-scale excursion with lengthy preparations, as for an Arctic expedition: the poppering and buttoning of multiple layers, thrusting of limbs into flaccid baby-shaped pouches of quilted plush or imitation lambswool, some of which came roguishly decorated with ears and even little rabbity bobtails. Then further zipping and hitching and swaddling and snapping of restraining buckles, until the baby lay like a fat, lace-knit primrose larva in the pram, with only his nose and his strangely watchful eyes visible between his woolly shawl and his knitted beanie hat.

And then bump, bump, bump of the pram up the area steps and trundle trundle to the shops around whose shelves-full of goods I manoeuvred clumsily. Everyone knows without thinking how much space their own body takes up, but it takes a while to get used to the idea of your personal space as being that of a pram with your body attached to one end of it. Then home again and by the time the pram had been wrestled down the vertiginous concrete steps to the front door and the larva unhitched from his restraining straps, stripped of his woolly layers, fed, cleaned and set to sleep or kick on the rug or whatever his routine demanded, I had the impression of having accomplished some considerable labour of physical and, oddly, moral satisfaction, like the swaddled explorers dragging their heavy sledges across the frozen terrain, making a few hundred yards of ground each day before retreating into the fragile shelter of their bivouac where the warmth and the light and the comforting human fug gave an illusion of protection against the cold vastness outside.

I didn't miss my vanished swiftness; I was fascinated by the lulling, repetitive routines of feed, burp, howl, wash, sleep. I liked the equipment that went with having a baby: the pram, the cot, the special baby bath, the wicker basket trimmed with translucent white flounces, like the ones that Mrs Tiggy-Winkle crimped so deftly with her goffering iron ('Smooth and hot, red rusty spot, never more be seen, oh!'). And I liked the business of being a mother, of smiling at the other mothers trundling their prams along the febrile, sharp-edged street, each wrapped in her own dreamy, slow-moving cocoon. The only thing I minded was when the outside world came rushing back in at the end of my maternity leave and I had to split into two people, the old, agile me by day and the new, drifting version by night. I did it badly and the baby noticed and became suspicious, refusing to sleep, then waking in the small hours and weeping inconsolably until dawn.

But that first painful severance was followed by other, more benign separations: some triumphant, some barely perceptible – walking, talking, first day at nursery school. Ten years on I had begun to entertain ideas of a partial return to something like the person I was before I became a mummy; to moving about, if only occasionally, freely and swiftly, uncoupled from the little dragging hand. That was what the riding lessons had been: hour-long assignations with my former self. But what had I done now? With some of the speed and lightness of ten years ago almost within reach of recovery, I had coupled myself again, this time to something the size of 50 babies, but apparently just as helpless, fragile and time-consuming.

To read some of the baby books, you'd think it a miracle that any baby ever managed to survive infancy, so numerous and terrible were the dangers that beset them, mostly concealed in the most harmless and jocund of disguises. To put them to sleep on their fronts was certain death, while laying them on their backs gave them the flattened heads of obscure tribal cultures. Duvets, domestic cats and taking them into bed with you could all cause them to smother. Warmth was a potential killer: extinction lurked in a fluffy lambswool mattress.

The cobweb shawl, painstakingly frame-knit by some twinkly-eyed Shetland granny in her picturesque hovel, could entrap tender fingers in its airy lacework (and then what? The books declined to say. Snap them off? Strangle them slowly, so they got gangrene and had to be amputated? Something bad at any rate). The kindly eyes, shiny noses and tinkly bells of those comfortable companions of infant life, their soft toys, could work loose and choke them. A crumb of peanut could close down their little systems in a matter of seconds. As for the murderous intentions of the banal household items with which they were surrounded – the stairs, the furniture, the seething saucepans and slicing knives of the kitchen – so dangerous were those that you'd almost feel inclined to surround the whole lot of them with electric fencing, if only electricity weren't so dangerous to tinies.

Horses, I gathered from conversation on the yard and in the tackroom, were equally vulnerable to the hidden perils of everyday existence. If you gave them cold water too soon after exercise, or rode them too soon after they had eaten, they were liable to go down with colic, a terrible malady involving desperate night-time journeys in the horse ambulance, cripplingly expensive emergency surgery and, at the end of it all, more than likely a visit from the knackerman in his van. (I knew all about colic. My son – and, by extension, I – had been a martyr to it in infancy.) A bite of ragwort could give them irreversible liver failure. They were piteously susceptible to passing viruses of flu and herpes and required constant dosing against a lurid bestiary of different sorts of worm.

Moreover, they sometimes did something really stupid called Getting Cast. A cast horse was one that had gone down and couldn't get up again. The deep banks of straw that I'd noticed piled around three sides of the stalls in the Royal Mews (and once spent an evening's practical stable management conscientiously levelling because I thought they were untidy) were a precaution against cast horses. Animals particularly prone to it – there was one at the Rooting Street yard, a luscious Irish cob called Billy who'd been fourth in his class at the Dublin Show – had to wear a funny little belt with a metal handle on top called an anti-cast roller. Though whether the handle was a contraption for winching them upright again once they'd fallen over, or was meant to perform a similar function to the cotton reels that my grandmother sewed into the backs of my grandfather's pyjamas (hers was an anti-snoring device) and make it too uncomfortable for them to lie on their backs in the first place, I had no idea.

Molly had a go at getting cast the spring after I bought her. I had just ridden her and went back to her pen with a carrot, looked over the door and saw her lying spread out on the stable floor, quite limp and flat and pallid, like a vampire's swooning victim in a Victorian Gothic novel. Jillie, who was passing, looked over the door too and suddenly began to talk very urgently, which was frightening in itself. 'Oh God,' she said, 'Your mare's cast.' She shouted to a passing livery to fetch some lunge lines (Why not me? I wondered. I know what lunge lines are – annoyed, in the midst of my panic, that she hadn't trusted me with this elementary task). Then she went very slowly and cautiously into the stable saying, 'Good Girl, Good Girl,' to the mare, and to me, 'Now I am going to sit on your mare's head while Deborah fetches the lunge lines.'

I had read about people sitting on the heads of fallen horses and a part of me, again oddly separate from the dread and fear that I felt about the cast mare, was extremely interested to see how this would work. Jillie began to lower her neat, muscular bottom towards the mare's head, at which the mare rolled one eye upwards, saw the descending behind and sprang to her feet as though nothing had ever been wrong. So that was the end of her getting cast.

Even when standing squarely upright horses seemed tragically easy to damage. They suffered from cold and even more from warmth. A rug incautiously applied to a horse that hadn't cooled down sufficiently after exercise could do untold harm to the animal's fragile constitution. There was the question of their legs and the things that could go wrong with them: outcrops of bone, known as splints, for which you were supposed to feel the legs at regular intervals; and an even more mysterious malady known as 'doing a tendon', which could come on for no very obvious reason, and the only cure for which, like consumption in the nineteenth century, was prolonged rest. The horse spent months on end alternately mooning about in a field or standing in the barn while its owner rubbed pungent unguents into its lower limbs or attached it to a machine that sent a cooling flow of water over the afflicted part.

Less devastating, though more disgusting, were their skin complaints: something called Sweet Itch, which gave them weeping bald patches in summer, and in winter, if you didn't keep their feet dry (so easy in the Somme quagmire that the yard and its surrounding fields became after rain), they developed Mud Fever, the symptoms of which were clustering scabs in the hollows of their heels, which you had to pick off before smothering the heel in Vaseline or some other sort of grease. Only once, halfway through a wet hunting season, Molly developed a mild case of scabby heels. When Mrs Rogers breezily announced the remedy I recoiled, but once you got going there was a curious intimacy in picking a horse's scabs: a sort of licensed return to the illicit schoolday pleasure of carefully levering a fat, juicy scab off your own knee with the edge of a thumbnail.

Once you had grasped the myriad different things that could go wrong with a horse, it was time to come to terms with the astonishing quantity of kit required before you could actually ride it. The shopping list for Molly's basic equipment – her layette, as I was beginning to think of it – ran to several pages, starting with the obvious things: saddle, numnah (a pad of quilted fabric or sheepskin that went between the saddle and the horse), bridle, reins, girth, but rapidly expanding to incorporate items that sounded as though they came from the kit list of the medieval war horse: breastplate, running martingale, brushing boots, overreach boots, elastic surcingle, French link snaffle, Cheltenham Gag. There were four different sorts of rug on this list, all essential (and supplemented on chilly winter days by a hollow-fibre single duvet, to be worn, Princess and the Pea-style, between the bottom rug and the two uppermost rugs).

The list for the grooming kit contained an equally lavish quantity of brushes: body brush, dandy brush, water brush, long-bristled soft brush, plus hoof pick, curry comb (which wasn't really a comb at all but a sort of vicious nutmeg grater for taking the fluff out of the body brush and the skin off the back of your hand), metal comb (also not for combing, but for wrenching hairs out of the mane and tail for the neatly depilated look favoured by human film stars). Two sponges, one for the face, one for everywhere else, a loofah mitt, hoof oil, a little brush for applying the hoof oil, plaiting bands and an extensive range of quasi-human cosmetic aids – high-factor sun cream for protecting pink noses on hot summer days, organic herbal fly repellent, baby shampoo for washing tails, baby oil for coating the (horse's) legs on muddy days, firm control hair gel (for mane plaiting), not forgetting a needle and a reel of thread for sewing in plaits, a roll of electrical insulating tape for taping up tails (essential in the muddy Ashford Valley country) and a packet of laundry blue for turning dingy grey horses whiter than white. And saddle soap and Neat's Foot oil for keeping the saddlery clean and supple.

Since I was keeping the horse in livery, I hadn't even needed to equip myself with a full set of the basics. I had not, for example, had to buy feed bowls, water buckets, brooms, shovels, forks and a wheelbarrow. Nor had I purchased (or learned how to use) a set of clippers. Shortly after the mare was due to emerge from the quarantine pen I arrived on the yard to find her all pale and naked and new-looking, like someone who had undergone a vicious haircut. The woolly, bluish coat of hair in which I'd met her had been shaved into a hunter clip: the hair left at its natural length only on the face, the legs, where it was shaped to an elegant point where the limbs joined the body, and a saddle-shaped patch on the back. Now instead of a slatey grey she was silvery-white with pink-brown nutmeg flecks: fleabitten grey, was the disreputable-sounding technical term.

The clipping had been a right performance, I gathered from some of the liveries who had formed an audience to the drama, with several people required to hold the mare's head, apply a twitch (a twist of rope tightened around the lip or ear, which has a mysterious calming effect on an agitated horse. You can also take a twist of the skin of the neck between finger and thumb, which is called a Tinker's Twitch), hold up her leg (to stop her from kicking) and so on while Tracy, Mrs Rogers's supernaturally competent head girl, applied the clippers.

Even allowing for the dispensation of not having to buy stable and clipping equipment, the sheer bulk of stuff that I'd suddenly acquired seemed preposterous. Ten years before I had wondered how, say, the Bedouin or equally light-travelling peoples managed their newborns without bumper-sized packs of super-absorbent Huggies, specially reinforced to contain 'soft poo', as the mellifluous female voice-over on the early-morning kiddies' TV adverts fastidiously put it, and

214

cardboard boxes of several gross of filmy peach-scented nappy sacks to encumber their nomadic progress. Now it seemed remarkable that the Mongol Hordes should have contrived their devastating sweep across the Eastern plain without so much as a black felt tailguard with royal blue ribbon binding, or a set of fully washable Velcro-fastening travel boots between them.

The trouble with all these devices was that I had no idea how to use them. Of course the same had been true of disposable nappies and Babygros which, when unpopped, looked more like the skin half of a recently flayed rabbit than a garment. The difference with a baby was that however slow and unhandy you were, the worst that could happen was that the baby might weep a bit, whereupon you would realize that something was amiss and – slowly, unhandily – put it right again. The chances of one of the parties involved emerging from a mishap with a back-to-front nappy seriously injured or even dead was small. A horse, on the other hand, could strangle itself in an ill-buckled head collar, break its leg by becoming entangled in an unsecured rein, lash out with a metal-shod hoof to the detriment of its handler's skull, teeth, or other fragile bits of skeleton. You could hurt it, and in consequence cause it to hurt you, just by doing up a buckle too tightly or too loosely, positioning a saddle carelessly, failing to spot a rabbit-hole on the track ahead . . .

The ignoble fact was that having bought this horse, I was frightened of it. Frightened that I might damage it, or it might damage me. Frightened of the amount of time and air it would suck out of my life and frightened of resuming, yet again, the dreary, infantilizing business of not being able to do something that other people found childishly simple. I might have considered all this before setting off on a horse-buying trip to Ireland but I didn't. I knew that I liked horses and liked riding and the logical next step seemed to be to find a horse of my own. But other people's horses are like other people's babies – utterly adorable, and you can give them back. It is quite different, having one of your own.

Fortunately, I was even more frightened of Mrs Rogers than I was of the horse. Or to put it more exactly: on balance, the idea of retreating from my present position seemed even more appalling than that of advancing. Evidently, if I really felt that I'd made a mistake, I could sell the mare for what I'd paid for her. I knew Mrs Rogers liked her. Someone told me that, having established that the mare had never seen an arena in her life and couldn't under any circumstances manage a left-hand canter around the rubber school, she had taken her into the sand school and put her at a series of ever bigger jumps. And the mare, according to gossip, had flown the lot – so willingly that Jillie had afterwards described her as 'brave' – a term of praise even higher than 'tidy' in the severely restricted Rooting Street lexicon of commendation.

What is more, I was a paying client. If I did retreat from the frightening responsibility of being this mare's owner, it wasn't to say that I was obliged to cut my connection with horses altogether, or with the yard. I could carry on with my lessons – which were themselves, let's face it, hardly stress-free. Perhaps that was as much as I could cope with, I thought, standing in the cold barn like a monument of confusion and misery. But I knew, really, that if I backed out now, the story would be over. I would be a silly woman who sometimes came for lessons and that would be it.

It was in this state of petrified gloom that Mrs Rogers's secretary, Jane, discovered me. 'What's the matter?' she said. So I told her that I thought I'd made a terrible mistake, adding, almost in tears, that I couldn't possibly catch up Molly, groom her and whathaveyou now. I'd come down from London expecting just an hour's lesson, I knew all the catching up and its sequelae would take me forever, I'd got an article to write and a deadline to meet and (shouting and snivelling now and wiping my nose on my sleeve) I simply couldn't do it all, whatever Jillie said. And if something had to go, it would have to be the mare, because it certainly couldn't be my livelihood. So there.

'Calm down, calm down,' said Jane, both naturally kind and not entirely displeased at happening across an interesting drama on this dreary winter's afternoon. 'Of course you don't want to sell her. You've only just bought her. Now, I'll catch her up and groom her. It won't take me a minute. And you get off back to London and write your article, and come back down here at the weekend when you've got more time and start getting to know her. All right?' 'Yes, all right, thank you,' said I, still sobbing, both relieved and ashamed to have been released so easily from the wrenching crisis in which I seemed to have entangled myself. I crept back to London and wrote my article and didn't bother wondering what Mrs Rogers would think when she heard, as she inevitably would, what had happened, because I already knew.

Jane was right about things seeming better at the weekend when I hadn't a deadline to meet. In the couple of days between feeling I had taken on too much with this mare and seeing her again I recovered my *amour propre* sufficiently to feel that I couldn't refuse the adventure that was beginning. And then I realized that – at last – I was thinking of the horse as My Mare. Which meant, I supposed, that the sense of attachment I thought I had felt in the thistly Irish field had survived her voyage across the Irish Sea. She might well turn out to be a problem, but she was my problem and I would keep her.

The hunter clip seemed to have made a psychological, as well as a physical difference. In Ireland I had thought, glancing back at the mare when we were leaving and she stood on the rutted track staring after us, that she seemed gawky and comic and almost in need of rescue. Clipped, well groomed and gleaming she seemed much more elegant and self-possessed. Dimly, I began to realize that she was very pretty, and that it wasn't just I who was struck with her looks. Standing in her pen or tied up in the barn she seemed to have developed the supermodel concomitants of extreme beauty. She appeared distant, haughty, wilful and uppish. In the same obscure way that I had begun to discern that I wasn't the only one to appreciate her beauty, I also felt the beginnings of a mismatch of talent set in. I hadn't really begun to ride her yet, but I started to feel small, clumsy and inept around her. I felt I was becoming the beautiful girl's inexplicable plain best friend and minded, as you would.

There were several early episodes of what (with hindsight) you could describe as Trying It On. Once I was standing about as one of the girl grooms brushed Molly's face. This groom, Jo, was a pretty, imperturbable teenager with the flower-petal pink and ivory skin, flaxen hair and small, sleepy blue eyes of an early Flemish Madonna. Her magnificent serenity made her a brave jumper and, perhaps because of that, or perhaps because she was naturally good with highly strung animals (she went on to a career as a veterinary nurse, for which she was evidently a natural) she loved Molly from the beginning.

Brush, brush, she went to the mare's face, while the mare, who had turned out, after being clipped, to dislike being touched almost anywhere, laid her ears back, rolled her eyes and pulled away from the brushing. Then all in a moment, she tugged so sharply at her rope that the loop of binder twine to which she was attached broke and freed her and she clattered back on her haunches in the barn, all bunched up with surprise and fright at what she had done.

I was appalled: crunched small with tension, panic and the anticipation of what would happen next (the mare would gallop off? Wreck the barn? Impale herself on a fork? Trample someone underfoot? Get onto the road?). I may even have uttered a small scream. Jo, meanwhile, reached up, took hold of the mare's head collar, observed mildly that she was a naughty girl, retied the loop of binder twine, reattached the mare's rope to it and continued to brush her face, both of them now apparently quite at ease with the process.

'I can't believe you did that. I would have panicked,' I said to Jo. 'Oh, well,' replied Jo, sweet, but evidently mystified that I thought there had been anything to be frightened of. Three years later, the same thing happened again, only this time it was me doing the brushing. I reached up, grasped the head collar as the mare plunged and clattered backwards down the yard, told her as I knotted her broken lead rope to the mended loop of binder twine and resumed grooming that she was a silly girl to act up when I was only trying to make her comfortable – all this as calmly (I thought afterwards) as though I knew what I was doing. And off we went again, brushing and being brushed in the state of companionable equilibrium that grooming is meant to induce. It wasn't until some days later that I remembered it wasn't an instinct, this partial ability to distinguish between a real crisis and a little bout of equine drama-queening, but a hard and imperfectly learned lesson which I would never really master, because I had started so late.

Tacking up was a trial. I wasn't used to it. I was accustomed to the horse for my lesson being brought to the mounting block with its girth already tightened and its stirrups dangling ready for me to put my feet in them. When I watched Jo or Tracy tacking up, the process looked perfectly easy and logical: heave the saddle on to the back, attach the girth one side, reach under the horse, attach it the other side. Pick up the bridle, catch hold of the horse's nose with your free hand, put your thumb into the handy gap between its front and back teeth so it opened its mouth, pop in the bit, slip the bridle over its head, do up a couple of buckles and there you were, ready to spring on and trot away.

When I did it, it was different. When it came to putting on the saddle, a horse's back wasn't just a back. It had withers and quarters, and my saddle was perpetually too close to one end or the other. I thought the saddle-shaped template of hair left after the clip might act as a guide, but it didn't seem to be much help. I'd be fidgeting about, trying to remember which of the three girth straps on the saddle were meant to be attached to the two buckles on the girth (and why three straps and two buckles in this inconvenient fashion? Oh, don't ask . . .) and Mrs Rogers, apparently absorbed in teaching at the other end of the sand school, 50 yards away, would suddenly bellow, with her extraordinary powers of voice projection, like Dame Edith Evans in faded purple breeches: 'Jane! That mare's saddle is too far back!'

I took to putting the tack on in the barn, in the hope of escaping the Seeing Finger, but it was no good. She'd come popping past on some errand and without slowing down, point out (how did she know, when nothing was visible beneath the saddle flap?) that I had failed to thread the girth through the slot provided for the purpose on the lower edge of the saddle pad. Also, my breastplate was on back-to-front (you mean there was a right side and a wrong side, like a vest?) and I had forgotten to secure the straps in their keeper rings. I was careful to wait until she was out of sight before attempting to put on the bridle.

Molly was head shy. Of course she was. I took a little comfort in the fact that she was like it with everyone, not just with me, but the business of getting a bridle on her was lengthy and exasperating. As soon as she saw you pick up the snaky tangle of reins, she pointed her nose to the sky, stretching out her neck as far as she could. It made her look quite extraordinary, like a star-gazing silver giraffe, but with something oddly predatory and insect-like thrown in as well. All you could do was wait quietly with the bridle behind your back until she forgot about it and lowered her head, at which you had to pounce like a jaguar, seize her by the nose and hope she would open her jaw slightly in surprise.

Once she had realized what you were about, she instantly clenched her teeth. They were impossible to unclench; she seemed impervious to the pleading pressure of one's thumb in her mouth. Helpful liveries would sometimes offer her little bits of carrot or apple, to encourage her to open her mouth, but she was expert at taking in the carrot and spitting out the bit in a single economical movement. I learned to allow an extra 45 minutes before my lessons were due to begin, just for getting her tack on.

Because she was being energetically schooled on the days when I didn't come down for a lesson, and because I knew nothing anyway, I couldn't feel the rawness that Jillie noticed and so wasn't especially bothered about it. She was nine years old and presumably quite set in her ways. If she had hunted all over Ireland with her head in the air, couldn't she just carry on like that, and hunt all over the Ashford Valley with her head in the air? Why did it matter if she wouldn't come soft – that is, arch her neck so that the line of her face was perpendicular to the ground as she moved? It mattered. That was all I needed to know. So I set about learning to make it happen.

Round and round the charcoal-grey rectangle of the rubber school I rode, twice a week and again at weekends, trying to crack the magical combination of leg and hand that would make the mare arch her neck and come soft, or at the very least, bend to the inside, so that her body, when seen from above, would appear to be curved in a gentle arc around my inside leg. I tried squeezing the reins as though they were a couple of sponges I was holding between my fingers, I tried gentle alternate drawing-back movements of the hands to make the bit move in the mare's mouth. In desperation, we even tried holding her head in the required position with draw reins, which made the horse pull against itself when it tried to raise its head, and then by physical force. None of it did any good. She continued to flounce around the arena with a ferocious adverse bend, head turned in exactly the opposite direction to the one we wanted.

'Hmm,' said Jillie. 'Not exactly a dressage horse, is she?' The problem was compounded by the fact that I didn't really know what it would feel like if she did suddenly come into an outline, so had only a hazy idea of what I was trying to achieve. It was like being a very average pianist and trying to tackle the 'Moonlight Sonata' from sheet music, without ever having heard it played by a really good pianist.

Ignorant though I was of the signals passing between the horse and myself, even I felt that something was really badly wrong one day, when the left rein seemed to turn to iron in my hand, with no flexibility at all on that side. No animal resisting like that could be happy, I thought, and my frustration at riding the mare badly was compounded by a more sinister feeling that my incompetence might actually be doing her harm.

It might be a bitting problem, Jillie reckoned, so we embarked on a protracted flirtation with different bits, each with a name more fanciful than the last. A sweet-iron Fulmer – an exotic-looking article with a mouthpiece made from two jointed, tapered bars of rusty-looking metal and long, pointed, silvery cheekpieces with metal bobbles at either end – seemed to alleviate the iron left rein for a while. After that we tried a Happy Mouth snaffle, a most basic bit made from a cylinder of pale yellow-green plastic which looked like a cross between a child's toy and a surgical appliance.

Keen to understand what was going on, I bought an austere volume called *The Horse and the Bit*, which made it very clear that, as I had uncomfortably guessed, an absence of subtlety in the rider was responsible for almost all problems of resistance. It contained a damning paragraph on the subject of non-metal bits: 'What happens,' it said, 'is that the horse just runs forward in little quick steps with a stiff back, throwing its head up and probably opening its mouth. If the rider avoids this, being very quiet and light, and the horse has the rubber bit, it may give the impression that it is going well, but in fact . . . it is not moving in its natural way but trundling quietly along . . . There is more to riding!'

Oh dear, I thought when I read this. Quick steps, stiff back, tossing its head, light, quiet, impression of going well . . . check, check, check. And the only reason she wasn't opening her mouth was that I had bought, on Mrs Rogers's advice, a Grakle bridle, with cross-straps running through a sort of little leather junction box perched on the bridge of the nose, which kept the mare's mouth buckled firmly shut. And there I had been, congratulating myself on how much better we had been doing since switching to the Happy Mouth bit. 'Trundling along' was a bitter blow. 'You're not just a happy hacker, are you?' Mrs Rogers once remarked. 'You're never going to be content just bimbling about the place.' It was the nicest thing she ever said to me.

When the vet came to the yard to administer some vaccinations, she called him over to look at the mare, in case there was a physical problem – though she had been vetted in Ireland. The vet watched her trot up and down, then we stood in the centre of the arena while Jillie rode her around in circles and figures of eight. Then he prodded her back and her legs, observed with interest the way in which she cow-kicked and tried to bite if you touched her belly or her inside legs, and at the end of all this, 'Nothing physically wrong,' said the vet.

'She's got an attitude problem.' And he departed to send in his bill.

I was perversely relieved by 'attitude problem.' I thought I knew all about those, having harboured a ferocious one of my own all the way through secondary school and beyond. If it was an attitude problem, then eventually I would get to the bottom of it, however long it took. In the meantime, 'Hard to love, your mare, isn't she?' said Mrs Rogers, whose own hunter, Camilla, had been kicked by Molly while they were out on exercise and bore, to my horror, the clear imprint of one of Molly's neat little shoes on her glossy, dark-brown behind. 'A gelding,' said Mrs Rogers, into the air, 'is always so much more loving, I find.'

I didn't find Molly unloving, or ill-natured, exactly. She was wilful, temperamental, quite often cross and occasionally frightening. But there was something else there as well – the quality that had made Mrs Rogers call her brave; a sense of partly-concealed willingness that might open up into something remarkable, if only one could find the key to unlock it. She seemed neither hard nor unwilling. She was so responsive to the leg that I was forever sending her by accident into a trot with my flapping limbs. On the other hand, she lacked the hysterical edge that had been so alarming during my lessons on the highly strung borrowed mare, Flossie. She was as easy to stop as she was to wind up and never felt like a runaway.

Learning to ride her was a process rather (I imagined) like picking a lock, or cracking a cypher: a frame of mind compounded of equal parts urgency and patience. I was unused to patience, having always found force of will a quicker and more effective substitute. Molly, however, was impervious to human willpower. (The cat, meanwhile, was turning out to be an equable and affectionate creature, apparently devoid of difficult character quirks. We loved him dearly and found it hard to imagine how we had previously endured the dullness of life without him.)

As the lessons continued Mrs Rogers started thinking aloud about when I should go hunting. Not the Boxing Day meet, she said, to my mixed dismay and relief. Too many people, too much milling about and excitement. Better start with something quieter. A nice little meet in the New Year, towards the end of the season, would be best. The Kennels meet was a good one. Lots of people went from the yard. We could hack to the kennels from there.

'Is there much jumping?' I asked nervously. 'None at all,' said Mrs Rogers firmly. It wasn't until halfway through my second season that I worked out this was the answer she invariably gave when I asked this question, even if she had spent a busy weekend directing a team of hunt jump builders and knew for a fact that there was a cross-country course halfway round the country we were to draw. She took an active interest in sports psychology.

In the meantime, would I let Jo, the groom, take Molly out for a day's hunting, just to see how she went (the horse, not the girl, who was known to be sound)? This was more of an instruction than a request, but I said yes anyway and came down to the meet, in the car park of the local pub, to see them off. I was quite unprepared for the furious surge of jealousy that overtook me at the sight of Jo, looking neat and nervous ('I'm cacking meself,' she said cheerfully) in a blue tweed jacket and a tidy hairnet, firmly settled (for the first time I understood the meaning of the expression 'a nice deep seat') in the saddle of my mare, who was equally smartly turned out in a sheepskin numnah and yet another new bit.

This one was a Happy Mouth gag – the same surgical arrangement of greeny-yellow plastic mouthpiece as the snaffle (it looked as though it ought to glow in the dark) but with side pieces offering three rings through which you could thread the reins. The lower the ring, the greater the stopping force you could exert, was the idea. Her mane was knotted into a tight row of plaited bobbles, her tail plaited into a sort of horsehair cosh and secured with three bands of white tape, her hooves gleaming with oil. She looked almost uncomfortably well turned out, like a bride who has been got at by a beautician and persuaded to go for full hair and make-up on her big day.

It was an ordinary Wednesday meet – a small crowd of horses and a few dedicated elderly foot followers in sensible shoes and quilted outer garments in practical shades of lichen, moss and bark. They were all grasping long knobbly thumb-sticks, which gave them a vague look of churchwardens and lent the car park gathering a ceremonial air. Trays of ginger wine and cherry brandy began to circulate, and plates of sausage rolls and sandwiches. I swallowed a glass of ginger wine, hoping that it would wash down the poison taste of envy as I stood at Jo's stirrup (my stirrup, actually), hearing what a good girl Molly had been to get ready; how she'd stood quite still to be washed and plaited (something like a miracle, that was, if true, given her usual routine of kick, bite, kick whenever you got near her with a brush or a sponge). 'They know when they're going hunting,' said Jo, fondly.

'Looks good, doesn't she?' called Mrs Rogers, impossibly grand and high up on Camilla in her black coat with a yellow collar, her fair curls clustering in well disciplined fashion around the edge of her black velvet hunting cap. She was Master that day and socializing vigorously, but there was something intent and absent about her, as though she were both preparing herself and listening for something.

There was a bold clattering of hooves from down the road and the huntsman came into view, leading hounds with the whippers-in, two men and a woman, behind. They must have unboxed and left the hound van at the yard. With their arrival – the men in scarlet coats with shiny gold buttons, carrying white kid hunt servants' whips, the creamy white, lemon, tan and black of the hounds, tightly packed in a sort of questing blanket at the huntsman's heels – the subfusc gathering in the car park, the little field of housewives and farmer's wives in black or tweed hunt coats and the foot followers in their anoraks, became suffused with drama and colour.

There was the expectant, buzzing, rustling noise of an audience before a performance begins. I had a vivid flashback of being a backstage assistant at the annual school productions of *Iolanthe*, or *Orpheus in the Underworld*, dabbling in a pinafore with sticks of Leichner no. 5 and no. 9 greasepaint while my friends drifted about in seaweedy green tulle fairy dresses, or sexy layers of can-can ruffles, remote and focused as the mounted field now seemed to be, separated from the ordinary rest of us by the characters they were about to become, waiting for their moment of transition into a different world of elaborately controlled excitement.

There was a stir, a shushing, restive, stamping silence as Mrs Rogers delivered her parish notices: thanks to the landlord of the Swan for hosting this meet and making us so welcome; atrocious weather, lot of rain, wet ground, good of our farmers to agree to have us, stick to headlands please. Thank you. Neil blew a sharp couple of notes on his horn and swung out onto the road, hounds close behind and the whippers-in, Master and field strung out in succession, trotting past the squat brick church with its collapsing flint wall, past the long, steep, grass bank topped with a high, rose brick wall – the boundary of what had been, until it burned to the ground in the fifties, Walter Winans's grand rented lodging of Surrenden Manor – and away towards the orchards and the first draw of the day.

It was bleak and grey in the empty car park with the sound of the hooves and the drama moving away at a brisk jog-trot.

I helped the handful of left-behinds clear up the drained glasses, got into the car and turned towards London and work, hating the ugly suburbs as I drove through them, as though it were their fault that I was in a car, heading for the city while my mare went hunting without me.

The mare, it was eagerly reported when I went to the yard at the weekend (it was Saturday, so Mrs Rogers was out hunting, but the non-hunting liveries seemed to know all the details) had been 100 per cent on Wednesday. Honest, willing, did everything asked of her. Stood like a rock when required, good among hounds, unfazed by traffic, deep mud or anything else; gave every impression, as well as she might, of having done this before and of being delighted to find herself doing it again. Nice little lady's hunter, just as Michael had said. I went up to find her in her pen at the top of the yard. I thought she looked happy and alert, almost relaxed: ears cocked forward, eyes round and bright. It seemed hard to be putting on her saddle for no purpose more exciting than that of practising circles and serpentines in the rubber school. As I tightened her girth I wondered if horses got discouraged, like humans, at having to keep doing something they weren't very good at. If so, it was no wonder she seemed happier now that she had been hunting.

The lessons were sharpened by a keen edge of knowledge that what I was doing now was about to be put into practice outside the arena, in the disciplined anarchy of the hunting field, which seemed at once so wild and formless and so elegantly controlled with rules and conventions. I was dismayed by how hard I found it to settle into the rhythm of a hunting canter, rising from the saddle as though at the trot to spare the horse's back (a back on which, after all, you were likely to be sitting for anything up to six hours on a hunting day). And of course I was worried about the jumping. I was jumping small courses now, of hunt-sized fences from about 2ft 3in to a maximum of 3ft. I would find very little bigger than that in the Ashford Valley country, said Mrs Rogers. And there was always a way round.

I had begun to repeat Always A Way Round to myself like a mantra ('always possible for non-jumpers to negotiate the country', was what it said in *Baily's*). My jumping was so inconsistent, it seemed inevitable that I should be making frequent use of this handy get-out clause. On good days, of which there were a few, the mare and I could tackle these courses with resolution, if not elegance. I knew that this was all to do with her, and nothing to do with me, but I also knew that it didn't really matter.

At this level, and for hunting purposes, my main duty was to refrain from being an impediment. If I could just do that – sit still, kick on and give with the reins as we took off – it would be enough. The mare was brave and clever enough to do the rest. The trouble was that I didn't reliably possess even these negative virtues. On bad days I was constantly behind the movement, jerking backwards just as I should have been leaning forward, interrupting the mare's arc over the jump and jabbing her in the mouth with the bit as she landed.

I knew what a good jump should look like. When I watched Jillie jump, I could anticipate every stage of the process. The turn, the approach, the slight folding-forward of the body as the horse took to the air, the return to vertical as the animal landed and was ridden away from the jump towards the next obstacle – all this was as clearly implanted in my brain's pathways as the operations of making a right-hand turn at a junction or negotiating a roundabout in a car. The difference was that on horseback, I couldn't make my brain force my body to carry out the necessary manoeuvres.

I had particular difficulty with the counter-instinctual

229

throwing-forward of my body as the leap began. I'd never been much good at doing things headfirst: diving, handstands, even the child's game of going downstairs headfirst, step by step on your hands, which my friends could do as lithely as lizards, all felt suicidal to me. Once, diving short-sightedly into what I thought was deep water, I had smacked my head sharply on the bottom of a concrete swimming pool and smartly detached both retinas. The resulting six-hour operation to stick everything back and sling a little silicon belt around one eyeball to hold it all in place had certainly been a powerful disincentive to doing anything headfirst ever again; even so, I couldn't really blame my wobbly jumping on it.

Long before that accident I had been a cautious and unathletic child. As an adolescent I played up my languid lack of physical co-ordination on purpose to enrage the school games teacher, which it satisfactorily did. Now it was I who became enraged with my own clumsiness as I lurched and jabbed my way around a course of jumps, unhappily at odds with my pretty, willing mare. The problem seemed to be partly inexperience but mainly a lack of balance. I could never quite tell when she was going to take off, didn't feel it until it began, by which time I was already behind the movement, leaning sharply backwards to counterbalance the sudden forward impetus, clinging to the reins and making the whole transaction twice as difficult for the mare as it should have been.

Even when I did manage to make the conscious effort (it was always conscious, never instinctive) to lean forward, I overdid it, hoisting my bottom out of the saddle in a fashion dangerously likely to tip me over the horse's head on landing, particularly since my legs were never thrust forward, in the approved hunting seat, but always trailing somewhere behind the girth, toes pointing earthwards. Russell, my teacher at the Royal Mews, said that I jumped 2ft jumps standing in the stirrups as though attempting a 6ft puissance wall. Even when he took my stirrups away I still managed, by clenching my thighs, to lift myself clear of the saddle. 'Don't jump the jump yourself. Let the horse do it,' said my teachers, in despairing chorus. Who would have thought the simple instruction, 'sit down', could be so hard to follow, particularly for someone who spent her entire life sitting down.

As for 'seeing a stride' – that magical incantation bandied about by showjumping folk, which was explained to me as the ability to place a horse correctly for take-off at a jump, so that if you put a fag packet in front of the jump at the optimum take-off position, the horse's hoof would crush it, every time it took that jump – I tried mentioning it to Mrs Rogers, and she simply shook her head. It was evidently as far beyond my present powers to see a stride as it would be for me to jump Russell's 6ft puissance wall.

About this time there was a new series of *Faking It* – a television programme in which people with no previous experience were trained very rapidly to pass muster at some quite demanding skill. One of the programmes starred a girl who earned a living as a podium dancer in a London nightclub. She had three months in which to learn how to showjump well enough to enter a competition. This girl had long nails, multiple piercings, a Medusa hairdo and an extensive wardrobe of cropped tops. She had barely seen a horse, let alone sat on one. Screaming at intervals, she bounced and cursed her way around the practice arena for hour after hour, regularly reduced to tears by the scary pair of instructors who had taken her on and kept hissing bitchy asides to camera about her bad attitude and general hopelessness.

But just before the competition date, something happened: she seemed to break through some mental or physical barrier. Suddenly, not only could she do what was asked of her, but the pleasure of her own success seemed to feed into a forward momentum of progress, so that even when something went wrong she had the reserves of confidence to feel it was the mistake that was the aberration, rather than the jumps she did right.

This was the point I could never quite reach. I could do the bouncing and the cursing (to Mrs Rogers's chagrin. She was unexpectedly ladylike in some ways and rather horrified by my nasty London mouth). But I could never quite make it to the confident plateau of knowing that I would get over a jump in reasonable style every time I tried it. Whatever I managed to achieve in one lesson seemed to vanish before the next, so that we had to start again from the beginning. Not that I should let that stop me from hunting. However discouraging, There Is Always A Way Round. On the other hand, though Mrs Rogers said nothing, I knew for sure she wouldn't think much of a pupil from her yard who took the alternative route when there were jumps on offer.

'It's just a matter of hours in the saddle,' said everyone consolingly. I was afraid it wasn't just that at all. Too old, too uncoordinated, no sense of balance – whatever the opposite of a natural talent for riding might be, I was afraid I had a generous dose of it.

I took my son to the Boxing Day meet, which was always held at the same pub, the Vine, in Tenterden High Street. The high street was edged with a row of metal crowd barriers, creating a narrow passage between a vast throng of pro-hunting people on the Vine side and a smaller group of anti-hunt protesters, some with children in pushchairs, holding placards or wearing cute Disneyfied fox masks, on the other. I looked to see if any of the placards bore a picture of the half fox-corpse that the antis had wrested from hounds in covert on my first day's Autumn hunting. I'd been assured that it would feature on a Boxing Day poster. There was, sure enough, a fair selection of limp fox bodies and trailing entrails on display, as though these things were somehow intrinsically disgusting or proof of cruelty. You might as well, I thought, put a picture of a lamb, halfway through the butchering process that transformed it from a woolly skipper in a field into a hygienic clingfilmed packet of supermarket chops, on a poster and carry that about as proof of inhumanity.

On the pro-hunting side of the street Morris Men skipped and jangled and the crowd shifted this way and that, calling Christmas greetings, hailing friends, visible but unreachable at a few yards' distance in the densely packed throng. There was an air of expectation and excitement, also perhaps of relief at being at last released from the family house arrest of Christmas Day. The Morris dancers subsided with a final hop and a stamp and sloped off, tinkling faintly about the knees, into the pub for a pint. The one veiled in a black cloth, topped with a shiny black horse's head with glaring painted eyes, snapped his scarlet jaws at the children pressing against the barriers as he passed. The festive chatter subsided slightly. Police in fluorescent yellow traffic tabards lined the road on either side, looking cheerful or fed up depending, presumably, on their private feelings about the hunt. 'This is well boring,' said Alexander. 'Can we go home now?'

'No,' I said. 'Look.' Down the narrow, police-lined channel left clear between the spectators and the protesters, a line of horsemen came riding. It was the Ashford Valley on the move: Neil with hounds, the whippers-in and Masters in scarlet, Mrs Rogers and the other Lady Master, Mrs Anderson, in their yellow-collared hunt jackets and behind them what seemed like an endless field, though it was probably no more than 30 people on horseback. Old men in bowler hats, children on ponies, the elegant Wednesday housewives on their nervy, fine-boned thoroughbred crosses, trotting sedately from wherever they had unboxed, then slowing to a walk as they reached the crowd and the barriers. I barely had time to register this scene for the hieratic spectacle it undoubtedly was – exciting, mysterious and intensely pagan – when it morphed into something quite different.

Neil got off his horse, led hounds on to a tiny triangular patch of grass just where we were standing and began introducing them to the surrounding children. The riders turned into a squarish enclosure fenced with metal barriers just outside the pub, and also began to dismount, handing their horses' reins to friends while they squirmed through the crowd towards the bar, flat-footed in their stiff boots. The sense of mystery that had surrounded them while they were riding through the clear channel between the two opposed armies of infantry dissolved into something domestic and convivial.

The force field of otherness that surrounds a person on horseback, particularly when that person is dressed in a uniform of some kind, is an interesting phenomenon, because it works only one way. Its effects are vivid to the person on the ground, invisible to the person on the horse. On later Boxing Days, when I was one of the long cavalcade clattering up the asphalt path between the barricaded lines of friends and enemies, I didn't feel other at all.

The first time I did it I felt nervous and slightly fraudulent, because the Ashford Valley hadn't yet resumed hunting after its suspension during the foot-and-mouth epidemic, and I knew that after parading hounds as though going on to hunt, we were actually going back to our horse boxes to take off our hunting clothes, change into civvies and go on a 'fun' ride across the country we should in normal circumstances have been hunting.

On the second occasion, by the time I found myself trotting just behind Mrs Rogers, who was riding her own horse and leading someone else's, towards the rest of Ashford Valley who were already assembled outside the Vine, I had been up since 5 a.m., had spent three-quarters of an hour walking Molly around a chilly concrete farmyard while the horse lorry was moved from the unboxing place to somewhere else, and had then been involved in a small flurry of activity when just behind me as we trotted towards the meet the hunt secretary's teenage son, Ned (on whom I tended to rely for a lead over jumps), had his knee smashed by a kick from the horse in front.

On my mind as we rode towards the pub was first, how was I going to do the jumps without Ned to follow over them? Second, that I had had no real idea how easy it was for a horse to pulverize human flesh and bone with one fluid movement of its hoof, and that I must make very sure in future both to keep back from the horse in front, and to keep Molly's rear well away from the people at this meet. Not that she was a kicker outside the stable, but evidently you never knew. And third, that I hoped with all my heart I was going to find someone I knew at the meet to buy me a stiff drink. I felt cold, tired, worried and rather sick from seeing Ned curled up on the ground in anguish. What I did not feel was proud, mysterious or in any way different from the crowds on whom I was looking down as I rode past.

Yet here is a photograph of me taken at that meet by my old college friend, the MP's wife Alicia, who sent it to me later. I am smiling quite nicely, as it happens, which is remarkable because in general nerves, especially hunting nerves, rearrange my features into a mask of blank ferocity. Despite the cheerful expression of pleasure and relief at seeing someone I recognize in the crowd, I have otherness written all over me to a startling extent: in the full-skirted black coat, the velvet cap, the netted bun into which my hair is coiled, the hunting whip with its stag's-horn handle and trailing leather thong.

Not to mention the fact that I am perched in the air at greater than human head height, with a horse between my knees and – there is no getting away from it, nice smile notwithstanding – the aloof, inward expression of a performer about to step on the stage. My mind may have been running on smashed knees and, longingly, on a double-strength whisky mac, but I look quite the little Diana.

There is something about the centaur partnership of horse and human that has an extraordinary effect upon the groundling psyche. I had felt it myself, standing earthbound at Jo's stirrup at the meet to which she took my mare, when I was overswept by an uncontrollable envy of her for being up there, on horseback, all ritually groomed and dressed and about to take part in a ceremony of power and risk and excitement from which I was dully excluded. It was quite irrational, because I'd willingly offered her the opportunity to hunt the mare. But I felt it all the same, and rationality had nothing to do with it. No wonder people who dislike the hunt do so with such quasi-religious extremities of fervour; that the opposition to hunting is characterized by an intensity of hatred more often associated with ancient sectarian conflict.

Anyway, here was Neil, centaur status forgone, off his horse and down on the ground with his cap off, transformed from the principal celebrant in a winter ritual of pursuit and death into a friendly bloke with a nice pinkish face and bright dark eyes, standing like a scarlet maypole in the midst of a whirling flurry of hounds.

Foxhounds give off *joie-de-vivre* and affection for human beings like a scent. This is partly a matter of blood. The Ashford Valley hounds had biddability bred into them, on account of the country, whose chopped-up nature, bisected by road and rail and areas where the hunt could not go, meant that they must be willing to allow themselves to be stopped, picked up and moved. 'It is surprising,' wrote Colonel Parkes, the Ashford Valley Hound Trustee, 'how some strains do not

236

like this (the so-called Old English of the Belvoir, Brocklesby etc tend to sulk if treated in this way). These requirements also ruled out Welsh blood. These hounds are bred to hunt independently in the Welsh mountains where hunt staff cannot get to them. By the same token, they are less than happy when interfered with.'

But the hounds outside the pub this Boxing Day morning were quite happy to be interfered with: their tails and ears pulled and their soft plush heads and wiry coats patted by strangers' hands. Besides being bred into them, their sweet natures must owe something to the centuries-old pattern of their training, which involves foxhound puppies being sent away from kennels at a few months old to spend the summer with local families of puppy-walkers who teach them their names and a degree of basic discipline before returning them to kennels to begin their training as a member of a hunting pack.

The practice of sending puppies out to walk was evidently well established when it was described by the poet William Somervile in *The Chase*, a five-book treatise on hunting, written in verse and published in 1735. Somervile, who was born in Warwickshire in 1677, had a great success with his poem. Even Dr Johnson, who couldn't be doing with hunting at all, said a kind word or two about it ('[Somervile] is allowed by sportsmen to write with great intelligence of his subject,' he wrote, adding that 'he writes very well for a gentleman'). And Peter Beckford, in his own great treatise, *Thoughts Upon Hunting*, called Somervile 'the only one that has written intelligibly on this subject'.

He came to a sad end, poor man. Oppressed by debt, he was 'forced', wrote his friend and fellow poet, William Shenstone, 'to drink himself into pains of the body to kill the pains of the mind'. He expired in 1742, poisoned by too liberal a consumption of a toddy mixed from 'rum, black-currant jelly and a very little water'. (A very nasty drink, this, responsible in its modern incarnation of rum-'n'-black for making underage schoolgirl drinkers of my own generation feel thoroughly poorly.)

Beckford, writing in 1781, sounds dubious about sending puppies out to walk – 'The distemper makes dreadful havock with whelps at their walks, greatly owing, I believe, to the little care that is taken of them there. I am in doubt whether it might not be better to breed them up yourself.' On the other hand, he adds, such puppies as survived the difficulties and dangers of being put out to walk 'were afterwards equal to any thing and afraid of nothing', by contrast with their unwalked contemporaries, which turned out 'weakly and timid, and had every disadvantage attending private education'.

Somervile's view of the boarding-school principle of sending young hounds to be educated away from home was a good deal more sanguine than Beckford's. He doesn't actually say, 'best years of their lives', but he paints a charming picture of the benefits of puppy walking for both puppy and walker. 'Unto thy choicest friends/Commit thy value'd prize,' he urges the would-be hound breeder, assuring him that 'the rustic dames/Shall at thy kennel wait, and in their laps/Receive thy growing hopes, with many a kiss/Caress, and dignify their little charge/With some great title, and resounding name/Of high import.' Which brings us back to Beckford and his fastidious dislike of high-flown names for hounds.

Not, Somervile is keen to point out, that puppy walking is all kissing and caressing by rustic dames. There is training involved as well: 'But cautious here observe/To check their youthful ardour, nor permit/The unexperienc'd younker, immature,/Alone to range the woods, or haunt the brakes/Where dodging conies sport: his nerves unstrung,/And strength unequal, the laborious chace/Shall stint his growth, and his rash, forward youth/Contract such vicious habits, as thy care/And late correction never shall reclaim.'

Of all the many habits of discipline that foxhounds are expected to acquire, probably the greatest is that of never, ever pursuing anything other than a fox. Chasing sheep, hare, rabbit, pheasant or anything else is known as 'rioting' (as in, 'We thought they'd found at last, but they were just rioting on a hare'), and is regarded, as Somervile says, as a 'vicious habit'. Along with the kissing and caressing, puppies at walk are learning to ignore all the other delicious seductions that make up the vivid scentscape of a hound's world. At the same time as being loved and cherished like a family pet, the groundwork is being laid for their transformation into a working foxhound.

Perhaps it is this combination of close human contact and the harnessing of their own animal instincts to perform a subtle and often difficult task — that of finding and following a fox by scent alone (the vagaries of scent in fox-hunting are legendary. You could write whole chapters or even a small book on the subject) — that turns out foxhounds to be so marvellously and attractively at ease with themselves and humans. Household pets — particularly dogs, because they are so emotionally responsive to humans, though it is true of other species as well — tend to evolve into a projection of their owner's personality and wishes. The neuroses and preferences of the owner are routinely transferred to the animal, which is in the process stripped of some aspects of its own nature, becoming, in the process, less than itself.

Hounds, while completely domesticated in the sense of being amenable to training and accepting of human authority, are also perfectly themselves. They are not neutered, they live together as a pack and are not required to adopt the quasi-human habits that people impose upon the pet animals who share their homes. As a result, they don't make good pets

239

and when their working lives are over, in general they are shot. This apparently ungrateful ending of a faithful servant's life is something else that upsets people who dislike hunting, though here again it is hard, if you are on the other side, not to feel that the huntsman's bullet in the head when a hound's physical prowess is declining might be a kinder end than that inflicted by their owners on some unfortunate old house pets, whose lives are prolonged past endurance by heroic veterinary intervention.

The overwhelming dread of death as the greatest possible evil, and the assiduous will to live in no matter what state of decrepitude and attendant humiliation is possibly the least humane of the quasi-human mores that people impose upon their unfortunate pets. I never see a novelty picture, in the tabloid newspapers that dote on such heartwarming animal stories, of a horse with a prosthetic leg, or a partly paralysed dachshund with its lifeless nether limbs supported on a little wheeled trolley, without thinking of the merciful huntsman's bullet that comes at a point when life is still relatively sweet.

Betty McKeever, the Kentish girl who was given her own pack of beagles, the Blean, by her father when she was eight years old and held the Mastership for 80 seasons, became as an old woman furious with the solicitor drafting her will when he refused to put in a clause saying that once she was dead, her body was to be chopped up and fed to her beagles so that she could have 'one last run across country' in their bellies. This 'one last run' line with its interesting combination of resonances – a mixture of the prosaic, the comic and the sacred – crops up more commonly attached to old hunters who have to be put down, and are taken to kennels to be shot and then fed to hounds.

This was the fate of Mrs Rogers's hunter, Sam, when he grew old and sick and stopped enjoying life. In fact it was from her, telling me that she had had to take him up to the kennels, that I first heard the expression. In the awful melancholy of losing an animal that had been both a friend and a colleague, the neat closing of the circle of life and death with this final ceremony of the last run – an animal version of 'dust to dust, ashes to ashes' – seemed a kind of consolation; more humane than the abattoir and more dignified than the sort of ersatz funeral rite, complete with quasi-ecclesiastical service and mock headstone, offered to the owners of defunct pets in the small-ads of country lifestyle magazines.

Looking now at the hounds frisking amiably on the grass, standing on their hind legs, their forepaws propped on the top bar of the barriers, pressing outwards towards the caresses of the crowd like a particularly extrovert bunch of pop stars greeting their fans, radiating charm, vitality, physical beauty and fitness and a delight in being alive and out of doors with their huntsman, about to go hunting, it was easy to understand how someone like Betty McKeever, who had lived with hounds all her life, might be keen for her spirit to live on in them after her death in the most practical way imaginable.

Football fans are notorious for wanting their ashes scattered on the sacred turf of their club's home ground (in fact, a version of this was what happened to Mrs McKeever in the end. They held a meet of the beagles at one of her favourite spots, scattered her ashes on the earth and drew over them), and hunts command the same passionate loyalty – with the important difference that hunt followers are active, rather than passive, spectators; not merely sitting in the stands chanting and criticizing, but following hounds as they follow the scent of the fox across country, with all the ingenuity and potential for comic (or even tragic) disaster inherent in picaresque narratives.

If the two foxhound puppies in *The Tale of Jemima Puddle-duck* are like football hooligans, with their up-for-it attitude, their cheery enthusiasm for the simple act of destruction whenever they find the opportunity, and their seamless segue from the chivalrous despatching of the fox who planned to devour poor Jemima and her precious eggs to the thuggish gobbling of those very eggs as a savoury chaser to the main course of raw fox, then a pack of properly trained foxhounds might be said to resemble a good professional football team with a manager they love. Same improbable peak of physical perfection and highly developed, instinctive athletic ability; same keen enthusiasm for teamwork and almost brutal super-fluity of high spirits.

Perhaps it was these qualities that attracted Alexander, who was indifferent to horses and as bored by hunting as I am by football, but inexplicably loved hounds, particularly the wayward Dreamer. He borrowed my camera now and took several pictures of them which afterwards came out unexpec-tedly well — arbitrarily framed abstract compositions full of arched spines, curved sterns and questing noses, suffused with the energy that foxhounds radiate like heat.

We hung around for a bit, patting hounds, hemmed in by the crowd. Besides the people I knew by sight — Mrs Rogers and her fellow Masters, Neil and the whippers-in — I could see Claire, who had lent me the pony to go Autumn hunting, on her little skewbald mare, Cornflake (Snowflake, the senior Master always called it, with an elaborate pantomime of being unable to remember its name. Snowdrop. Corncrake . . .), which was shivering convulsively. But there were several yards'-worth of people and a metal barrier between her and us, so we couldn't go over and chat but could only wave and stay where we were, onlookers to the spectacle, involved but detached.

Neil was back on his horse now, hounds gathering around him, the stragglers being rounded up by the whippers-in who called their names in a distinctive sing-song, garnished with roars and growls of admonition: 'Lattice, Lat-ice! Come on up! Good old girl. Come on then! Dreamer! Dreamer!' The senior Master, standing in his stirrups, cap off, delivered a brief speech of exhortation and defiance, urged us all to turn out for the Countryside Alliance march to be held in London in a couple of months' time, thanked us for our support, wished us a Happy New Year and set off at the head of the field, following the huntsman and his hounds to wherever they were going (where were they going? Wasn't it all antiques shops and dinky weatherboarded cottages off Tenterden high street? Evidently not), to cheers and clapping from the pro-hunt side of the street, jeers and waving banners from the antis.

They left behind a palpable absence, a hunt-shaped hole in the gathering which swiftly began to finish up its drink and dwindle away towards the plates of cold turkey salad and reheated Christmas pudding waiting at home. Alexander was keen to get to the grandparents' house, where there was to be a rerun of Christmas Day, which we'd spent at home in Greenwich, with presents under the Christmas tree and crackers before the cold turkey and stuffing. We joined the drift towards the car park. I felt flat and oddly pointless but not as bereft as I had on the day my mare had been part of the press of horses trotting away to the first covert. Quite soon now it would be my turn.

The new year began in a flurry of dreadful weather. The wind blew and the rain fell and the Ashford Valley's country, notoriously the sinkhole of Kent, weltered in mud so that the farmers were reluctant to let the hunt cross their land. Meets were cancelled, rearranged and cancelled again. In mid-January the House of Commons voted by 399 votes to 155 in favour of a ban on hunting. I felt sick, and thought the Ashford Valley would be desperate but was surprised to find them cheerful, almost sanguine. They seemed to be of the opinion that the awe-inspiring effects of the Countryside Alliance march, plus the disinclination of the House of Lords to endorse a ban and the distraction of the forthcoming election, would see off the threat to hunting, at least for the time being.

I began to feel anxious about when Molly and I might finally go out – but not overwhelmingly. The Kennels meet wasn't until February and the weather must surely improve by then. But on February 20 a group of animals infected with foot-and-mouth disease was discovered at an abattoir in Essex and two days later fox-hunting was voluntarily suspended by its governing body, the MFHA. After that, everything seemed to collapse quietly in on itself.

It was odd, travelling back and forth between London and the Ashford Valley and seeing how differently the foot-and-mouth epidemic made its impact in the two places. In the city the imagery was stark and shocking. The front pages of the newspapers and the television screens were filled with scenes from an inferno: farmyards full of bewildered stock, lowing cows, bleating sheep, slaughtermen in overalls with bolt guns in their hands, their faces like masks, stiff with the awful weariness of repetitive slaughter. And standing by, angry and protesting, weeping or frozen with distress, the farming families whose lives had lost their accustomed rhythm and fallen into a cacophony of disorder.

There were aerial shots of greyish lines scrawled across the familiar green patchwork of the countryside which proved, when the camera approached more closely, to be mass pyres, tens of yards long – the greyish mass made up of hundreds of dead bodies of mostly sound and healthy stock, culled as an unsuccessful – and increasingly, it seemed, panic-stricken – effort to stop the spread of the disease. When the pyres were lit and the flames shot up, the crisping limbs of animals were silhouetted in their lurid, intermittent light.

There was pathos and indignity in those upturned hooves. Cows and sheep and pigs the right way up look massive and immovable: solid features of the landscape like the trees and hedges and buildings that surround them. Flipped upside down by death, their incongruously slender legs and elegant cloven hooves pointing towards the sky, twitching as the cooking muscles contracted in a poisoned simulacrum of the traditional British roast, they were as disturbing an image of ruined lives as the odd, naked room sets you sometimes see in pictures of the London Blitz, where a bomb has demolished part of a terrace of houses but left one almost intact, its protective outer walls ripped off and its intimate insides, the chintz sofas and frilly-skirted dressing tables, the candlewick bedspreads and kitchen implements and bathroom toothbrushes and sponges all exposed to the air and the indifferent perching pigeons.

As winter turned to spring a malign pattern set in – more outbreaks of disease, more killing, more pyres, more discussion by politicians and scientists and farmers on whether the right thing was or was not being done – spiked occasionally by catchy feature stories of grisly cuteness: a calf was pulled alive from a pile of dead bodies. It was granted a stay of execution and named Phoenix. Two years later, it made the headlines again when it had a calf of its own. An Easter lamb also made the front page of the papers. It was weltering in mud and certain to die, because DEFRA regulations forbade it to be moved from the field where it had been born. It, too, was given a name, Lucky, and reprieved for a life as a family pet.

These stories of redemption seemed somehow to obscure the reality of all the other calves and lambs who hadn't been plucked from the piles of dead cattle or the freezing mud soup but had perished and burned. Their extinguishing became a commonplace; another digit in the cloudy mass of statistics that began to lose its impact as the election campaign gained momentum. The progress of the disease and the ensuing slaughter continued to be reported, but its power to shock diminished by degrees. It was like watching the story of some interminable disaster going on in a far distant land – awful, but oddly detached and a bit repetitive. 'I'm bored with foot-and-mouth,' said the editor of a newspaper section with whom I was having lunch one day. 'I wish the bloody farmers would just shut up whingeing. They're getting compensation, aren't they? It's time to move on.'

Fifty miles from London it felt quite different. Kent was almost untouched by outbreaks of the disease, so there were no pyres in the fields on the way to the yard, no drifting stench of burning flesh, no clouds of smoke by day and leaping flames by night. It looked and smelled much as before. But the effects of the disease were present nevertheless. What you felt at once were the restrictions on where you might go. The south-eastern toll rides organization had a network of bridle-ways and farm tracks that fretted the land all around the yard. At the Rooting Street yard you could ride down the narrow grass path between the rubber school and the sand school and at once you were on a toll ride track that led round the margin of a cornfield, then into another field and another; past the cross-country field, along the bank of the Great Stour – more of a stream than a river at this point – along the edge of woodland and into orchards. You could ride for hours off the road and see almost no one – the gamekeeper sometimes, a tractor ploughing or spraying, or a combine harvester in the season.

As you moved along the track, grassy in summer, rutted mud and ice puddles in winter, you were encircled by a small forcefield of disturbance: a contained ripple of activity that kept pace invisibly with the horse, beginning a few yards ahead of you and settling again as you passed like the wake on a river as a boat goes by. In winter it was mainly birds that warned of your presence: pheasants bursting from the bare thickets in a flustered bundle of feathers with their hysterical, rattling klaxon of a call; partridges, suddenly bolting onto the track and running in a dither straight ahead of you, almost under the horse's hooves (they did the same thing on roads in front of the car. The only thing to do was stop until they had calmed down sufficiently to totter back into the safety of the hedge).

There were magpies everywhere and small birds too, though the magpies were supposed to prey so viciously upon them: robins and sparrows, blackbirds and thrushes. In the spring, the hedges were full of finches – greenfinch, goldfinch, chaffinch – and wrens and bluetits flew into the air as they heard the sound of approaching hooves, and you could hear jays and woodpeckers in the coverts, though they showed themselves less.

Once I came upon a big green woodpecker standing in the middle of the track and instead of flying away as we came near, it began to walk, plodding along rather doggedly as though its feet hurt. I thought it must be sick or injured, and began to wonder whether I could find a place to tie up Molly safely while I went to look (and also whether, once on the ground, I'd be able to get back up again, possibly with an ailing bird about my person). Still wondering, I rode alongside the trudging bird, giving it a wide margin. It didn't look at us as we passed. It was very striking, with its green back and yellow waistcoat and head marked with red, white and black. I stopped the mare some yards ahead of it and looked back. It was standing still again, and at last it seemed to notice us. It took unhurriedly to the air and flew away into the wood and that was the last I saw of it.

In summer when the air and the ground were warm and there was plenty to eat the inhabitants of the field margins seemed to grow more negligent about showing themselves.

You could ride out in the afternoon sunshine and find rabbits languidly nibbling the short grass at the edge of the path who barely troubled to heave themselves back into cover as you rode by. One field at the back of the farm was a particular haunt of young foxes. Often you would turn into it and see a cub spring from the crop where it had been basking or hunting, bounce across the track and disappear into the wood. We took one by surprise one day: it was hidden among the wheat and either didn't dare or didn't choose to make the dash into the open to reach the wood on the other side. It began to move away, very quietly and stealthily, crouched low and almost invisible except for the trace of its movement marked by the swaying greeny-gold wheatstalks like a current running through water.

All the banks were pocked and cavernous with badger workings, but I never saw a live badger, except occasionally late at night when I'd catch sight of one shuffling along the roadside, blinded by the car headlights. They were too nocturnal to meet out riding by daylight, and so were hedge-hogs, though there were masses of them around, to judge from the pathetic flattened bodies with which the roads were regularly encrusted.

I never saw a nightingale, either – though I probably wouldn't have recognized one if I had, since they are nonde-script small brown birds – hard to distinguish, unless you are well up on these things, from any other generic small brown bird. But Mrs Rogers's husband, James, said they could be heard singing in the woods near the Hothfield petrol station, and after he said that of course I thought I heard them all the time, especially when I was refuelling the car, propped against the dirty silver paintwork, trying not to breathe the fumes from the petrol gun as I filled the tank before driving back to south-east London where no nightingales sang, at the petrol station or anywhere else.

What happened once the foot-and-mouth restrictions came into force was that a veil, like the gauze at the theatre which is invisible when lit one way, but with the lights differently angled looks like a solid backdrop, fell between the land and the people who were accustomed to pass over it for recreation or their livelihood. Every stile and signpost suddenly sprouted a piece of white paper with black writing on it, covered against the weather in a clear plastic bag, announcing that rights of way were suspended. You might not cross the country on foot or on horseback. You could look, but you couldn't touch. You could ride the roads, but not step on the path. It was like visiting a museum of agricultural life, perfectly authentic and utterly unreal.

The effect was heightened by the absence of life in the fields. It wasn't something you noticed at once, because the disease began in late winter, when the stock would ordinarily be indoors in any case. But as the spring and then the summer came, the unaccustomed asepsis of relations with the land as you rode by gained an extra dimension: a peculiar feeling of something so familiar as almost to be invisible having gone missing.

It was like stepping into your grandparents' house – where the squashed old armchairs, one with a crocheted rug draped over its sagging shoulders, had stood in the same place since before you were born, drawn up close to the fireplace where the grey Chinese rug lay, pocked with little scorch marks from falling cinders, and above the mantelpiece the eighteenth-century silhouette of a man with a foppish arrangement of curls clustering about a sort of French loaf pompadour, framed in black lacquer with a bunch of ormolu oak-leaves by way of a hanging ring, which had hung there so long that a pale patch showed on the wall underneath. There was the feeling that something had changed – but what? Had they had the rug cleaned, or the walls repainted? Bought a new set of fire

249

irons or just moved the armchairs a couple of inches off their accustomed marks? Hard to say, but hard, too, to account for the curious sensation of unease, of something's being out of true.

In the end it was April before I realized that the subliminal sense that something looked and smelt and sounded wrong emanated from the empty fields. No lambs played on the big expanse of pasture by the turning from Charing to Pluckley (where an ominous billboard announced 'This land sold for Attractive Development'); no mixed herd of cattle grazed on the other side of the hedge as you came into Little Chart. The uncropped grass grew rank and the absence hung in the air, not apocalyptic like the pictures on the telly, but infinitely unsettling all the same; the barely perceptible tremor of a distant earthquake.

In fact there was plenty of road hacking around Rooting Street that didn't involve too much confrontation with fast traffic, but I didn't know the area well, apart from the roads I regularly drove, and in any case was only just growing accustomed to the idea of owning a horse that I could ride when I chose, without having to make an appointment a week in advance. The first time I rode Molly out of the yard on my own felt very odd, almost as though I were stealing her, or bunking off school while the Argus eye of the headmistress was momentarily closed. I realized, like a child who has never been taught to play, that I didn't really know what to do on a hack. Presumably you were supposed to walk a bit and trot a bit. I must not canter on the road, I knew that much. But how long should I ride for? This hacking wasn't just for my amusement. It had a purpose, to exercise the horse, which was particularly important now that the fields and toll rides were closed and the horses were arena-bound.

The traffic on the road outside the yard was relentless.

Twenty years ago, said Mrs Rogers, when her elder son was in his pram, it had been so quiet that she used to have to get parents to drive up and down in their cars during the Pony Club traffic proficiency test so as to give the children some real experience of handling their ponies around vehicles. But now cars came barrelling past in both directions every few minutes, rarely slowing as they came to the yard, though there was a road sign warning of horses. I didn't know what Molly was like in traffic and didn't want to find out quite yet.

It was true that I'd ridden horses regularly around Hyde Park Corner on the way back from the Hyde Park manège to the Royal Mews, but that was in a stately crocodile, with fluorescent Sam Brownes and flashing lights to strap to your boots and a brace of prefect-like Civil Service Riding Club ladies fore and aft to whip in the stragglers and hold back the impatient traffic with imperious hand gestures. I hadn't considered in detail – in fact was obstinately refusing to consider at all – what might happen if I got into trouble when hacking on my own. But I was keen to avoid getting mixed up with cars.

A few yards up the road from the stable was a turning to the right marked Little Chart Forstal. A narrow, potholed lane led past a mock-Tudor house with metal gates and a dense, dank shrubbery of leathery-leaved rhododendron and laurel behind which a pair of Rottweilers rampaged, barking savagely at imaginary threats. Molly, on her first outing down the lane, walked unmoved past this horrible pair of snarling Cerberuses, continuing placidly past an ancient, crooked brick house with a strange little tree outside, clipped into a lacy umbrella of twigs, and out into the open space of a cricket green with a pavilion at one end and a margin of white stones.

It was the white stones that began the long list of things Molly didn't care for – a list that, in the summer months (she was afraid of nothing during the hunting season) ran, when I wrote it down, to several sides of a small notebook. White or pale things generally were appalling: plastic carrier bags, discarded Styrofoam coffee cups, fence posts, the foot-and-mouth notices nailed to the stiles, the pale undersides of burdock leaves and sheep all brought on a sudden flounce to one side, or if she was especially startled, a sideways leap of several feet. She had a strong prejudice against geometry. Square metal manhole covers and the wedge-shaped, brick-edged culverts with which the Council was conscientiously attempting to improve the drainage of the waterlogged roads around Little Chart both got the flouncing treatment. The road from the yard to anywhere you might want to hack out was interrupted by manhole covers or culverts every few feet, so our progress up it became a ballet of overstrung nerves.

It wasn't just angles that bothered her: she objected equally to cylinders. A pile of drainage pipes, a fallen log lying idle and harmless in the bracken by the roadside, sent her into fits of the vapours whenever she passed them, while a field dotted with large cylindrical bales wrapped in black plastic sheeting alarmed her so much that she didn't even turn round to retreat, but began running backwards at high speed up a narrow track.

These frighteners were at least predictable. In the early stages of our relationship, I used to think of bracing myself as we approached a culvert or a log, though in fact what you had to do to avoid falling off was the opposite of bracing – a sort of counter-instinctual floppiness was the best hope of sticking in the saddle. Once I had mastered the rudiments of what disturbed her, I thought, I should be able both to prepare myself and reassure her. But beneath the straightforward vocabulary of alarm of which I was slowly compiling a lexicon there lay a deeper stratum of dismay that I found it impossible to decipher.

When I was a teenager my parents owned a gloomy cat

called Marcus who spent most of his time huddled in the airing cupboard. On rare occasions, he would emerge from his cosy nest of clean underwear to join the rest of the family in the living room. But not for long. After half an hour or so of sitting by the fire with his paws curled under him like a normal cat he would rise, arch his back into a taut bow of horror, bristle all his fur up like a dandelion clock and, eyes fixed on some dreadful sight in the corner of the room – invisible to the rest of us – would retreat, spitting fearfully, to the airing cupboard. It was an unsettling habit, particularly if you happened to be alone in the house when he did it, but I had almost forgotten it until Molly began to exhibit her own version of the Invisible Terror.

We'd be trotting along, as peacefully as you could when alertly on the lookout for round, square or pale things that might give her a nervous turn, and then for no obvious reason, she'd throw in a *grand jeté*. Afterwards, you might hear the faint rattle of a pheasant taking off far inside a wood, or see out of the corner of your eye a whisking rabbit-scut. One spring day we were riding past a newly sown field on which a quantity of oddly still pigeons were sitting, and I was trying to work out why they looked so fixed and immovable when she sprang into the air and hit the ground running. And when I contrived to stop her and glanced back, I saw a short, squarish man with a bundle of leafy branches fixed to his hat rise slowly from behind a small screen, also decorated with branches. He was holding a gun. The frozen-looking pigeons were decoys. We had been in the way of his shot. Molly had sensed him, and I had not. Probably I ought to have felt grateful for her swift reactions, but an aggrieved part of me still felt that it wasn't quite fair to jump about like that at invisibilities.

The things that didn't frighten her were equally unpredict-able. Half a field after the pigeon incident we were passing an overgrown pond and a heron took off underneath us – a great, labouring heave into the air with much effortful flapping of ragged grey wings. I wondered if that mightn't send us leaping straight into the pond, particularly with our nerves still jangling from the pigeons, but she didn't even quicken her stride.

She was just as calm about a stray sheet of plastic blown by the wind across a cornfield, which came writhing and twisting towards us like the murderous drapery of M. R. James's horror story, 'Oh, Whistle, and I'll Come to you, My Lad.' To me it looked evil enough to terrify the sedatest old carthorse: there was a nightmarish, inexorable quality about its twitching progress across the stubble, but the mare appeared not to notice it. And at a point-to-point, when the whipper-in, to whom I'd lent her for the day, noticed a couple of hounds engaged in some florid misdemeanour and cracked his whip right by her ear, she stood as still as a police horse: ladylike, perfectly behaved, an inexplicable monument of steadiness and calm.

The road to Little Chart Forstal became our regular hack all through that strange, silent spring and summer. After the cricket green it ran between hedged arable fields, downhill to a crooked humpbacked bridge over a stream, then up again, past houses and sheep pasture and a deep, dark pool where moorhens swam, through high, tunnel-like hedges on either side to a cluster of cottages before coming out onto the main road just by the petrol station where the nightingales sang.

From the top of the rise, just before you plunged down towards the stream and the little bridge, you could look out over the valley and its neat, irregular patchwork of fields in multitudinous variants of green and tawny, bordered with narrow lines of darker green hedges, like piping. Beyond the invisible stream in the valley bottom the land swooped upwards again in the long, low line of the hill on whose flank lay the point-to-point course. The big road ran along the bottom of that hill. You could hear it, if you listened hard – a low rattling whoosh, like waves over pebbles. But you couldn't see the cars, only the grass and earth spectrum of the land with its trees and hedges, and the little brick farmhouses crouched in its sheltering contours.

The first few times I rode this route, it felt as though I were undertaking something quite interesting and intrepid. I hadn't been out on horseback unaccompanied before. I didn't know how the mare would go. Every expedition had its moment of alarm. My particular private terror was the humpbacked bridge with its low parapet. Each time we crossed it, I had an idea that she would take fright at the water and leap over the parapet. But the real water obstacle came later, at the moorhen pond, where there was an outlet contained within a smart new red-brick culvert with sharp angles.

Molly's first sight of this arrangement was also the site of our first real battle. Ears back, eye rolling, she refused to go forward. First she stood still, then she began to retreat. I didn't know what to do about this. My instincts were developed for dealing with children, not horses. If it had been my child who was suffering from an irrational terror, I should have coaxed it past. But Molly was beyond coaxing, and too big to coerce. Dimly, I thought I remembered reading or being told that you mustn't lose a battle with a horse, or it would think it had the upper hand and start to bully you. I already had the idea that her bad stable manners were a form of bullying, so I thought I had better kick on briskly past the culvert. Nothing happened. I kicked some more. She turned round and began to trot out smartly towards home. I turned her back towards the culvert and kicked again. She sidled reluctantly towards it and then stopped.

I could feel her seething unhappily beneath me and realized that I couldn't let this go on, that even if I had no idea what to do, which I hadn't, I had to take charge of what happened next. Until now there had always been someone to tell me what to do, but now there wasn't. I kicked on, and when she stopped again and began to turn, I hit her smartly with the whip. I hadn't hit anyone, or anything, since I was 14 years old and found that the girl sitting behind me in Latin class had spent the entire period poking the end of my pigtail down the inkwell with the end of her fountain pen. I thought I had an aversion to hitting, which I associated with uncontrollable rage. I didn't want to be in a rage with this mare. I wanted her to be my friend. Nevertheless, I hit her, with misgiving, but without rage, and it worked. Bridling slightly, she trotted crabwise past the awful culvert and on up the road. On the way back, I kicked hard and we passed it without resistance, beyond some expressive eye-rolling.

The next time we went that way, I anticipated, and got her past it with no more than a tap of the whip. After that, I began to be bored with this hack. It was late winter. Everything looked dreary and bedraggled in shades of sodden brown and grey. There was nothing to look at, and nothing going on. Every detail of the route – the fields, the hedges, the potholed road, the houses with their obstinate suburban plantings of forlorn Pampas grass and bare, gnarled standard roses in orna-mental beds – was burned into my memory in a way that become less, not more interesting with repetition. I didn't know where else to ride that would be as quiet and safe as this. What's more, it was the right length – about 40 minutes of trot and walk, out and back, and not all on the flat. But every time I did it, my resistance grew a little. It felt like eating a meal devoid of flavour. The mare was getting a modicum of exercise, I was getting a little experience of handling her; beginning to realize that riding was more than just sitting on a horse and making the right moves. At the same time as not falling off, I was having to learn to interpret the horse and even to think like it. Slowly, we were becoming accustomed to one another. The rudiments were being established, but they lacked savour.

After a while there came a shift in the season, almost imperceptible at first, but then the signs of spring began to accumulate. Snowdrops and helleborus came up in orderly clumps on the verges opposite the cricket green. Over someone's garden fence I could see aconites opening like scattered gold coins against the dark earth. Primroses and violets and wood anemones grew on the steep banks that led down towards the stream. The bare wet twigs bore greenish-yellow lambstail catkins and pussy willow scuts of silvery fur. The raw, chill winter air that scorched the inside of your nose when you breathed it warmed and began to smell of wet earth and growing and, faintly, of flowers.

The violets and primroses withered. Now when the breeze blew in the right direction, it carried the fragile wild-hyacinth smell of the bluebells that spread a shallow lagoon around the boles of the straggly wood of nut trees. The hyacinth faded and was replaced by the fleshy, pointed leaves, starry white flowerheads and forthright kitchen reek of wild garlic. Before the buds on the wild roses were open the election had been held and won by Labour, on a manifesto promising, among other things, to 'reach a conclusion on hunting with dogs'. There was still a foot-and-mouth epidemic, and large parts of the countryside remained under restrictions. People wrote articles in the newspapers about the effects on the economy of the loss of tourism revenue, but politics had knocked the epidemic off the top slot in the headlines. The papery interdictions nailed to the stiles grew faded and tattered in the wind, the sunshine and the rain, and the empty, glassed-in feeling of looking over the hedges into the ungrazed pasture was as strong as ever.

In the late spring we began to spend the weekends in a rented flat on the top floor of one of the farm cottages. Earlier in the year I had been driving through Wye when I saw a To Let sign on a building at the railway station which must once have been the stationmaster's house. It was a nice, Victorian red brick cottage with pierced white wooden boarding around its gables like a narrow lace edging. It seemed to give directly on to the station at the front, and from the car window I thought I saw a bit of garden bounded by cast-iron railings at the back.

I parked and hurried towards it, very excited by the To Let sign. Alexander would love it, I thought. For years when he was very small he had been obsessed in a thoroughly trainspotterish way with Thomas the Tank Engine and his bickering collection of crosspatch railway chums. If I were to rent this cottage we could lie in bed at nights and listen to the mail trains rushing past. On warm days, we could take our elevenses onto the platform and wave to the carriages full of daytrippers on their way to Margate or Broadstairs. It would be like *The Railway Children*. And perhaps, if he spent the summer in Kent, he might lose the intense suspicion of the country that made him drag me away from Estate Agents' windows in Charing and Canterbury whenever I stopped to look in them.

But as I drew close I saw that the cottage was derelict. The net curtains hanging at the upstairs window were grimy and hanging sluttishly askew. The little back garden was full of rubbish, the white-painted woodwork rotten and peeling and the lower windows sealed against break-in with padlocked metal grilles. It needed someone to care for it – but not us. It was too big a project for me to take on alone.

I was on my way to the yard and all the way there I thought about that abandoned station cottage and what fun it would have been to have stayed there, with the companionable roar of the trains rushing past the front door and a tidy little stationmaster's garden with marigolds and raspberries and sweet peas growing up a framework of hairy string at the back.

When I got to the yard I told Mrs Rogers about it and asked if she knew of anyone with a place to let, not too expensive. If she did, I'd be interested. She said she'd bear it in mind and the following week, rather diffidently, she said it might not be what I was used to, but there were a couple of flats in one of the farm cottages. One was empty and the other about to be. I could look at them if I liked.

We walked across the paddock at the top of the yard. She heaved open a gate of rusty metal spears and put a key in the back door of a semi-detached brick cottage. The downstairs flat was a single room, painted *eau-de-nil* with a flowery border at waist height. There was a little shower room and an oddly shaped kitchen. Off the kitchen was a cold, whitewashed walk-in larder with a deep, north-facing window-sill faced with a slate slab. I'd always wanted a larder with a slate slab.

The upstairs flat was bigger and painted in a riot of assorted distemper: custard yellow all the way up the stairs, which were carpeted in a ferocious design of chocolate and orange swirls. The bathroom was pale green, the bedroom peach and the living room, which was large and very light, with arched-top Dering windows on three sides, a modest harebell blue. At one end of the living room was a sink and some kitchen cupboards, and from the window by the sink you could look out over the paddock to a view of fields and woods as far as the horizon. (By night, this charming pastoral scene was lit with a lurid orange glow from the distant sodium lamps of Ashford. But there were no street lights in the road to the front, so if you looked up at the night sky from that side of the house you saw nothing but infinite expanses of blue-black space, pierced with stars.)

I struggled briefly with a desire for a walk-in larder but the upstairs flat was a better size for the two of us. Alexander was a restless and talkative sleeper and I didn't fancy sharing a room with him. Mrs Rogers named her rent and I said I'd think about it, but I knew I'd take what fate seemed obligingly to have lined up for me. I spent the next few weeks fixing the place up so that (I hoped) Alexander wouldn't take against it when he saw it. Then I bought a large-scale Ordnance Survey map of the bit of East Kent that took in Rooting Street and a big chunk of the Ashford Valley country and stuck it to the wall.

We spent every weekend of the summer laying down our tracks across that piece of country. We went in the car, but in my mind's eye I saw the places where we had travelled marked with a wandering chain of footsteps, like the arrow-print of birds' feet on sand, or the maze of snowy footprints that bewilders Pooh and Piglet in *Winnie-the-Pooh*. We began to sink into the early stages of an intimacy with the places within a semi-circular sweep from the yard to the coast; to recognize their names and characters and learn the routes between them as though picking up a foreign language.

Mainly it was towards Dymchurch that the car wheels turned as we left the lane from the cottage. I'd been there once before, on a strangely satisfactory family holiday which we spent in a rickety, black-tarred wooden hut, like a large garden shed. It was panelled with wood inside, painted a hospital green. There was an iron bedstead with a fat, pink-flowered eiderdown which I had to share with my sister, to our joint horror, and no bathroom. The hut stood in a large grassy field, just over the road from the sea and densely populated with rabbits. Its rawboned blackness was decently veiled by a leggy tangle of salt-bitten rosebushes with cruel thorns and small, bright pink flowers.

The lav was contained in a second, smaller hut, a little walk down a narrow trodden path from the house, with a tunnel of overgrown roses overhead. Underneath the iron bedstead was a china po, but I had a disagreeable memory of a discoloured white plastic potty sitting unemptied on the bath-room floor at home and a nine-year-old's disdain for peeing into some kind of overgrown mug. Besides, when you woke in the early morning, when the sun was piercing the thin curtains, and slid out of bed, you could let yourself very quietly out of the front door into the fields where the coarse grass was silvered with dew on which your bare feet left dull green footprints. There were other footprints there already: the neat oval pawmarks of the rabbits who clustered around the hedges at the field's margin and ignored the passing of a child in a skimpy blue bri-nylon nightie on the way to the lav with its long iron chain, its loud, indecent, groaning flush and its enveloping, *Sleeping Beauty* thicket of rose branches, beautiful and menacing, like the ones that scratched out the prince's eyes in the fairy story.

My memory of this holiday was not so much a narrative as a series of disconnected flashes: the pale-blue plastic kite with a yellow tail that they bought us and we let go, so my father had to chase it for miles over the fields and dykes of Romney Marsh. Learning to swim in the cold, brown sea, so shallow and reassuring as long as your feet were on the firm ripples of the sandy bottom; so boisterous and unreliable as soon as you tried to allow it to support you. A sweetie shop in the town which sold seaside rock in all sorts of marvellous shapes: not just bright pink peppermint or striped tutti-frutti sticks with Dymchurch written in glassy red letters all through their white middles, but huge sugar dummies hanging from a loop of satin ribbon, too big to get into the mouth of anything but a giant baby, sugar pigs with scarlet smiles and little piggy black eyes, and most remarkable of all, a set of false teeth in bright pink and glittering white rock.

The sugar teeth looked so very like the teeth that my grandfather and grandmother kept in glasses of water at night time, one each on the small tables on either side of their matching beds (they looked like a couple of old tortoises when you went in for a drink of squash and a story first thing in the morning, their faces shrunken and sharp and their voices all different and gummy), that I thought it would be kind and amusing to buy them a set each as a present. My mother disagreed and headed me off in the direction of some less controversial keepsake.

We only went to Dymchurch once. After that we reverted to more conventional holidays in National Trust cottages in Cornwall, or respectable family hotels in Normandy, but the prickly, rackety, makeshift flavour of the place lingered, and when I saw how close it was to Rooting Street I thought we must see what it was like now.

We didn't go directly, but sidled up to it in a series of oblique excursions. We took the miniature steam railway to New Romney where there was a strange railway museum in an upper room at the station, around the margins of which was built a miniature track with elaborate landscaping: hills and fields and halts and level crossings populated with tiny models, sheep and cows, diminutive milk churns and poultry hampers, tiny porters pushing hand trolleys laden with cases, little passengers waiting decorously on the station platforms and small but robust hikers toiling along the cliff paths where, concealed in the steep folds of the plush grass hilltops, there lay in wait anarchic colonies of sharp-toothed plastic dinosaurs.

The train ran through New Romney to Dungeness, through a level, shingled landscape like the end of the world, dotted with inconsequential houses with odd gardens like fetish shrines: arrangements of tyres and artificial flowers and eyeless dollies with naked plastic limbs and matted gold nylon hair. There was a black lighthouse at the terminus with a winding staircase hung with charts of offshore wrecks and a round cabin at the top entirely full of a vast lens like a fly's eye. A sign at the entrance said 'lighthouse kittens' and we

262

thought we'd take one home, but they turned out to be toys. The sea was a bright sandy brown and it rattled irritably at the bottom of steep shingly banks sparsely sown with thorny, grey-green plants bearing starveling flowers in arid yellow or a bleached mauve.

High summer came. In the hedges hard, greenish black-berries and sloes and elderberries began to flush winy red and purple. Clusters of unripe cobnuts showed like milk teeth on the nut bushes and lay abandoned on the ground with toothmarks scraped in them where the squirrels had tried gnawing them, found them empty, or full of a bitter, immature fluff, and thrown them away in disgust. The combine droned in the wheatfields at the back of the farm. The morning light would wake me very early, shining into the peach-distempered bedroom through the curve of the uncurtained windows and I'd sit up in bed and look out across the paddock, caught in early-morning stillness like the moment before the curtain goes up at the theatre, the turf burnished and glittering with dewdrops not yet burned off by the sun and my silvery mare quietly cropping the sparkling grass like a grazing unicorn.

In the white glare of August I at last stopped sidling about to either side of the Dymchurch beach, packed our swimming things and drove us straight there, down the fast road through Ashford and then by a meandering slow road that crossed the bleak ambiguous collaboration of sky, land and water that was the marsh – sheepless and empty now, the flatness interrupted by the poking spires of ancient small churches – then skirted the coast with its squat, suspicious punctuation of Martello towers.

As we drew into the town I thought that none of my scraps of memory had survived. There was no rough field with untidy rose bushes and a black tarred hut; just the usual tawdry seaside accretion of cheap houses. The high street looked desolate. No sweet shop with grinning sugar dentures, no general stores selling Anchor butter, salad tomatoes, sliced bread, tinned ham, evaporated milk and fishing nets to a queue of people in shorts with sand stuck to their legs and angry sunburned shoulders daubed with white cream. Just a strip of tired-looking cafés and souvenir arcades with inflatable dinghies and rubber tyres festooned outside. When we got out of the car there was a strong smell of fish and chips and the air was filled with the urgent twangling of slot machines.

'Great. An arcade,' said Alexander. 'Can we go?' 'We can not,' I said. 'We are going to the beach.' Though not for long, I thought privately. I was beginning to regret this excursion into a vanished past.

We walked up the gritty track that led from the car park to the road, skirted the town hall, opposite which a cock was crowing insistently in someone's back garden, crossed the road by the municipal lavs and fetched up in a little paved square in which the Hythe Town Concert Band, sweltering in its natty uniforms, was puffing urgently into trombones and clarinets. Up some concrete steps, a scramble up a steep, grassy slope and there, at the top, was the Dymchurch I remembered. A concrete retaining wall descending in a sharp curve to a long expanse of hard, wave-rippled sand and shingle patched, I now remembered, with secret quicksands of disgusting mud, which looked almost the same as the ordinary sand until you stepped into a soft, treacherous sinking underfoot and felt your legs engulfed in squelching murk, inhabited by things that wriggled slimily under your clutching toes.

Clustered around the concrete slipway was a busy encampment of windbreaks, beach chairs, cooler bags, heaps of towels and ambitious sandcastles with dry moats. A donkey van was parked on the sand, and patient donkeys were giving rides to excited children in bathing suits. Two large yellow buoys were moored off-shore and beyond them a swarm of jet-skis droned up and down, buzzing like lawnmowers. The shallows were full of jumping children and their parents. On either side, the coast swept round in a sheltering curve. In the distance to the south you could see the pale industrial glitter of Dungeness and the nuclear power station. Northwards the houses beside the beach wall became steadily older and more substantial as the sandy beach ran out into shingle; then the shingle ran out as well and there was only sea.

Black wooden groynes partitioned the beach. A long drift of interesting objects lay at the water's edge: fish-egg cases like parchment bubble wrap, dead jellyfish in translucent mottled purple and tortoiseshell brown, dismembered crab claws, greenish ribbon strips of seaweed and shells: empty razor shells, large, ridged creamy clam shells and smaller, fragile, flattish shells in pale, appetizing colours like sweets – lemon yellow, striped orange, cream and black, Parma violet and rosy pink. The further you explored from the slipway by the ice cream shops and the loos, the fewer the people (and the more frequent the patches of sinking mud).

We spent the afternoon idling on the beach, digging holes and watching the water come up in them, paddling in the shallows; even, briefly, taking our feet off the bottom and swimming a few strokes in the chilly water, which looked a delectable deep turquoise shading to indigo from the beach, but an opaque, glaucous non-colour once you were actually in it. Then we went to the arcade and fed twopenny pieces to a slot machine like a glass case at a museum, containing six rickety brown metal horses which jerked spasmodically along a green baize racecourse and you had to bet on the likely winner.

After that we bought chips and went back to the beach and ate them slowly, sitting on the sea wall, swinging our legs as the donkey man led his donkeys – a snuff-colour with dark crosses on their backs (which I'd been taught at school was because of Jesus Riding on a Donkey) or chocolate brown with paler rings around their mild eyes; large clumsy heads with flapping ears and delicate little hooves – up the ramp of the trailer and drove away just ahead of the incoming tide. Then we carried our bundles of damp, sandy towels back to the empty car park where the evening air was cool and moist under the hawthorn trees and turned for the motorway and London and home.

That was how we spent the remaining weekends of late summer: among the sand and shingle, the mud and the creeping tides, the donkeys and dead jellyfish, the slot machines and the chippies. I took to making circuitous approaches, through the narrow roads and scattered villages of the marsh – Ivychurch, St Mary in the Marsh, Newchurch, Hamstreet. The landscape was a shifting, evasive mixture of the domestic and the wild. Once we turned a corner and came across a man in blue workman's overalls and a straw hat, walking alongside a large, piebald horse with feathered hooves, which was tearing placidly at the long grass on the roadside. I slowed and he took off his hat to us as we passed. In the rearview mirror I saw the horse toss its head and trot away down the road, with the man strolling easily behind. I began to feel as though I had rediscovered something mislaid a long time ago; but after a while I thought that was wrong: I hadn't retrieved anything; I had found something else, with a fleeting resemblance to the thing I had lost, but really it was quite new and different.

The summer felt as though it might go on forever – a succession of sunny days poised on the expanding and contracting strip of shore between the sea wall and the water. But then with brutal suddenness the holidays were almost over. The shop windows were crowded with grinning midget mannequins in blazers and satchels, hoisting signs in childlike letters reading 'Back to School!' as though that were something

266

to celebrate. The last evening on the beach the air felt chill and clammy as we sat eating our vinegary chips, and a white mist blew over the pure blue line where the sky met the sea.

This time last year I had been going to my first Autumn hunting meet. This autumn there would be no hunting. Foot-and-mouth, which had fluctuated all summer, the numbers of new cases seeming to diminish, then increasing again, flared up at the end of August and the restrictions on hunting remained in force. Hounds were shut up in kennels but we began to get the horses fit, riding out for an hour or more at a time, ten minutes walk, five minutes trot, then back to walk again, along narrow roads where the trees met overhead and grass grew down the centre of the tarmac.

In place of a normal meet card, the Ashford Valley published an Events Meet Card. There were a great many events. Not as many as there would have been meets, but at least one a week: a hunt breakfast to begin the season; cross-country schooling followed by yet more breakfast, a sponsored ride, a start-of-season coffee morning at the kennels ('Come and meet your sponsored hounds and sympathize with them'), a Pony Club Mock Hunt, a bonfire party, mounted Remembrance Sunday, the Hunt Ball, the annual hedge-laying competition ('the hedge is at the Three Chimneys end of Dig Dog Lane. Help is required cutting stakes and binders') – all the trappings of hunting, lacking only their *raison d'être*.

Claire and I took our mares – her Cornflake and my Molly – on the sponsored ride through Bedgebury Forest. It was quite fun – a long hack on a pleasant October day through pretty wooded countryside, following a route marked by yellow chalk arrows. It felt a bit like the sort of wholesome outdoors activity I'd been obliged to participate in during my time as a reluctant Girl Guide, though more interesting, because horses were involved and the sausage and bacon brunch at Yew Tree Farm at the end was accompanied by a decidedly un-Guidelike quantity of whisky and cherry brandy. We did it quite fast, at a steady hunting canter, because Claire was expected somewhere for lunch and her boyfriend kept ringing her mobile to find out how long she'd be. Even so, there was nothing alarming about it, or even very exhilarating. The country was attractive, but our presence in it had the same flat, aseptic quality of the road hacking I had been doing all summer. Only the fittening work had felt interesting, because there was a point to it — it wasn't just wandering aimlessly about the lanes.

As the autumn drew on there began to be rumours that fox-hunting might resume under license in uninfected areas. By early November, the newspapers had begun to give a date of 3 December for a resumption. On November 20 the MFHA met Alun Michael, the minister responsible for hunting at DEFRA and representatives from the NFU in a consultation process that was to continue until December 7. The date set for a resumption of hunting was 17 December, leaving a little over a week for hunts to apply for a permit. The permit conditions were stringent. The date, time and place of each hunt, 'together with details of the likely area to be covered by the hunt and the likely numbers of participants' were to be sent to the local DEFRA office, two working days before the meet. A permanent record was to be maintained of each hunt. Within three working days, a post-hunting Certificate of Compliance had to be posted to the hunt's DEFRA Divisional Veterinary Manager. Records were to be kept of all country crossed, and any movement of hounds to and from kennels. Once a permit was issued, checks would be made at the initial meet and at random meets thereafter.

People attending the hunt must disinfect vehicles used to move 'horses or dogs for the purpose of a hunt'. The document explaining the system of permits added helpfully that 'dog' in this context 'means any hound, beagle or other dog'. People attending a hunt must wear 'clean outer clothing and footwear' and disinfect the 'outer surfaces of their footwear before and after the hunt'. A distinction was made between 'spectators' and 'participants'. A participant, explained a letter from the MFHA to Masters of Hounds, 'is anyone who wishes to leave the road and must be a Hunt member, Hunt guest or Hunt staff, whether mounted or on foot. Anyone else following the Hunt is a spectator and best endeavours must be taken to encourage them to follow the progress of the Hunt from the public roads.' One curious side effect of this stipulation was to make Masters apparently responsible for the behaviour of their own hunt saboteurs.

The Times, for which I wrote, wanted to publish an article on the first day's hunting after a gap of almost ten months and I was commissioned to write it. I was to hunt on the 17th, write my piece by lunchtime on the 18th (if I survived, I thought, but did not say aloud) and the article would appear on the 19th. The only difficulty with this was that the Ashford Valley had decided not to begin hunting on the first possible date, but to wait until the New Year, to allow hounds to get fit, and give the Masters time in which to visit the innumerable farmers over whose land we needed to ask permission to hunt. So I joined a long queue of journalists whose editors had told them to go hunting, and were now pleading with the MFHA, the Countryside Alliance Campaign for Hunting and any other likely sounding organization to fix them up with one of the 30 or so hunts that planned to go out on December 17.

A piece of good fortune matched me with the Bicester, a hunt with country in Oxfordshire, Buckinghamshire and Northamptonshire, which its then Joint Master, Ian McKie, described to me when I visited as a 'non-smart, four-day a week pack'. I wasn't entirely sure how to decode this description, which lacked the admirable directness of Neil Staines's summary of the Ashford Valley as a 'good third division hunt, of four divisions'. Four days a week was a lot. The Ashford Valley hunted two, but the Bicester country was larger than ours; they kept two packs of hounds, a bitch pack, hunted by Mr McKie, and a dog pack hunted by Patrick Martin – 54 couple of hounds to the Ashford Valley's 30.

The hunt had a long, narrow country running from Daventry to Aylesbury – about 50 miles long, though only 20 or so miles wide – the result of an amalgamation in 1986 of the Bicester & Warden Hill with the Whaddon Chase, 'Mainly plough country,' said *Baily's*, but with 'much grass in the southern part, with flying fences and much timber.' The Whaddon Chase had been hunted by the Selby Lownes family (a member of which had been the long-serving Master of the Ashford Valley's neighbouring hunt, the East Kent) for almost 200 years, from the eighteenth century until the 1920s.

'Non-smart' I took to be a classic English inversion, meaning – approximately – fiercely local and rather private, lacking the brash invasion of outsiders more interested in showy riding over fences than the finer points of venery that the fashionable Shire hunts still tended to attract. I guessed the difference between the Bicester and what its Joint Master might have considered a 'smart' hunt was probably the difference between some hidden, private jewel of an old English country house, and the more emphatic attractions of a Chatsworth or a Blenheim with their insistent freight of important Old Masters and exigent day-trippers in search of organized entertainment and facilities.

One of the lucky elements in my having drawn the Bicester in the lottery of hunts starting up on December 17 was that I could claim a tenuous connection with them. One of my former employers was a literary agent who as a young man had been keen on hunting. Now he lived in the Bicester country and knew another of the Joint Masters, Mrs Tylor.

When I told him about my day out with them he promised to make certain they understood that my description of my riding skills was not a decorous piece of false modesty, but strictly true. The hunt was providing a horse, as well as the day's hunting. I hoped very much it would turn out to be the brain-dead gelding that Mrs Rogers had originally reckoned to be my ideal mount.

She, at any rate, seemed rather impressed that I was going to hunt with the Bicester. She suggested a couple of jumping lessons on Big Molly, to get me used to the idea of riding something other than my own mare. But I couldn't get the hang of the other Molly at all. After my mare she seemed impossibly vast and ungainly. It was like straddling an elephant, and however much I kicked on, I couldn't get her to move at any pace faster than a languid trot, although I knew that in a recent fit of high spirits at the Pony Club Mock Hunt she had jumped, unasked, a metal five-barred gate. In the sand school we approached a tiny crossed poles at a slatternly shamble and I fell smartly off over her head, landing on my feet with the reins still in my hand.

'That's clever,' said Mrs Rogers's friend Bridget. 'Let's try it just once more, shall we?' 'Oh dear,' said Mrs Rogers. 'Oh well. Never mind. You'd better just stay at the back with the non-jumpers. There are always some of those.' She didn't actually add 'and for God's sake don't tell anyone you were taught by me,' but the thought hovered in the air.

The MFHA's special instructions for the resumption of hunting were for a low-key start in ratcatcher, as for Autumn hunting. The situation – picking up again after two lost half-seasons – was unusual. Never before, not during previous foot-and-mouth outbreaks, not even in wartime had the fox-hunting season failed to begin at all, throughout the entire country. Now horses and hounds were unfit, young hounds who should have learned their job during Autumn hunting in September and October were still unentered, the fox population, which in an ordinary year would have been dispersed and reduced by December, had been untouched by hunting (though not, it was safe to assume, by other forms of control) since February and no one quite knew what changes FMD might have wrought to farming patterns and farmers' feeling about the hunt crossing their land.

After my dispiriting performance on Big Molly, I was clinging tenaciously to the notion of a low-key start. I hoped very much that I shouldn't be encountering the flying fences and timber mentioned by *Baily's*. The meet was on a Monday at midday. The Friday before that I drove to Bicester, to meet Ian McKie and the huntsman, Patrick Martin. The kennels were extensive, neat and extremely picturesque: brick-built, with primrose paintwork. Mrs Rogers's word 'tidy' came to mind. Hounds were just coming back from exercise as I arrived, escorted by the huntsman and Master, mounted, in old red coats. Everything involving the hounds was very quietly and economically done, but trailing about after Patrick as he finished his kennels chores before sitting down to talk into my tape recorder, I thought there was a gravity about his movements that lent the mundane kennels tasks a certain ritual quality.

'Watch this,' said Mr McKie. The huntsman opened a gate from one part of the kennels where the pack was gathered to the adjoining yard and called, 'Dog hounds! Dog hounds!' At which there was a sort of simmering movement among the pack, then half of it detached itself and filed through the gate that Patrick was holding open, while the other half – the bitch hounds – remained where they were. It was a remarkable sight. 'How do you do that?' I asked. 'Oh,' said Patrick, 'It's just a way of splitting up the hounds. You have to have an affinity with them. It's hard to explain.'

I hadn't met a huntsman before, or not to talk to. Neil was always doing his job when I saw him, and much too busy for conversation, even if I'd dared try and engage him, which I didn't. In any case I had from my reading the idea that huntsmen were a taciturn breed, often charismatic, but rarely given to idle chat. I was afraid once Patrick was out of the kennels and sat down in his drawing room (a corner of which was occupied by a large Christmas tree) in front of my tape recorder that he would have nothing to say. But I was mistaken. The prospect of his way of life's being reclassified as a criminal activity had unlocked his reticence. He was passionate and articulate when describing the fine details of his job – a job that is equal parts delicate nuance and punishing physical slog.

'It's an old art,' he said. 'An inexact science. You can read every book in the library, but you can either do it or you can't. It's all down to your experience and your knowledge of fieldcraft. It is what happens out hunting that people know you for – your handling of hounds and the way the hounds hunt and your personality. It is a very lonely place, because whatever the huntsman is doing, his mood – how good or bad it is – filters back through hounds. If they are having a really good time and the huntsman is on top form and he's got a bit of personality or character, he can make it fun. You've got to have the standard, it's got to be done properly, but within that framework you can have a lot of enjoyment.

'People say "enjoyment" and flick you back to killing a fox, but to me it is the enjoyment of breeding hounds, looking after them, seeing them do what comes naturally to them. Some are better than others. A pack of hounds is a union of all these different characters: a pack made up of different individuals. They come together and until you hunt hounds you can't understand it. When you walk into a kennels and see the hounds, they are an extension of the man that looks

273

after them. Their characters, the way they are – everything in a kennels says everything about the huntsman that looks after them. It is something you can't hide.

'Handling a pack of hounds, it is the invisible thread. You have this link with them – the horn is an extension of your voice. The voice is used to control them on the road, or when drawing a covert, to encourage them: "Leu in there" – every huntsman has his own expressions. You could say, "Go in that wood and find a fox," if you said it musically.

'You always use the same calls, starting off with a long drawn-out note, for collecting hounds up; then a short, sharp note is when you want hounds in a hurry. They can tell if you are excited or if you are calling them out of covert. They react to the mood of the day. It is an evolved thing. Hunt servants all have different ways of doing it, but the end result is the same. As long as what you do is the same every day, they get used to it.

'Obviously, when a different huntsman moves to a different pack he has different calls, different voicing. Hounds are remarkable animals and they can adapt. One man leaves, another comes in. We've got a hundred hounds in kennels: you walk in there, and they don't know you, but you have this affinity with them. They are a pack animal, they look up to you, and you dictate what they do. And then suddenly [out hunting] you say, "Go in there," and it's down to them.

'At the end of a day's hunting you should be mentally knackered, because you never stop. You become so focused on what you are doing, focused on the invisible thread, linked to hounds, even if they are two, three fields away. Where's the wind? Is he coming across the wind? That chap's got his hat off – is that the fox? You're sat on that horse, but you don't even realize it. If someone said, "You've been going for five hours on a horse," you'd be amazed.'

Jane Ridley, in her history *Fox Hunting*, wrote of the nine-teenth-century Belvoir huntsman, Will Goodall, that 'he treated his hounds like women, never bullying, deceiving or neglecting them'. The tenderness of Patrick Martin's descrip-tion of his hounds brought that passage to mind. I wondered what it might be like, being married to a huntsman.

On the other hand, what was he saying about his job? 'It is a way of life, isn't it? To me it is the most important part of my life. I've got a family, but I spend more time with hounds than I do with my family. That's the way it is. Because of the way I was brought up. I'm a stickler for detail and having things done the right way. And I take a great deal of pride because the hounds reflect the hunt. At the end of the day it is what hounds do on a day's hunting that gives the hunt a feeling of togetherness.'

I thought there was something very enviable about this (unless you were the huntsman's family, I suppose): the techni-cal mastery of hunting hounds on the one hand – satisfying and fascinating as any highly developed craft skill is, from plumbing to embroidery – and the intensity of a huntsman's attachment to his pack and the country they were hunting. Then, too, the seamless absorption of life and work and the inextricable attachment of both to place; not a job that you did for a set number of hours and then gratefully shrugged off to resume the 'real' life that must be lived within the meagre allowance of one's spare time, but a fusion of one's liveli-hood with what one found most interesting: a vocation, like acting, the priesthood or medicine. (Aspects of all three occupations were involved, I thought, in the rich mixture that was the huntsman's role, along with farmer, butcher, athlete, genealogist, housewife and PR man.)

The other side of it was (I thought, driving home to begin a weekend's uneasy contemplation of the fact that I was about to go hunting for the second time ever, with an unknown pack, on a strange horse, in unfamiliar country) that it had an unsettling, receding-to-infinity quality. You opened one door – the one marked 'riding', say – and that turned out to lead to all kinds of other doors, each leading to some additional branch of knowledge without which a proper grasp of the first subject was impossible.

Although you could argue that all knowledge was like this – one work of literature or historical fact or scientific discovery linked to others and yet others in a vast mesh of influence and consequence – the difference was that this particular subject was so hard and slow of mastery, and so relentless in its demands on your brain as well as your body. It wasn't like the kind of academic or journalistic work I was used to, which involved ideas or texts whose essential elements you could absorb in a burst of intense concentration over a few hours or days.

The integration of the physical demands of riding with the emotional and intellectual calculations of venery – training yourself to think as the fox might, and as hounds would, while keeping the larger picture of the hunt in focus and at the same time anticipating the shape it might be about to take – was a process more like the growth of a tree than the mastery of a text. It would take years, as far as I could tell, just to grasp the rudiments, and there was little you could do to speed it up. You just had to wait for it to take root. Yet by Monday I must somehow contrive to draw together the horse and the riding of it with some sense of the fieldcraft and venery that it had taken Patrick Martin a working lifetime to learn. I was not at all convinced I could think and ride at the same time. I hoped they would find me a very dull horse.

Monday morning in London was dull and cold. The meet wasn't until midday, so I didn't leave Greenwich for Bicester until just before 8 a.m. Because I was embarking on this adventure with so little experience of hunting, I had no idea what a luxury this was. My normal hunting days, once I began having them, started well before dawn, at a quarter to five in the morning, with an hour's drive from London and a further couple of hours' anxious grooming and plaiting in the freezing dark of the yard. This one would involve no grooming, no loading, no responsibility at all, other than that of turning up in the right clothes.

The alarm rang just before 6 a.m. (but I was already awake and worrying). I got up with intense reluctance, thought about breakfast, decided I couldn't manage anything except a cup of tea with a lot of sugar in it, and began to pull on the multiple layers of thermal vests and long johns, woolly tights and thick socks over which, eventually, would go the tidy outermost layers of a woman who looked as though she knew what she was doing in the hunting field: a pair of fawn breeches, a starched white shirt and navy spotted tie, my tweed jacket with the bronze hunting-horn buttons and my beautiful shiny black Schnieder hunting boots. I had a peculiar feeling of slippage, as though something had gone wrong with time: as though the person inhabiting my body wasn't really me.

The feeling sharpened as I drove along the Embankment from Pimlico towards Chelsea. Every mile I drove towards Oxfordshire felt forced and reluctant, as though I were pressing through dense undergrowth. It would be very easy to stop. The seduction of letting go, turning the car around and letting myself be carried back by the tide of commuters, drifting southwards all the way home to the safety of the warm bed from which I had so fearfully emerged was almost irresistible. In a trance of reluctance, I passed Earl's Court and Kensington, circumnavigated the Shepherd's Bush roundabout and joined the M40 to Oxford.

The anaesthetic quality of motorway driving with its bland herd momentum had a lulling effect on my nerves. So did the fact that I knew this route well and my brain was accustomed to recognizing it as a benign journey – towards the excitement of the new university term at first; then visits to friends and periodic affectionate returns to a place that had formed me. By the time I came to the great cutting in the Chiltern hills, the point from which you look down on the Oxfordshire valley spread out in front of you – the squat-towered churches set in an irregular chequerboard of hedged fields and invisible streams fringed by leaning willow trees – the balance between curiosity and terror had shifted a little. Not enough to say that I was looking forward to the day ahead, but enough for me to be interested rather than paralysed by the thought of what might happen. As I drew closer to the Oxford junction I could see the grass blades on the verges were dull silver with frost. If the ground was frozen, they wouldn't be able to go. I suppressed a shameful twinge of hope and drove on.

The kennels office was a small room with the same cramped, comforting qualities of the Rooting Street tackroom. On the walls bloomed a dusty herbaceous border of ancient, faded rosettes – thickly clustered green and yellow, red and purple and pink. The floor was boards and there was a plain wooden table in the middle of the room, with a pile of printed forms on it. At one end was a sink with a jumble of coffee mugs and teaspoons and jars of instant coffee and whitener. At the other hung a rail crammed with brown kennels overalls, red coats in various stages of smartness and decay and a writhing population of horn-handled hunting whips. There was a coal-burning stove in one corner and a delicious, soupy fug of horse, leather, mud, hot wool, hound and coffee.

There seemed to be a great many people gathered in this confined space, of whom I recognized only two: Patrick and Mr McKie. Besides them there was a quantity of stout men of various ages, from youngish to oldish, with brownish clothes and reddish faces, one of whom was introduced to me as the terrier man, and a fine-boned, formidable person, recognizably from the same school of deportment as Mrs Rogers. This was Mrs Tylor, another of the Bicester's Joint Masters. It was her sister, Sally, who was lending me a horse. No one was saying much, or appeared to be doing much, but the room was full of a firmly repressed anticipation

It felt like the fragments of dead time before a performance at the opera, when the house lights are still up and the orchestra is filing by dribs and drabs into the pit, the musicians still functioning as separate entities in the moments before they become the single organism that is an orchestra – getting out their instruments, blowing into them, fiddling with strings and pegs and slides, rubbing them with dusters, wiping rosin along their bows, raising and lowering the music stands and fidgeting to get comfortable in their chairs in preparation for the moment of whirling stillness when the conductor raises his baton and the performance begins.

The whisky finished, we stepped out into the yard, where a horse lorry was parked and a lean, dark-haired woman in a greenish tweed jacket and a dark-blue foulard stock with white pin-dots was unloading a chestnut horse. 'You're not riding that, are you?' said Mr McKie to me, making a face of comical dismay. I certainly hoped not. It was huge and had nostrils flared like giant commas. Mrs Tylor took its reins and led it to the side of the horse box. So it wasn't for me, then. It was her Master's horse. Thank goodness. The next horse down the ramp was smaller, about the same size and build as Molly, and seemed to have a milder disposition. At any rate, it wasn't flaring its nostrils or tossing its head as much as its predecessor. This was Sparkle, a 12-year-old bay mare, and her owner, the woman in the foulard stock, was Mrs Tylor's sister, Sally.

Sparkle, said Sally, knew exactly what she was doing, and would look after me. There was no need to worry (from which I concluded that my friend the literary agent had done as I asked him, and laid it on thick about how nervous and incompetent I was on horseback). The only thing was, she suffered from a dislocated larynx. On no account was I to try and hold her back if she started to go fast. I was to sit tight and let her stretch out on a long rein, and all would be well. If there were jumps, and Sally didn't know whether there would be or not – there was a red run and a black run, but she had no idea which, if either, we would be doing that day – I needn't do anything at all. Just sit still. Sparkle was an eventer and knew her business.

I said in what I hoped was a resolute voice that if there was a choice, I personally should be doing the red, rather than the black, run and Sally nodded neutrally. She had definitely assumed the task of nannying me, but she was absurdly unlike the bawling, big-bosomed Pony Club bossyboots I had been afraid of encountering in that role. Instead she was slender, bookish and kindly in a cool, assessing way that made me worry that my inexpertly netted bun was falling down and wish that nervousness didn't make me chatter so.

Having taken the mare's rug off I suffered a vivid moment of panic about not being able to get on from the ground, before someone advised me to lead her round to the ramp of the horse lorry and climb into the saddle from there. Thanks to the disembodied voice of Mrs Rogers inside my head, reminding me just in time to tighten the mare's girth before putting my boot in the stirrup, I contrived to complete the mounting process more or less without ignominy.

The view from on top was almost like being on Molly. Different colour, but the same distance from the ground; the same neat, slender proportions. I had expected – hoped – to be given something huge and stolid like Herbie or Big Molly, but this was better, because it felt familiar: a narrow, clever, responsive little mare, just like the one I was used to. Suddenly

I felt much happier; almost as though I knew what I was doing.

I followed Sally to a big paddock next to the kennels where everyone was assembling. A smaller field than usual, said Sally. About 30 mounted followers and 20 on foot, compared with the usual Saturday field of 80 to 100. This was, in effect, Autumn hunting, though we were a month and a half into what would ordinarily have been the full season, so there was no 'meet' – none of the odd but convivial alcoholic elevenses that precede a full day's hunting: a mid-morning cocktail party of nerves and gossip, fuelled with discordant but invigorating combinations of food and drink: sausages and ginger wine, cheese sandwiches and port, mince pies and cherry brandy, ginger biscuits and sloe gin. The field gradually drifted together at midday on what had turned out, after a frosty start, to be a dull, watercolour day in shades of blue and grey, and after a bit the huntsman gave a toot on his horn and we set off down the road behind him towards the first covert.

He was hunting the bitch pack – a mixture of experienced old girls and unentered new bugs who took a keen but undiscriminating interest in a blackbird, a pheasant, a hare and a small bounding brown thing which I took to be a particularly large and athletic hare, but Sally said was a Muntjac deer. Each time they were patiently called off, collected up and cast again. To my eye, informed by the expertise of a season's-worth of tutorials with the Ashford Valley foot followers, this looked like promisingly foxy country: plenty of brambles and low cover. At one point, we watched at a field margin while hounds vanished into a dense expanse of long, parched grasses and withered docks, their movements traceable only by the vague stirring and brittle clicking of the dry stalks.

Suddenly something happened. I didn't see what, and I didn't hear hounds hunting. Whatever it was, it swept us at a fast canter along the side of a hedge, over a shallow ditch and halfway along the side of another low, gappy hedge, where we checked. And then I saw the fox: quite large, the colour of dead beech leaves, trotting warily along the other side of the hedge. His head and brush were down. Sally and I were standing alone for a moment; he raised his head, turned to look at us and I caught his gaze. He looked hunted. I thought he looked like the fox in the anonymous fourteenth-century poem of *Sir Gawain and the Green Knight*, who doubles along a hedge, listening for hounds, then creeps along a valley by a wooded covert, hoping to lose the hounds by guile before running straight into three of them, big and fierce and grizzled in the undergrowth. He draws back quickly and jumps aside, then, 'With all the woe in the world,' writes the poet, 'he went away into the wood.'

The swift flashing back and forth of perspectives and sympathies in the poem – now the poet makes us see the hunt from the fox's point of view, now from the hounds', now from that of the uproarious Knight who is the Master of the Hunt, bounding about the woods in pursuit of game while his guest, Sir Gawain, remains at home in the warm, conducting a more sedentary drama of flight and pursuit with his seductive hostess – conveys with eerie exactness the fluid, filmic emotions of following a hunt; the flitting succession of momentarily overwhelming sensations: melancholy, exhilaration, excitement, pity, dread; the peculiar conviction that at different moments one is the fox, the hound, the horse, the woods. And at the same time as one's sense of self is swept away by all these other feelings, there remains the ice-chip of mindfulness, the calculation of what one knows or can guess: the direction of the wind, the lie of the land, the telltale flight of birds or movement of stock in the fields, the technical business of getting over the country and the fences: mental transactions as simple and as complicated as a poem.

The fox ran low to the end of the hedge and vanished. Sally

turned away and I cantered after her. 'If you want to slow down,' she called over her shoulder into the wind, 'push your heels down.' I didn't want to slow down, but I thought this probably meant I was committing my usual sin of drawing my legs up and pointing my toes at the ground. The mare was moving fast, but even with the loose rein it didn't feel as though she was running away. I pushed my heels towards the ground and turned my toes to the sky and she steadied. Ahead, Sally had checked at a low wall around a villainous-looking enclosure: dense brambles, a nasty tumbledown barn, a derelict woodpile.

The huntsman was in there, off his horse and on the ground. There must have been noise – the cry of hounds and the sound of him urging them – but I don't remember it, only the scarlet of his coat among the ragged brambles and the woodpile, and then that he came forward from the woodpile and stood silhouetted against the skyline, the slope of grass and the bare branches of the trees with the grey-blue sky behind them, holding the body of the fox high in the air. And then the soundtrack, so to speak, starts up again and he is cheering and whooping to his hounds before throwing them the body to break up.

In the poem, the Green Knight dismounts from his horse as hounds fall on their fox, snatches the carcass before they can tear it to pieces and raises it high, hallooing as hounds cry around him in 'the rich clamour that there was raised for Renard's soul'. And then, writes the poet, having made much of their hounds and stripped the pelt from their quarry, 'thay helden to home, for hit was niegh nyght.'

It wasn't yet night in Oxfordshire, but the light was failing and the temperature beginning to fall. That dip in warmth, the chill of evening dropping slowly through the air, some- times meant that the scent suddenly improved. Once I got going with the Ashford Valley, I used to hear them talk about the 'three o'clock fox', meaning the fox whose scent you pick up just before twilight. (There was also something called the three o'clock flask, produced mid-afternoon by well prepared men with lots of pockets in their hunt coats, and handed around just as one's courage began to falter and one began to think gloomily about what a long way home it was, and what a lot of bad-tempered washing and grooming and rugging up in the freezing dark of the barn and scraping of gouts of adhesive mud off encrusted saddlery lay between one and a cup of tea with plenty of sugar in it and a nice hot bath.)

Anyway, having killed their first fox the Bicester hounds picked up an afternoon scent and hunted it up and down for a bit. The field, meanwhile, had picked up the news that the neighbouring hunt, the Heythrop, who had started earlier, when the frost was still hard and the scent less good, had had a blank (that is, foxless) day, thus casting our own day into a flatteringly successful light.

The second fox failed to come to anything and when I found myself trotting decorously down a farm track I thought I recognized from the beginning of the day, I thought we must be moving on to draw the next covert, and gave myself the first of what would turn out to be an infinity of small hunting sermons on the need to keep going when you thought you'd done enough for the day and were beginning to feel all cold and cross and to think with longing about the lifestyles of people who spent their leisure time sensibly parked in front of the telly. But it was over. We had had our outing, so had the hounds and the surrounding foxes. The ones who had done it before had settled into their work again; the rest of us now had an idea of what was expected of us, and that was enough.

Patrick blew for home (that delicious sound, welcome as the bell at the end of school, signalling that you have survived to the end of another day's hunting and can now, just as soon as you've cleaned and fed your horse and put him to bed, peel off your clammy shroud of sodden clothes and frisk like Sir Gawain in an ermine-trimmed blue velvet dressing-gown before a bright hearth. Or at any rate, claim some modern version of those elegant medieval comforts). And we turned back to the kennels. 'Look,' said Sally, as a pale, flitting shape flew low overhead, 'a barn owl.' He was setting out on his hunt just as we were returning from ours. The nights at Rooting Street were clamorous with owls and the despairing squeaks of their prey, but I had not seen one so close before.

The Bicester seemed a nice, dry country and the little mare was barely muddy, certainly not by the weltering standards of the Ashford Valley. I helped untack her and put her rug on, then went to the office to say goodbye and thank you before starting for home. They were all standing about in the comfortable trance of warmth and relaxed tension that takes over when you get off your horse at the end of a day's hunting. The day wasn't over for any of us: most people had horses to do. Patrick had hounds to see to: the ones that had been left behind as well as the ones drawn for the day's hunting. I had 50 miles and more to drive before I could take off my boots and sit down to my supper. But here was this small cabin, full of sparse comfort, warmth and light, like a shepherd's hut on a bare hill when the night is closing in. There were tea mugs on the table, a scattering of spilt sugar crystals, a teaspoon marooned in a puddle of slops on the corner of a discarded Compliance Form. The low buzz of conversation didn't stop when I looked in, but swarmed across the room (it seemed) to include me.

I came in, took off my hat and gloves, put down my whip and, taking alternate sips from the mug of tea and the plastic cup of whisky that had been pushed towards me across the table, slowly let slacken the tight lacing of nerves and excitement that had been holding me together all day. 'Hunting,' wrote the American David Itzkowitz in *Peculiar Privilege*, a scholarly and admirably straight-faced account of the oddities of early English fox-hunting, 'is by definition something that happens at the boundary where the human domain confronts the wild.'

For half a day we had been skirting that boundary; now we were beginning to withdraw again into our own domain. I drank up my tea and my whisky, gathered up my things and began to leave. It was too soon to feel exhilarated. I hadn't had time to give shape to the inchoate sensations of the day and besides, I had the drive ahead of me, and the piece to write in the morning. For now I was in a dreamy state of animal comfort: warm and safe, and that was enough.

'Just a moment, before you go,' said Mr McKie. The terrier man shouldered out through the door and into the dark, returning with something curled in his enormous hand. 'For you,' said Mr McKie and the terrier man handed me something soft and a bit muddy. For an instant I didn't know what it was. Then I saw that it was the brush. Oh, I said. Oh. Afterwards I thought it could have been an understandable piece of theatrics to encourage a visiting journalist to write a sympathetic piece, and perhaps it was. But just in that moment I thought it meant that I'd done all right, that I'd passed a test and was part of the tribe: no longer quite on the outside, looking in.

'Put it into a jar of meths for a month or two. That'll cure it,' said the terrier man. For the time being I coiled it into my hard hat (where it gave the cat a terrible turn later that evening when he discovered it while I was in the cupboard, looking for meths) and went away into the starry darkness. I put the hat on the front seat next to me and drove home, following the snaky double lines of orange lamplight all the way to the city, with this strange, damp trophy curled up next to me, filling the car with the smell of fox while I half-listened to the workaday rise and fall of the Radio 4 news-presenter's voice telling me what everyone else in the world had been up to that day. I wondered, driving back down the road by the river in Chelsea that I had followed with such misgiving that morning, whether I was the only person in London making her way home with a fox's tail for a companion.

The second after this thought came to me, it struck me as silly. Plenty of people were moving about the city clutching carrier bags containing flesh of various sorts, neatly butchered into chops or rashers, drumsticks or self-basting roasts, hygienically wrapped in supermarket plastic. Quite a few people were probably lugging home the feathered spoils of a day's shooting in the back of their Range Rovers. And, since it was a winter's evening, quantities of women would be setting out for an evening's diversion at the ballet, the theatre or a dinner party, draped in the neatly matched pelts of entire families of foxes. By these standards my brush was just another insignificant body part.

But it didn't feel so to me. It felt like a talisman. In the story of Sir Gawain, his adventure leads him to spend Christmas in a magnificent castle, owned by a mysterious Lord and his sexy wife. The Lord proposes a bargain with his guest, who is cold, hungry, exhausted after a long journey and nearing the conclusion of a quest at whose end lie trouble and danger. This, says the Lord, is no state in which to go hunting, which is what he has planned for the next three days. He will go out early on his hunts, but Gawain shall rest and recover at home, where the Lady of the castle will entertain him. Then at the end of each day, they will exchange whatever prizes the day has brought them.

In this way they divide between them the twin constituents

of chivalry, love and arms (or to put it another way, love and death, though the chivalric convention is that each contains its elements of danger, of which love's peril may well be the greater, since a false move in that pursuit may place in jeopardy not just your mortal and mutable body, but your honour and your immortal soul).

On the first day, the Lord's quarry is deer; on the second, boar. The fox, as vermin, is a lesser quarry. Nevertheless, it is the 'ignoble' fox that is the object of the third day's pursuit, and on which turns the emotional crisis of the poem.

Gawain, having resisted with an heroic effort the high-octane flirting of the Lord's wife, confining himself (despite her reproaches) to chaste kisses, which he duly passes on to the Lord when he comes in from hunting, laden with venison and great slabs of boar flesh, weakens on the third day and eventually succumbs, not to unchastity but to a moment of cowardice: he evades her caresses, but accepts the offer of a belt of green silk (green being the colour of magic generally, and in particular the hue of the alarming opponent, the Green Knight, who waits for him at the end of his quest) that is promised to preserve him from physical harm.

At the end of the day the Lord returns to find a fire on his hearth and sitting beside it his guest, who springs guiltily forward and kisses him three times (there is a faint, mixed echo of the kiss with which Judas betrayed Jesus, and the three denials with which St Peter distanced himself from Christ after His arrest). These three kisses (and absolutely nothing else. Nope, not a thing. In particular nothing with magical properties) are his day's haul, says Gawain, when the Lord says that he's had a good bargain for his day at home.

I can't match that, says the Lord, 'for I have hunted all day and got nothing but this miserable fox-skin, Devil take it. A poor exchange for such precious things.' And with the resonances of this exchange humming in the air like the sound of pealing bells that have just fallen silent, they settle down to that most fascinating and boring of conversations, the details of the day's hunting.

The psychological intricacies of this are complicated to unravel. The fox may be vermin, but of all the beasts hunted by the Lord of the castle, it is the only one to which is attributed a quasi-human foreknowledge of its own death. The 'woe' with which, faced with the three hellish grey snarling hounds, it turns away into the wood is an echo of Gawain's fear for his own life; perhaps even of the dread with which Christ himself prayed to be allowed to avoid the fate that lay ahead of him. More than the gentle deer or the angry, defiant boar, the fox in the poem – intelligent, resourceful, calculating – mirrors the hero's fallible humanity; the gift of the fox skin is a symbol of his mixed nature, compounded of courage and gaiety, cowardice and guile.

Though I didn't analyze it in quite those terms, I felt the brush, now pickling in a Kilner jar of meths in the kitchen cupboard, meant some of those things to me, too. I knew that in several fundamental ways, hunting was a reckless thing for me to be doing. It was costly both in time and money. You could argue that it was diverting attention and funds that would have been put to better use doing something I could share with my son. And it was dangerous. Far better horsemen than I had been badly hurt, permanently maimed or even killed out hunting. My riding was amateurish, my jumping a joke, my knowledge of horse behaviour sketchy.

There was, of course, Always A Way Round, but I didn't necessarily plan to take it. Even if I stuck to the flat, it could be argued that I was deliberately putting myself in harm's way. What would happen to my son if I hurt myself so that I couldn't work or look after him, even for a short time? The whole weight of our household rested on me. No one would help us if I damaged myself so badly that I was no longer able to bear that burden. We would be shipwrecked.

Balanced against that bleak thought was the infinite variety and fascination of fox-hunting, which had seized my imagination in a way that nothing (other than a book or a love affair) had done before. It wasn't the danger, or even the riding that interested me – I felt absolutely no wish to take up drag-hunting, or blood-hounding, or eventing, or to do anything else in the slightest bit risky. If legislation were passed to ban fox-hunting I should have to become the happy hacker that Mrs Rogers had once accurately observed that I wasn't. (What was more, I should have to sell the mare, since she wasn't a hack either and a life spent ambling about would make her bored and sour.) What interested me about hunting was the adventure: the shifting, unpredictable play between the characters – the human and the animal – the setting in which their drama unfolded and the chance events they might encounter in the course of the day.

At home I lived a life that was as demanding, as lonely and exhausting as an Arthurian quest, but without the coherent narrative shape, the companionship or the excitement that go with an adventure. That was the missing element that hunting offered, of which the scrap of fox fur curled in my hat felt like a talisman: its magical properties, like the fox pelt in the Gawain poem, were not to be compared with the dull, unresonant fur coats and carrier bags of pork chops and chicken breasts or even dead pheasants with their feathers still on, dodging all around me as we made our way through the London streets.

The Ashford Valley sent out a meet card on which the opening meet, on The Green, High Halden, was set for January 19. This meant that we shouldn't hunt on Boxing Day. Instead we paraded hounds in the high street dressed as though to hunt, then returned to our horse boxes, took off our hunt coats, changed into waterproofs and anoraks and went on another fun ride across some of the country that in other circumstances we should have hunted. It was a fine, clear day and a beautiful ride, high on grassy banks between watery channels at the verge of the Marsh. The odd thing was that for the mass ride across country without hounds, the strict hygiene regulations seemed no longer to apply. There was no form to fill in, no trough of disinfectant in which to dip our boots. We just got on our horses and went.

If ever the sensations of my first season's hunting seem in danger of growing blunt and indistinct, there is a photograph that brings them rushing back, as sharp and pungent as when I first felt them. It is a picture of me at the opening meet, at High Halden. By some trick of perspective I seem to be sitting isolated on Molly in the middle of a ring of people, like a child at the centre of a game of The Farmer Wants A Wife. The photographer is standing to one side and slightly to the rear of me. My face and Molly's are turned aside, so you can only see our quarter profiles. Our expressions are unreadable, but the body language is eloquent.

Molly's mane is scrunched into a line of eleven bristly love-knots; her tail is plaited, doubled, secured with white tape into a short, blunt horsehair knout and decorated with a bow of green ribbon, which is meant to signal to other riders that she is inexperienced and unpredictable. Despite this, she is standing square and easy, neck arched and ears cocked: the stance of an experienced hunt horse that knows, because it has just spent the previous two hours being washed, groomed, plaited, boxed up and unboxed again, that it is going hunting.

Poking out from the back of my velvet crash cap is a doubled loop of fairish hair, savagely pinned and netted, that echoes the brutal club shape into which the horse's pretty tail has been subdued. It is to this ponytail that the green ribbon of inexperience should more fairly have been attached. Molly is calm, alert, relaxed. I have already been sick once, from nerves, and now I am concentrating hard on not heaving again in front of everyone. My ankles are locked at right angles, my arms straight and stiff as chairlegs, the muscles of my behind clenched so tightly that it feels like sitting on a couple of the pointy bits from the inside of an eggbox. Which must be murder on poor Molly's back, only I am not thinking about Molly, I am thinking about me. What I have just done, and what I am about to do.

It is 10.45 on a mild morning, more like early spring than January. The sky is fragile blue; the sun shines strongly. The shaggy, end-of-winter grass of High Halden village green is tiger-striped with dark, elongated shadows of horses and foot followers. People keep coming up and talking to me. The hunt secretary asks for my riding money, which I somehow manage to fumble out of my pocket and hand to her. Peter Deacon, who began teaching me the rudiments of hunting when I went out on foot last season and whose meet this is, comes up and says Hello, and am I now too grand, up there on my horse, to give him a kiss? Someone else offers me a sausage roll, which I decline with horror (it will be almost the end of the season before my stomach unclenches sufficiently for me to tackle solid food at meets).

After spurning the sausage roll I look round and see that Claire, who gave Molly and me a lift to the meet and has promised to nanny us through the day, has vanished. There are familiar faces all around – on the opposite side of the green I can see Mrs Rogers, deep in conversation with the lawyer from the office at the end of my road in London, who has exchanged his subfusc pinstripes for a full-skirted scarlet coat with a green velvet collar and a natty pair of tight white breeches. But there is no comfort in the sight of them. They are much too important to be bothered with me. It is Claire who was supposed to be my security blanket, and now she has disappeared.

With all my heart I wish that this was a dream and I could wake up and find myself pushing a trolley round Sainsbury's. As I am thinking this ignoble thought Claire reappears, managing adroitly to keep a hold of Cornflake's reins as well as two plastic glasses of viscous brownish liquid and a ham sandwich with a big bite out of it. 'Here,' she says, handing one of the glasses to me. 'Drink this; you'll feel better.' I take a gulp and wait for the corresponding lightening of my spirits to kick in.

I haven't been as bad as this all morning. Buoyed by the success of the Bicester outing I bounced out of bed when the alarm rang at 5 a.m., resolutely, if not quite cheerfully, set off for Rooting Street before dawn, a little late, but still feeling fairly uppish, and arrived at the yard a few minutes before 8 a.m., just in time to hear Mrs Rogers say sharply to Claire, 'What time did you tell Jane Shilling she was supposed to be here?' At which my Bicester bravado evaporated quite quietly, like a little wisp of steam, and an ominous vision came to me of all the innumerable tasks I had to accomplish before I would be ready to load the mare and set off.

On an ordinary riding day it took exactly half an hour between the moment when I untied the lead rope that secured the metal gate of the mare's pen at the top of the yard and the moment when I actually got onto her back. That involved bringing her down to the barn, assembling her grooming kit and tack, swiping a damp sponge at the worst of her stable stains and a body brush over her back in a perfunctory version of grooming, then putting on her saddle and bridle and leading her out to the mounting block.

I had just heard Mrs Rogers bawl to Claire (in a voice evidently meant for my ears also) that we should leave the yard at 9.45. 'Nine forty-five?' I said to Claire in dismay. 'For an 11 o'clock meet?' 'Unboxing,' said Claire. And then, serenely (nothing ever seemed to rattle Claire's sweet nature, not the rough blasts of Mrs Rogers's hunting-mornings wrath, not getting lost on the way to the meet, not even being shouted at by fierce old Ashford Valley ladies while backing a trailer into an intractable parking space in a muddy farmyard in the driving rain. It was a quality for which I felt a helpless envy and admiration), 'Don't worry. You'll be fine.'

Well, I was worried. It was now 8.20, which meant that I had just under 90 minutes in which to fetch the mare, wash and brush her into a state of gleaming whiteness, plait her mane (which I'd never done before), smear her legs and underside in baby oil (against the mud), oil her hooves, get her tacked, rugged and booted for travel, fill and hang a hay net, load her onto the trailer, then tidy myself into a state of immaculate neatness to match the mare's. In my uppishness about surviving the day with the Bicester, I had overlooked the fact that I hadn't had to do any of the preparation. That little mare had been produced for me polished and ready to go, like a new toy with the batteries fitted. This one I was expected to assemble for myself.

An acrid atmosphere of urgency filled the barn, where Claire's pony, Cornflake, and Mrs Rogers's hunter Camilla were already tied up, shivering with nerves and squirting loose green droppings onto the concrete floor while Claire and Tracy, the head girl of the yard, stood on little stepladders at their sides, knotting their manes in concentrated silence. Shrivelling inside with a cocktail of different fears – fear of humiliation because I didn't know what I was doing, of being shouted at for keeping everyone waiting, or more likely, just being left behind while they rattled off to the meet with their perfectly prepared horses neatly ranged in the lorry like a tidy row of sardines and, muted but not quite stifled by the more immediate getting-ready-in-time panic, the rumbling obbligato dread of what might happen during the day ahead, assuming I got that far – I clumped off in my ungainly gumboots to fetch Molly, hoping that she wouldn't have acquired too many stains in the course of the night.

She was waiting impatiently at the gate of her pen, ears pricked, aware from the lights and the activity that some excitement was going on. And she was filthy. When I brought her into the barn and took off her rug she looked under the flickering strip lights as though someone had smeared her with gouts of khaki camouflage cream. Half her face was brown – had she spent the night with her head comfortably pillowed on a heap of warm dung? Her legs were blotched and there were matted greenish splotches on her flanks and belly, where the dirt had somehow managed to work its way under three layers of rug and a duvet. 'Oh, Molly,' said Tracy, in muffled outrage, through a mouthful of plaiting thread. 'And we spent all that time giving you a bath yesterday.' I got a bucket of water, squirted in some baby shampoo, and began scrubbing at her with a sponge.

The worst of it came away quickly. The water in the bucket turned bright brown and the stains faded to a ghostly pale green. Faded, but didn't disappear. Scrub, scrub, scrub, I went with my sponge, Lady Macbeth in cleated gumboots. The mare rolled her eyes, strained backwards the length of her lead rope, cow-kicked irritably. I squeezed a blob of shampoo directly onto my sponge and applied it neat to the green bits. Murky suds dripped on the floor. On her body the marks seemed mostly to have gone, as far as I could tell in the dingy light, but the side of her face was still lurid as Hallowe'en ghost make-up. It was 8.39. Barely an hour before we set off and I hadn't started plaiting.

'I can't get the green off,' I said to Claire, almost in tears. 'Dog chalk,' said Tracy, indistinctly. She had finished plaiting and was sewing up Camilla's tail. 'In the box on the top shelf. Rinse the shampoo out and rub the place with dog chalk.' The dog chalk was a powdery white lump. I rubbed it over the green bits of the mare's face and stood back to get the effect. She now had a head half grey-white and half the colour of almond icing, with a brown ring around one eye where I hadn't liked to rub with the chalk for fear of hurting her. The effect was not, I thought, what Mrs Rogers would call tidy, but too bad. If I didn't start plaiting now I'd never be finished.

Tracy had already showed me how to plait a mane. I wasn't attempting the advanced version, with plaits stitched in so firmly that they would have to be cut out with scissors at the end of the day. My plaits were going to be secured with rubber bands which would, with luck, hold firm for the duration of the meet before they started pinging off. After which I hoped it wouldn't matter if they came adrift. To plait you needed a comb, a tube of hair gel and a bag of elastic plaiting bands in the same colour as your horse's mane – then you needed something to stand on, so you were raised above the level of the horse's neck and could get a proper grip on the bristly hair.

You began by sectioning the mane into an odd number of clumps, each the width of the palm of your hand, and securing each section loosely with a band. Working from the base of the neck you took the rubber band off each bunch in turn, ran a small blob of gel through the hair to make it easier to work, divided the bunch into three equal bits and, pulling as tightly as you could, made a firm plait, turning the end over when you had finished and holding it with a plaiting band. Then you doubled the plait over on itself once, and once again, and secured the resulting knot with another band. Then you did the next one. When the whole neck was plaited, you did the same thing with the forelock, which left the horse looking like the Little Girl in the nursery rhyme, who had a

Little Curl, Right in the Middle of her Forehead. The whole enterprise had strong overtones of My Little Pony.

Teetering on the curved lid of the plastic box that held my grooming kit, with a bag of bands and the hair gel in one pocket and the comb in the other, I was braced for a struggle. The reason everything to do with Molly took so long was that she treated all attempts to lay hands on her, to groom or put on tack, as hostile manoeuvres, to be resisted with all the strength and ingenuity at her disposal. I didn't think she'd take kindly to being plaited. But I was mistaken. As soon as I started to section her mane she dropped her neck into an accommodating arc and seemed to go into a kind of trance from which she did not stir, however hard I tugged on the coarse strands of hair. Unlike Cornflake, who kept tossing her head and twitching the plaits from Claire's gel-slippery fingers and had just aimed a loose green splat right into her grooming kit.

'Now, Jane,' said Mrs Rogers, rushing through the barn like a comet with a fiery tail. 'If I may just advise you . . .' (Mrs Rogers advise? Whatever next?) 'Oh, yes please . . .' said I. 'These plaits,' said Mrs Rogers, 'should not stick up like a row of bottlestoppers, the way you've got them. No, they must bend along the neck, like rosebuds.' She reached up and twitched some of my stiff knots, which bent obediently in the approved rosebud manner, then she shot off again on her original orbit. I carried on rolling the row of stiff dreadlocks into drooping flowerets.

The sweet, synthetic, tropical fruit smell of the hair gel wafting from the mare's mane joined the comforting back-ground smell of horse and straw, manure and baby shampoo. I looked along the line of three horses, tethered along the barn wall in various states of dishabille, each standing at ease with eyelids drooping, resting a back leg with the tip of the hoof just grazing the ground, with a female handmaid in attendance, hard at work on some grooming process or another: I was still plaiting, Tracy was securing Camilla's doubled-up tail with a roll of brown insulating tape, while Claire was brushing Cornflake's hooves with a viscous green oil that smelt of the dreadful embrocation in a brown glass bottle that my grandmother used as a cure-all for any random ache or pain.

Something about this scene – the idle, glossy beauties lounging in a somnolent row, each tolerantly accepting the attention of a busy little acolyte, the pungent mixture of chemical fragrance mixed with the smell of living bodies – gave me a sudden flashback to the hairdressers where I'd spent the afternoon earlier that week, having my own mane painstakingly twiddled in much the same fashion as I was now fussing with Molly's, while my neighbours had their nails varnished and their pre-dinner party chignons welded into place. Michaeljohn goes to Rooting Street, I thought. But then I happened to check my watch and it was 9.05 and there was no time to spare for jokes or flights of fancy because I hadn't even started getting her tack on yet.

The more I tried to hurry, the more clearly I could see that getting a horse ready for hunting was a matter of precision, like making mayonnaise or a soufflé. There were no shortcuts. It took as long as it took, and if you tried to hurry, it would all go wrong and you'd have to start over. This particular *aperçu* came while I was trying to fill a hay net, a task as prickly and intractable as stuffing a pair of fishnet tights with dry vermicelli. The faster you tried to do it, the more ineffectual you became. Already that morning I had put the breastplate on inside out, so the buckle pressed into the tender flesh of the mare's chest, then strapped on the foam leg supports known as 'boots' back to front, with the fastenings all facing the wrong way. The trouble was, inside out for horses wasn't just a matter of aesthetics. All this fiddling with tiny intractable hooks and buckles and mysterious straps and loops of tape was more like packing a parachute than getting dressed in the morning and accidentally putting both feet through the same leg-hole of your pants.

My son, when getting ready for school to a backing track of me shrieking that we ought to have left ten minutes ago, had a maddening mantra which, delivered in a drawly voice of studied languor, went: 'I can take as long as I like. I've got all the time in the world . . .' When Mrs Rogers began stamping up and down the barn – boots on, the decorously furled knot of a gold-pinned stock just showing above the neck of her Ashford Valley sweatshirt – demanding to know if we were ready to load, I thought (twiddle the reins and catch them up in the throatlash; tighten the girth so the saddle doesn't slip off in the lorry; knot the hanging ends of the martingale so it doesn't get hooked on anything in transit, all this with a sense of rising panic, like a narrow strand of wire being steadily twisted around my temples), that 'I've got all the time in the world' might have its uses as a mantra for hunting mornings as well as school mornings.

Claire and I were following Mrs Rogers and the horse lorry to the meet with our mares in a trailer. I had never tried to load Molly before and didn't know whether she would cooperate or not. This didn't feel like an ideal time to find out. I wished I had thought of arranging a rehearsal or two beforehand. The trailer had two narrow compartments separated by a plywood partition, with a thick metal bar at chest height across the front end of the compartment. Cornflake was a bad loader, so Molly was to go on first.

The trick was, said Claire, to walk confidently up the ramp, towing the horse by its lead rope, as casually as though you were leading it into its pen, and then at the last moment, duck under the metal bar at the end and lash the lead rope to the loop of string dangling from the wall. She would stand by with a lunge line in case Molly tried to run out at the last minute. Some quirk of equine eyesight which I didn't wholly understand seemed to mean that they interpreted something as insubstantial as a lunge line as a significant barrier, so if you tied one end of the line to the trailer, and stood at the other end of it, holding it taut, the horse would think it was a fence of some sort, and not swerve towards it. That, at any rate, was the theory.

Plaited and oiled, with a travelling rug slung over the austere black leather geometry of her saddlery, Molly seemed remote and horribly strong, like a gladiator ready for combat, or a boxer in the moment before he flings off his dressing-gown and steps into the ring. I had a vivid flash, almost an hallucination, of what it would feel like to be crushed by her against the metal bar at the end of the compartment. (That vision never quite went away, even after I'd got quite nifty at loading. Almost two years after this meet, Claire and I went on a sponsored ride across country, ten miles or so of pretty bridle-paths with a few little jumps, as a gentle pre-hunting rev-up. We parked in a large field, crammed with horse lorries, and tied to each lorry was some immense muscular animal mis-behaving in some way or another – baring its teeth at the next-door pony, pawing the ground, steadily kicking in the side of the lorry, and so on. Every so often someone, nearly always a woman, would pop out of one or another of the lorries and bellow in a furious voice, 'Don't do that!' The sight was so absurd that I began to laugh. 'Look,' I said to Claire, 'this whole field is full of massive horses being told off like naughty toddlers by little cross women. Why do they put up with it? Why don't they just break their loops of baler twine and kill us with their iron hooves?')

As I led the mare down the yard to the trailer, my knees

were shaking, the hand clutching the lead rope was trembling, and I was afraid that my vision of being crushed would somehow jump from my brain to Molly's. But her contrariness had its benign moments; perhaps the affable trance into which she'd sunk while being plaited hadn't worn off; more likely, she realized she was going hunting. Whatever it was, she stepped into that trailer as graciously as a duchess. Cornflake went on the other side, and we were on our way.

I'd been so slow getting the horse ready that I hadn't even started on myself. As Claire followed Jillie, who was driving the lorry at a cracking pace along the winding route to High Halden, I was doing quick-change contortions in the front passenger seat, squirming out of the mucky over-trousers and jumper that I was wearing on top of my clean shirt and breeches, fastening my tie (no stock for me. I was still in novice ratcatcher), pinning my hair into a net and applying lipstick with the help of the wing mirror. 'How do I look?' I asked Claire, when I thought I was ready. 'You look fine,' said she, eyes firmly fixed on the lorry, now whizzing through a tricky junction up ahead. A cassette of some vague, flutey new age music – the sort of thing they play in the changing rooms of shops for rich hippies – was burbling on the car stereo. I wondered if it was meant to calm me down.

'Now then,' said Claire, negotiating the junction with a flourish that made the horses stamp in the trailer, '(Stand still, ladies!) There are quite a few little stick jumps and ditches in the woods at this meet. Nothing to worry about. Just sit down, heels down, let the reins slip through your fingers.' 'Jumps?' said I. 'Oh no. But Jillie said there wasn't any jumping at this meet.' 'Did she?' said Claire, surprised. 'Oh. Well, there is, but nothing to worry about, I promise you. Oh look, this must be where we're unboxing.'

I couldn't speak. I wasn't even really frightened any more,

but filled with rage and contempt for the vanity and self-delusion with which I had convinced myself that after three years of riding for no more than a couple of hours a week, and with no natural aptitude, I was ready to go hunting. Well, it was too late to do anything about it now. We unboxed the mares. Muttering something to Claire about needing a pee, I found a nasty secluded corner full of brambles and rusty wire and threw up a mouthful of bitter froth. Then I went back, got on the mare, and followed Claire down to the meet.

Apart from me, the small black cloud at the party, the atmosphere was ebullient, full of relief and happiness that the season was beginning at last: people on foot and on horseback greeting one another with the ease and pleasure of old friends at a reunion. Jillie now had someone's baby perched on the pommel of her saddle and was laughing as loudly as she had earlier been shouting. There were a few bored police dotted about the place. I got off the mare to dip my boots in the trough of DEFRA disinfectant (why – since my feet weren't going to touch the ground? Unless I fell off, of course) and Boyd, grinning as though he'd just heard some good news, gave me a leg-up so exuberant that I flew into the saddle as neatly as a jockey. It was a change from the usual disorderly scramble of my leg-ups and made me feel better.

So did the whisky Claire had gone to find, which loosened the knot of self-loathing clenched in my stomach, leaving behind a vague and not unpleasant sense of detachment. As a child, I used to hide in the angle of the stairs to peer down through the bannisters on the guests arriving at my parents' rarely held parties. With the whisky came an echo of that curiosity and fascination at a scene where I was both present and apart.

The pleasant illusion that it wasn't really me sitting up here in the wintry sunshine with a view of the world framed by a pair of expressive grey ears persisted all the way through the senior Master's Parish Notices – a business-like affair of reminders about forms and boot-dipping – and continued as we left the green for the first covert. And then we turned off the road and onto farmland and I snapped sharply back into the present: a present in which it was disagreeably clear that I couldn't make Molly stop.

The horses ahead of us set off along the edge of the field at a canter and we rushed after them, out of control in the mass of horses and riders. I had a confused impression of one of my son's video games, in which Homer Simpson and his family, at the wheels of various vehicles, career in reckless fashion the wrong way around roundabouts, over central reservations, through car parks and shopping malls, hurling aside anything in their path. I looked up for just long enough to see that ahead of me they had all stopped, and were standing by a wood in a clump – into which I seemed about to plunge at speed. With a desperate wrench of the right rein, I managed to circle away and bring the mare round again. The wild canter or gallop or whatever it was changed down to a swift but more manageable trot. I saw Claire, laughing and chatting as though nothing was wrong and edged towards her, trembling. I was just getting up to her when they all rushed off again.

All the elementary fieldcraft that Peter Deacon had spent the previous season patiently trying to teach me fled from my mind. I had no idea whether hounds were hunting and we were following them, or if this was simply the Ashford Valley's usual means of moving from one covert to another. I couldn't have told you the direction of the wind, the whereabouts of the huntsman or anything else. The only thing I was conscious of was that I was caught in the middle of this mass of horses, with no means of exerting control over the one I was sitting on. There was nothing I could do, beyond doing my best to hang on and hoping that her herd instinct would encourage her to stop when the rest of them came to a halt.

As a feeling, it had something of the voluptuous abandon that I'd felt when I was first learning to ride and fell off Herbie – the recognition that there was nothing you could do to influence the trajectory that you were now following. Your only option was to allow whatever happened, to happen. On the other hand, that fall had all been over in a matter of seconds, whereas this wild flight might – for all I knew – continue all day, until darkness fell. I wasn't sure my physical stamina would endure until then. I began to see why Mrs Rogers regarded falling off with the horror usually reserved for grave moral lapses. You wouldn't last long if you fell off in the middle of this.

On the other hand, there must eventually come a point – mustn't there? – where your muscles simply wouldn't work any more. Weeks, months, even years of my adult life passed without my ever having to make a physical effort that required all my reserves of strength. I was quite wiry, with the low-level domestic fitness that you get from housework and heaving bags of groceries out of the car boot and running about with an active child, but my only experience until now of using all my strength to accomplish something had been lifting a heavy suitcase off an airport carousel. That exertion, like falling off Herbie, had been over in a couple of seconds. But I'd now spent ten continuous minutes using every bit of strength in my arms, back, fingers, thighs and calves to make this mare stop, and she wouldn't. All the soft tissue in my back felt as though it might any moment peel cleanly away from its skeletal attachments, like tugging the breast off a chicken carcass. I was sure Claire had no intention of going home early, so this could easily last for another five or six hours.

Musing thus, gripping with my legs and leaning back on the reins with my full weight, I looked up for a moment and found the field had stopped again. The only people still moving were the huntsman, the two whippers-in, the senior Master. And me. It was already taking all my strength just to keep from going any faster. I'd got nothing left to stop with. Sorry, I gasped, as we swept past the Master. Sorry, sorry, sorry.

As we came level with the whippers-in I loosened my rein sufficiently to give it a vicious yank and either that, or the fact that the mare had seen there was almost no one ahead of us, made her stop at last. She came back into my hand, turned and we began the long, awful walk back to where the Master was standing and behind him the field, goggling and thanking their good luck (and superior riding skills) that it wasn't they who had just over-ridden the Master in the first ten minutes of the opening meet.

In Patrick Dennis's delicious confection of 1950s frivolity, *Auntie Mame*, there is a memorable scene in which the Yankee Mame, having incautiously claimed a keenness for riding that she doesn't entirely feel, is manoeuvred by her husband's jealous ex-fiancée into a day's hunting in the Deep South, where she is ignominiously run away with and over-rides the Master. At which everyone gathers round and exclaims at her courage, magnificent seat, extraordinary horsemanship and so on.

I didn't think that was likely in my case. I'd read enough hunting stories to know that over-riding the Master was, along with kicking a hound and heading a fox, one of the classic hunting misdemeanours. There would now be a fearful telling-off with lots of shouting, at the end of which I would be sent home with my character in shreds.

Well, I was past caring. I thought it a low trick of fate, to have made me waste all that time worrying about falling off when actually it was my destiny to be sent home. But so what. I'd had enough. I'd done my best, and it wasn't good enough, and now I could stop. I would go back to the trailer and wait there until Claire had finished and I would never come hunting again. The only thing I really minded was that I hadn't brought a book with me, so goodness knew what I was going to do for the next few hours. Fat tears of self-pity fell on my gloves and the pommel of my saddle. 'I'm sorry, Master,' I said, as I rode up to him.

'Ah, Jane,' he said. 'Have you brought your tape recorder?' Eh? 'Were you perhaps trying to interview my whippers-in?' What? I looked up. He was smiling. He had made a little joke. There was going to be no telling-off and no sending home. My hunting career was not yet over.

'Have some sloe gin,' said Claire, as I crept to the back of the field. I was afraid that Mrs Rogers might take the opportunity to deliver the sharp smack of reproof that the senior Master had unaccountably failed to deliver, but she said nothing. Only the next hunting morning, when I went to fetch my bridle, I found that the bit – the toy-like, banana-coloured Happy Mouth gag – had been replaced by a ferocious torture-chamber object, hung about with hooks and chains, with a dense black mouthpiece as thick as my two thumbs and great shafts of metal by way of cheekpieces. 'It's a stopping bit,' said Mrs Rogers, by way of explanation. Which it certainly was.

The absolute authority of Masters of Foxhounds in the field is hard to explain. People who were once unquestioned figures of authority – parents, teachers, doctors, politicians, the police, the judiciary, the priesthood and football referees – now find their activities viewed through a spectrum of scepticism in shades from questioning to resentment, so the ability of an MFH still to command a field that has already paid heavily, in money, time and effort, for its day's hunting, seems an extraordinary anachronism. What is more, hunting tends to attract just the sort of strong, argumentative characters that are hardest to control (the Ashford Valley AGMs were lively proof of this).

I was not at ease with authority figures. As a child I had devoted a good deal of energy to the small-time subversion of such soft targets as schoolteachers and Girl Guide leaders. As a grown-up, I avoided authority as much as possible, by finding work in those safe houses for timid and ironical anarchists – the jobs of secretary and newspaper sub-editor.

It felt odd to be back as an adult in a schoolroom world of hierarchy, uniforms and coded jargon, where the wrong sort of hairnet could provoke a public rebuke and a failure of skill or knowledge attracted the same opprobrium as a sin (more so, actually – I got the impression that all sorts of dodgy social behaviour might be excused if only you were a brave and elegant rider). But my imagination was engaged now as it had rarely been by an institution. In this frame of mind the rules seemed, unexpectedly, less a restriction of liberty, more part of the architecture of an odd but intriguing edifice that I was intent on exploring.

All this thinking and talking and reading about hunting before ever I got round to doing it had given me a sharp sense of the invisible intricacies of what to an incurious or censorious onlooker must seem a disorderly spectacle: Wilde's unspeakable in pursuit of the uneatable. Though I was too flustered at the moment to make out its underlying pattern, I knew the apparently inchoate swirling across country in which I was involved represented the apex of a great pyramid of labour, diplomacy and imagination. Hounds had been bred, whelped, sent out to walk, retrieved and trained. Farmers and land-owners had been cajoled for permission to cross their land, hunt jumps had been built, horses made fit, schooled, clipped and shod, the country walked by the Master and huntsman, the coverts to be drawn decided and the shape of the day planned, as far as it could be, given the vagaries of foxes and weather and scent.

On the morning of the meet, all over the hunt country and beyond people had been rising before dawn to groom their horses and then themselves. I spent far less time getting ready for London parties (at which – who knew – I might find the love of my life) than I did getting myself and Molly ready for hunting, where I knew perfectly well that we would both be covered in mud five minutes after leaving the meet (so if the love of my life happened to have taken a notion to come hunting, he would certainly not recognize me as his future sweetheart under the stippling of Ashford Valley clay).

The wilful convention of perfect turnout varied a bit among the field in general. Not everyone plaited, and sometimes they even wore waterproofs if it was raining. But neither of these dispensations was allowed if you came from the Rooting Street yard. If it rained, which it did, insistently, you sat there in your sopping jacket and breeches and got an elegant case of rheumatics – which was fine by me. Elegance had always seemed to me a form of self-control. Buttoning my hunt jacket just before I got on the horse felt like a ritual preparation for the test of stamina that lay ahead. I should have been less brave in a Barbour.

On the other hand, I was now beginning to feel that my stamina had been tested to its limit. I was relieved not to have been sent home. But I still didn't see how I was going to make it through the next five hours. My strength was exhausted. I'd thrown up what little breakfast I'd had, so my stomach was empty, apart from a toxic hangover mixture of whisky and sips of sloe gin. Since getting out of bed this morning I'd been through emotional extremes sufficient to make most operatic heroines think of throwing themselves off the battlements. And it wasn't even midday. What I needed now, I thought, was a rest.

And a rest, with the capricious generosity of a hunting day, was what I got. The first cavalry charge wasn't the pace for the entire day, it turned out. Once the edge was off their animal spirits and excitement at finding themselves out hunting, most of the horses settled into a steady hunting canter – a lovely, powerful, rolling gait, like the up-and-down swoop of the gilded wooden horses on an old-fashioned steam roundabout – that was comfortable to sit to and fairly easy to rev up or calm down. What's more, you didn't spend the whole time on the move. There were frequent checks while Neil vanished with hounds on foot into the obscure depths of a wood, leaving his horse behind ('There goes Neil, beagling again,' said a foot follower.)

The field, meanwhile, got out its hip flasks and began the serious business of catching up on gossip. The London solicitor lit a small cigar and smoked it under an oak tree, looking like Lord Ladythorne in Surtees's *Ask Mama*. Claire was working the field like a conscientious hostess at a cocktail party, introducing me to a blur of faces whose names I instantly forgot. The light was pure as water, the air smelt of damp earth and dead leaves; the relief at being alive and still in the saddle and not lost was delicious. But I had no idea where hounds were, or what they might be doing, and after a bit I began to feel guilty for my deficiencies of observation.

Among my haphazard fox-hunting library were several little volumes of advice for the fledgling fox-hunter. They were often written by military men and inclined to address the reader, kindly but firmly, in the hortatory first person plural: 'We will make up our minds as to when we will get out of bed, catch, feed and dress our pony, giving ourselves plenty of time for breakfast and saddling up, not forgetting to arrange for some sandwiches or rations to take with us.'

Besides a Captain Hook-like obsession with Good Form ('Button-holes are theatrical and unworkmanlike'), the authors of these manuals had an insatiable appetite for list-making of a macabre and pessimistic nature. One such list, of Things the Fox-hunter Should Have In His Pocket, anticipated disaster with unseemly enthusiasm. It advised a handkerchief, for use as a bandage; a boot-lace, for mending broken reins; a 'small, solid, well stoppered glass bottle of iodine' for pouring 'into the jaws of a greedy wound'; and several small safety-pins, for holding torn breeches together.

In my pocket at the opening meet were none of the above, though I began to carry safety-pins after tearing my jacket on a branch. Instead I had a roll of Extra Strong Mints (good for numbing a stomach pinched by nausea or starvation), a spare hairnet and a powder compact. I was teased for the powder compact, which was felt to be a ludicrous piece of London vanity. But I reckoned there was no need to look like death, just because you were feeling like it. And I noticed that casualties of the wooded country quite liked borrowing it to admire their scratches in when we emerged from the forest.

Hidden among the gung-ho language of my hunting manuals – R. S. Summerhays's *Elements of Hunting* (with Preface by Dorian Williams, MFH) and Colonel the Hon. C. Guy Cubitt's Pony Club publication, *Riding To Hounds*, with its marvellously *de haut en bas* disclaimer, 'This booklet is intended solely to help those who have not the opportunity of adult guidance in their own home' – was one instruction that I took to heart, which was to Look About You.

A Summerhays-educated child, chancing to see a fox break covert, would automatically check his sturdy wristwatch, simultaneously noting the time and the exact spot where he saw the fox go away, rehearsing to himself meanwhile a verbal description in astringent telegraphese of the fox's movements ('Twenty yards to the left of that tree in the hedge', or 'Dropped in the ditch at the bottom end of the hedge in front'), ready to pass on ('in a strong, clear voice') to the huntsman or whipper-in, should he come thundering up, demanding, 'Which way did he go?'

Summerhays children, when moving at speed on their game little ponies, did not cling to the mane with their eyes shut, or wish silently that it would all stop. Instead, they kept one eye on the horizon and one on the ground and, should they 'come upon a nasty rabbit-hole or broken ground which is likely to bring a rider down', they resisted the impulse to scream or whimper, and smartly followed the Summerhays code: 'Fling your head to one side and shout over your shoulder, as loud as you can, "Ware hole!", pointing to it if you have a spare hand.'

The notion that one might, while galloping over broken ground, have a spare hand with which to point to a rabbit hole was sufficiently exotic for me to realize that I was not Summerhays material. His children – plucky, good-humoured, competent, keen – were evidently amateur whippers-in, or even amateur huntsmen in the making. I had no such grand ideas. My only ambition for today had been to avoid falling off, getting shouted at or over-riding the Master, and even that was now reduced to two of its three elements.

On the other hand, there was a clear distinction in my mind between riding and hunting and that distinction had to do with the way I looked at my surroundings. On the rides across country that we had been doing as a substitute for hunting, the landscape existed mainly as a backdrop to the chat. I had learned from Claire to look at the quality of the ground (because of what it might do to the horses' legs if it were hard); I might even, if the pace were steady, contrive to watch for holes or wire. We would note, in a general sort of way, the prettiness or otherwise of the landscape and we cast a sharp eye over the houses that we passed, discussing in detail which ones we'd like to own. But we were gazing at the country from outside, as though it were a picture, rather than sinking into it, as I felt I should be doing now, as though the lie of the land were a text on my understanding of which I should be examined before I might come hunting again.

There were big gaps in what I knew. I had no idea what was signified by any of the patterns of notes on the hunting horn that flew like birds from the woods where Neil and his hounds were invisibly searching for a scent. I knew that you must not holloa unless you were sure that what you had seen was the hunted fox, but I didn't really know the sorts of places where foxes might appear, how to tell whether they were hunted or not, nor what the alternatives might be – if there were any – to a holloa. I wasn't even sure what a holloa was. But then the charm of hunting, the antidote to its dread and harshness, was that sometimes you found things out, just by sitting quietly and doing nothing in particular.

Standing at ease by a grassy bank one fine day later that season, I found out what a holloa sounded like when one of the foot followers saw the fox skirting the hedge in the far distance ('Where? Where?' said I, failing to spot it at all) and holloaed right underneath me: a full-throated shriek, half lament, half war cry, with a particular, heart-stopping quality that is shared by the sound of a hunting horn, the cry of a fox in the night – and perhaps also the pealing of church bells and the song of the nightingales in the spinney by the Hothfield petrol station.

Another day I was parked at a cautious distance from the Master in a neat mown ride in Bedgebury forest when a fox popped out of the woodland to our right, trotted across the ride and vanished into the tangle of leaves to the left of us.

After a while there was a small commotion and the huntsman appeared, with some hounds. With a gesture at once economical and magnificent, the Master took off his hat and pointed with it, at arm's length, towards the place where we had seen the fox vanish. 'Tally Ho across!' he said. The huntsman nodded and plunged into the wood.

It was the first time I had ever heard the words 'Tally Ho!' spoken for their proper purpose. I felt a sort of triumph at the sound, much as Cecil Sharp must have done, crouched at the fireside of some ancient who was croaking out a folk-song half-remembered from the days of Boney's wars.

Now that I'd caught my breath on this turbulent first morning with the Ashford Valley, I wasn't sure what I should be looking for. I couldn't see any hounds and I needed Peter Deacon to decode for me the significance of the flight of the birds and the direction of the wind. I gazed at a patch of moving colour in the middle distance that resolved itself into the figure of Rick, the whipper-in, cantering down a grass track between two fields, jumping what must be some sort of little hurdle at the far end, travelling on to the far corner of the field, then turning back to the point from which he'd set off. Some singularity of the way in which he and the horse moved together made it appear as though they were not really moving at all, but standing poised, like the statue of a horseman while the landscape shifted around them. There was something inevitable about the way they covered the ground and flowed over the jump – not like riding at all, as I understood it: more like breathing.

That beautiful partnership, a degree more relaxed than effortless, was what I wanted to look like on Molly – one of these days. I unclenched my bottom and tried to sit down in the saddle. I glanced around at the rest of the field, who were lounging in their saddles as though sitting on so many comfortable old chintz-covered armchairs. I was the only one with a straight riding-school back and primly pinched reins. I dropped my hands, loosened the reins, took my toes out of the stirrups and let my feet hang down.

'Is this your first time out?' said a man next to Claire. I said yes, and that I'd been riding for three-and-a-bit years, and he said, very nicely, 'That is quick.' I was just uncurling in the warmth of this scrap of approval when Claire said, 'There's a little post-and-rails just ahead. Are you up for it?' So I said yes, very fast, not letting myself think about it even for a moment, and we set off. It was a tiny, rather decrepit uphill jump, the only way into the next field, covered in moss and lichen and crumbling gradually into the surrounding leaf-mould.

All the real jumpers had already done it and were vanishing into the distance; it was surrounded by an irresolute rump of the middle field, muttering about other ways round. The nice man hopped it and fell off on the other side. Then Molly gave it a sniff and walked over it very deliberately, one foot after the other. 'Well done, well done,' said Claire, unduly generous. But at least we were on the other side of it and catching up with the rest of the field, and suddenly there was a whole series of jumps at irregular intervals: a nasty one with – as I saw when I looked down in midair, as I had been told I must never do – a curl of wire across the top of it, and another that loomed high and solid and was surely bigger than anything I'd ever jumped in my lessons, but it was coming up so fast that before I had time to think about not jumping it we were over. Then there was a twiggy log that Molly jumped unexpectedly high, so that I caught her in the mouth as we came down, and another small post-and-rails and then we'd pulled up under trees at the top of a field at the opposite side of which, on a rising slope, the tiny figures of hounds, huntsman and whippers-in streamed in silent procession.

'That's a very forgiving mare,' said the man who had fallen off, which was true enough, if not quite tactful. In the distance, the gravedigger figure of the terrier man was crossing the slope at an angle, his leaf-shaped spade propped on his shoulder, his coupled terriers capering alongside.

'There's the fox,' said Claire, pointing. 'See?' As usual, I couldn't, but for once it didn't matter, because at last I'd understood how you might ride and think at the same time and the secret seemed to be exactly what everyone had been telling me, that you did nothing. You sat still and made your mind go empty and let the horse do the work. That was something I had never been able to do over the jumps in the sand school, however often I repeated to myself the formula that I might know the jumps had just been made three inches higher but the horse didn't. I could never get rid of the feeling that it was only by prodigious feats of my magical willpower that we were able to leave the ground at all. But now the hidden truth of jumping had been revealed to me, and it was that you simply put your trust in the horse – which left you plenty of spare time in which to interpret the coded narratives of venery concealed among your surroundings. Amazing.

'Your blood was up, I dare say. It's like that, out hunting,' was what Tracy said when I excitedly reported the phenomenon to her on the yard a few days later. I was a bit crushed to learn that my marvellous discovery was old news, and equally dismayed to find that the Revelation of the Secret of Jumping was fairy gold and had vanished by the time I got back into the sand school, where it was lurch, bump, grab, worry all over again. But I'd had the feeling now, I knew it was real, that astonishing, fluid curve at speed over solid timber, like water running fast over boulders. I might not be able to recreate it in my lessons, but at night-time, in my dreams, it happened over and over again.

It was dark when we hacked back to the hay-barn where

the trailer was parked, and very cold. Claire's car had a flat tyre and as we strained to loosen the wheel nut it came on to rain. We missed our turning on the way back and led our mares, muddy and tired, into the barn just as Mrs Rogers was putting the rugs on Camilla. 'What happened to you two?' she said, and then, 'So, Jane, did you have a good day?' I said I wished I hadn't over-ridden the Master ('I didn't see that,' said Mrs Rogers, very firmly) but apart from that I'd had a wonderful day. The mare was fantastic and I couldn't wait to go out again. There was a small silence. I thought she might say something about my jumping, but she didn't. Dizzy with sloe gin and exhaustion and triumph, I thought I'd chance it. 'Oh go on, Jillie,' I said, 'it may not have been pretty, but admit, it was brave.' 'Hmph,' said Mrs Rogers, but not unkindly.

Reading books about hunting while curled up in a warm bed had done nothing to prepare me for the brutal physical grind of it. In Nancy Mitford's novel *The Pursuit of Love* the narrator, Fanny, gives a vivid description of the discomforts of a hard day's hunting in bad weather: 'The rain was pouring down by now. An icy trickle was feeling its way past my left shoulder, and my right boot was slowly filling with water, the pain in my back was like a knife . . .' concluding, 'After hunting we were kept in bed for at least two hours.'

The Rooting Street version of *après*-hunting did not involve bed rest. What happened when you got back to the yard was that you spent almost as much time cleaning your horse and making it comfortable as it had taken to prepare it in the morning. If we were lucky we might find that Tracy had left buckets of warm soapy water in the barn with which to wash off the worst of the mud. If not, we had to do it with cold while the temperature outside the barn was dropping towards zero and, if it were a clear night, the frost crackled in the air.

Most days ended with the horse half-encased in a carapace of encrusted mud that covered its legs, its belly, breast and face. One way or another, with a brush or a sponge, you must get it all off, or the horse would be sore the next day, and the scabs of mud fever would form on its heels.

I was slower at grooming than the others, and in any case Molly, made even more irritable than usual by fatigue and excitement, kicked like a kangaroo when you tried to wash the mud off her belly and legs. Most nights I would be left alone in the barn after the others had finished, dancing a solitary fandango in boots and shirtsleeves around the kicking mare with my sponge and my cooling bucket of muddy water. And when she was clean at last, and rugged and resting safely in her pen, I must scrape and wash the dried mud off my tack, and saddlesoap it all, so that it would be clean for the girls to use when they came to school her the following week.

Depending on how far we had to travel home from the meet, and how lost we had become on the way, it could be eight at night – 12 hours since I'd arrived on the yard – before I eventually got into my car, frozen, muddy and stiff, to drive home. The tiredness and fading excitement that made Molly irritable coagulated in hard lumps in my knees. When I first got off the horse I could scarcely bend them; once unbent, it was hard to make them flex again.

I imagined that I would feel lots of things after hunting: I thought I would be exhausted – physically wrecked, emotion-ally drained – and hungry. I thought I would sleep as though drugged and wake blooming and rosy-cheeked from all the exercise and fresh air that came from sitting in a saddle from eleven in the morning until five in the afternoon. But I was mistaken. I wasn't tired, or rather, I was meta-tired: so far beyond tired as to have come out the other side – animated by an emergency reserve of lurid energy that made everything seem flickering and greyish-iridescent, like the world seen by strip lighting or with detached retinas. This unnatural vitality made sleep elusive – and what with the wakeful nights and the dehydration of hours on horseback with nothing to drink but a cocktail of sips from people's hip flasks, the following day I generally looked like the Undead.

It would have been nice to come home to someone who would hear my footstep on the path and begin to make toast and scrambled eggs, sitting me down meanwhile to drink a glass of something (sherry? cocoa? egg nog? hot sweet tea? – at any rate, something comforting and stimulating). But I found I wasn't hungry – or at any rate, I wasn't hungry for anything I might cook for myself. In any case, as soon as I got back I must collect my son, and in the moment that he saw me I was transformed, like Cinders on the stroke of midnight, from someone who had spent six hours in the saddle following hounds into a suburban mother, embarrassingly got up in muddy boots and filthy breeches, with a scratched face, tangled hair and an excruciatingly uncool checked waistcoat.

'I think housework is far more tiring and frightening than hunting is,' says Nancy Mitford's heroine, Linda, in another passage from *The Pursuit of Love*. 'Yet after hunting we had eggs for tea and were made to rest for hours, but after house-work people expect one to go on just as if nothing special had happened.' For me, a day's hunting shaded seamlessly into a brisk dose of housework – the polishing of the horse and its saddlery followed without a pause by the ordinary chores of getting tea, washing up afterwards and supervising bathtime – exactly as though nothing special, or even mildly interesting, had happened.

I found it hard to settle for this. In fact I found the transition from hunting back to ordinary life hard to manage with any grace at all. I was as excited and voluble as a person in a state of minor shock, and I should have liked someone to ring up and tell about my day in boring minute detail. There wasn't anyone, though. My London friends thought my new passion a comic or deplorable eccentricity. They didn't love me any the less for it, but they didn't much want to spend whole evenings hearing about it.

Quite soon I learned to treat the lonely aftermath, washing the horse in the empty barn and cleaning my tack after everyone had finished, then the hour's drive home in the dark, with my aching knees slowly unlocking in the grateful warmth of the car heater, as a sort of post-match debriefing. Sometimes I turned on the car radio (on the way back from the opening meet, I switched to Radio 3, where they were in the middle of Mozart's 'Hunt' quartet, which I thought a pretty gesture from some kind of tutelary deity). More often I drove in silence, not thinking, just following the glowing trail of red brake lights curving ahead of me, half my mind on the road, the rest floating at random in a dream-like pool of images from the day just passed.

There were 19 meets in that truncated season – Wednesdays and Saturdays. I went to eight of them and each time it seemed as hard as the first. Familiarity and habit didn't seem to blunt the sharp edge of dread that began on Friday nights, when I was cleaning my boots and brushing my coat, and kicked in hard when the alarm began shrieking that it was five o'clock and I must come out from under the warm bedclothes and plunge into the cold house, where the central heating hadn't yet begun the tubercular coughing that was its morning rev-up, and even the cat was still asleep with his tail wrapped over his nose.

What happened eventually was that the dread became not less, but more manageable. I began to recognize its habits: it gathered in waves that swelled towards panic, then leaked away to a shallow disquiet. Noticing this didn't make me feel any braver, but I made up a technique of fear-surfing to get

319

over the worst of it. From being the sort of little girl who sticks her fingers in her ears and carries on reading with desperate concentration when the teacher leaves the room for a moment and a classroom riot breaks out, I had grown up to be the sort of adult who is scared to go on the white-knuckle rides at funfairs and finds the fight sequences, even in movies rated suitable for children (*Star Wars*, *Lord of the Rings*), too horrible to watch.

I thought fear an emotion without redeeming qualities. It was what you felt on waking in the darkness to the sound of an unknown footstep on the stairs and an inexplicable smell of cheap tobacco wafting under the crack at the bottom of the bedroom door; it was the feeling that went with losing control of the car in the fast lane of the motorway, whirling round and around and hitting the central barrier; or when you were summoned to the office of someone who not only intended firing you, but had clearly been saving up the moment as a titbit of pleasure for himself – a succulent little reward for a constructive morning's work. I could think of nothing good about being frightened. On hunting mornings it tensed my muscles, froze my brain, made me clumsy, forgetful, angry, spiteful and prone to humiliating physical collapses. I kept having to find dark corners in which to shed tears or be sick.

I thought this was cowardice, and that eventually I'd get over it and be like everyone else: calm, methodical, cheerful and on top of things. After a bit I realized that I probably wouldn't, but at the same time it struck me that there might be other things I could do with fear, besides being paralysed by it, or exhausting myself by fighting it. There was a line I liked in a book by Adam Phillips, a scholar and psychotherapist: 'We make things bearable by making them interesting,' it went. I thought that what I hated most about being frightened was the way in which, like sadness, it flattened every nuance and tainted all experience with its own metallic flavour. So I began to plot the patterns of my fear.

It was worst in London, the night and the morning beforehand. I'd go downstairs in the dark and see the trappings of the day's hunting all laid out, clean and polished as I'd left them the previous evening: the coat and velvet hat steamed and brushed, the breeches, polished boots, hunting whip and the mare's sheepskin numnah, smelling sweetly of washing powder and horse. They all looked unreal: as little to do with me as fairy wings and a wand. At such moments I found it hard to believe that the yard, Molly, the day's hunting, existed, or that I'd be missed if I simply didn't go. It took a convulsion of the imagination to put on the fancy dress, get in the car and turn the key in the ignition.

The start of the journey always made things seem better. There was the comfort of activity; the sense that the adventure was beginning and besides that, the secret joy of possession that comes with getting up very early. The dark sky shrinks and the stars dissolve in the creeping tide of light. Some mornings it looked as though there were a battle going on up there, with towers of cloud and great gouts of crimson and bruised violet separating the blackness in the west from the brilliance in the east. At other times I would be driving in the dark, then in an instant the sky above had turned a colour as fragile and pure as a blackbird's egg, pierced by the stars' faint points of light. All this was interesting, and the more so for seeming unobserved. The road was abandoned, the windows of the houses along the route unlit, the dew heavy on the grassblades, the world still asleep, apart from me (and the huntsman, his hounds and the foxes. And who knew what lay ahead of us all in the next few hours?).

Arriving at the yard, breaking out of the warm, egg-like capsule of the car into the chill stink, the hurry and racket of the stables and the barn was another bad moment. Eventually I saw that the worst points came during the transition from one state of being to another: turning from my London self into my hunting self; emerging from the dreamy cocoon of the car to the fierce concentration of the yard; loading the horses onto the lorry, then unloading them, going through the final button-fastening and girth-tightening before trotting to the meet. After that the drama was beyond my control and the pattern changed. There was no more time for anticipation or dread; all my powers of imagination were concentrated on trying to keep up and not fall off.

There was more, of course. There would have to be. However timid a person might be, the unadorned business of testing one's nerve couldn't remain interesting for long. I found the sharp edge of fear matched by a keen equivalent sense of intellectual engagement. It was a long time since I had tried to do so many impossible things at once. Not since university, a quarter of a century before, had I felt such a passionate sense of engagement with a subject. I carried it with me wherever I went. On the bus and the school run, in the grocer's and hanging out the washing, I thought about hunting.

Mrs Rogers's shrill cries of 'Kick on!' seemed to have extended beyond my legs to become an injunction for the conduct of my life. At various moments that seemed to have nothing much else in common – sitting in a smelly schoolroom to write the examination paper that would be my exit visa, if I passed it, from one kind of life to another; translating Virgil in the syrupy light of a library on a late summer afternoon; walking the wide-awake new baby up and down the moon-path in my bedroom in the small hours, singing nursery rhymes, Christmas carols, lullabies, old Janis Joplin blues; anything that might send him to sleep for the few hours remaining before I had to go to work – I used to feel a sense

322

of physical effort, as though I were pushing with all my might to open a door that some opposing force was trying to keep closed. I felt it now: that kicking on towards a knowledge that would be worth the struggle, if I ever got it.

There was something else as well. Something that came gently, without fighting or prodigies of concentration; something more like a gift than a prize. It was that Molly started to like me a little better. If I had thought about it, I might have worked out that if you spend 12 hours a day, once a week for a couple of months, in company with a fellow creature, half that time spent brushing and grooming it, and the other half sitting on its back with your leg pressed against its warm flank, your view of the world framed by its ears, you are liable to end up a good deal more intimate, whether you like each other better or worse than you did before. But she was my first horse; she had an aloof and complicated nature, and I knew nothing about the ways in which horses communicate. I was better at reading Virgil than I was at reading her, and I hadn't guessed.

Nothing came off Molly normally. She bit and kicked on the ground, was brave and competent as soon as you got on her, did her job honestly but entirely without signs of attachment to anyone, like a very efficient and self-contained temporary secretary. If you offered her a carrot she ate it nicely, then laid her ears back and gave you a rattlesnake look as you tried to fasten her rug an instant later. Nevertheless, after the first couple of hunts I did notice that the glory and gratitude I felt at being carried so bravely and safely over hedges and ditches, up banks and across posts-and-rails seemed to be producing an echo, the faint cheep of a sonar sounding taken from somewhere a long, long way down. It wasn't love, and it vanished, like the Revelation of Jumping, as soon as hunting was over. But there it was. It was not nothing.

There was a season of this, and then a summer and another season, in which some things were different and some the same. Two things that were different were that I wore a black coat now, with a full skirt and a starched white stock, and I had a proper hunting whip with a stag's-horn handle and an interesting past. I had not wanted to buy one raw and new, but as the start of the season drew close I despaired of finding an old one. I took my son to visit my parents and as we were leaving my mother said that an elderly friend had been turning out some things, and she had wondered if I would like this. If not, it could be thrown away.

She was rattling the walking sticks in the embossed brass umbrella-stand as she spoke, and I thought she might produce the sort of silver-mounted ebony cane that I recalled the Miss Havisham figure of my grandfather's ancient foster-mother leaning on one day when I was taken to visit her when I was nine and she was ninety-something. Or perhaps a parasol with a carved ivory handle and a cover of Victorian silk gone papery and insubstantial with age? Then she found what she was digging for and drew it out and it was a hunting whip, short and neat enough not to be too heavy for me, with a silver collar and a covering of plaited leather, a little worn from being carried in somebody else's hands and exactly what I had hoped I might find when I was unsuccessfully searching junk shops for old whips.

The other thing that was different was that Claire had a new boyfriend, so she was busy and hunted less often, which meant that I no longer had a permanent nanny and pilot, and could not continue to shelter behind her or rely on her to tell me how to take my jumps, but must try and find my own place in the field. It was much harder, and towards the end of the season bad cracks appeared in the partnership with Molly that had given me such confidence all through my first season. She began to stop at her fences and I didn't know why (though

I knew it must be my fault) nor how to retrieve the fleeting moment of glory in which I realized that if I sat still, she would jump anything.

The season ended in an ignominious muddle of stoppages and fallings-off and a fearful public shouting-at from Mrs Rogers for cantering across an open field instead of sticking to the margin, as an elementary grasp of fieldcraft should have shown me that I must. 'Why didn't you follow the footfalls?' bellowed Mrs R, silhouetted on horseback against the skyline at the brow of a hill while I and my fellow criminals sat hunched on the slope beneath her. 'Oh dear,' said Boyd, offering his flask of cherry brandy while I snivelled into the sleeve of my hunt coat. 'Jane in full cry. Again.'

I kept a sketchy hunting diary. Not a proper one with details of where we drew and where we found and where he ran to, and how he was accounted for, but a breathless scrawl of whatever I could remember and wasn't too wired to write down when I came home. When I looked back at it, I thought that the pattern of the hunting days it recorded had inadvertently taken the shape of a medieval Book of Hours.

In the Books of Hours I had seen in museums a single image – an incident from a bible story, a saint's life, or just a seasonal activity such as reaping or sowing, brewing, hawking or threshing – was framed by a decorated margin, busy with inconsequential activity, sometimes grotesque or ignoble, sometimes beautiful: flowers and birds and butterflies all mixed up, without regard for proportion, with little gargoyle faces of dismay and wrath and small figures performing base or comical functions – playing the bagpipes with an expression of intense melancholy, or sitting back-to-front on a donkey while poking it energetically up the bottom with a stick.

That was what I seemed to have made, from words instead of pictures, placing a border of odd fragments around a single image that rose from nowhere (you never needed to look for it. It came and found you, wherever you were) into which the essence of the day was magically distilled. Around the edges there tumbled swags of the nightshade berries that threaded the autumn hedges, juicy and red as coral beads or drops of blood, next to a little expostulating homunculus, shaking drops of real blood from the finger that it had just stabbed on the buckle of its stirrup leather and now was leaking red stains onto its clean white horse.

There was the terrier man, making his stately way between clumps of early primroses in answer to the huntsman's call. A Pony Club child, disappearing with a shriek into a crumbly, pony-sized badger-excavation; a paddock full of Shetland ponies, fuzzy and fat as bumblebees, snorting and tossing their heads and racing along the hedge as the field cantered by on the other side. A car, parked in a charming glade, deep in Bedgebury forest, the windows steamy, the chassis faintly rocking, rhythmic movement just visible within, the Pony Club mothers brightly diverting their children's attention with a chattering edge of desperation in their voices. Me, taking off my soaking breeches after a sodden New Year's Day of hunting round and round a dreadful wood in pouring rain and diminishing circles to find that my bottom had been stained a deep navy blue by the leaking dye from my saddle. Mrs Rogers in vaudeville frills, corset and fishnets, kicking up her heels as a saloon-bar hostess in the hunt revue.

Frozen at the centre of all this small incident were infinitesimal gaps of stillness. Momentary pauses before the tape began rolling again. Mrs Rogers, belabouring the fat cob Billy with her whip, squeaking, 'No! Billy! Billy! No!' as he sank comfortably to his knees, a luxurious roll in the soft grass on his mind. A check on the marshes at the top of a grassy bank above a dyke; a rude creaking noise, like the sound of a person bouncing on a very old mattress, then two swans flying low above the water, white arrows down the dead centre of the dyke. Molly and me on Boxing Day, scrambling up the steep bank of a stream over which hung the low branch of a beech tree, turning to see that the tiny, exquisite showjumper just behind us had failed to duck, and now hung swinging by one arm from the branch like a tiny, exquisite orang-outan, while his horse stood apologetically off to one side. Rick, the whipper-in, riding Molly at the point-to-point, scarlet coat and white coat in the bright spring sunshine, frozen at the gallop while the world whirled around them. Hounds, plunging like dolphins in a foam of white violets and wood anemones on the very last day of the season.

There are few foxes in these still moments. They haunt the margins, bouncing out of copses, bursting from cover between people's legs, trotting down grassy rides, creeping along field margins, lying limp and beautiful and dead from a gunshot in ignoble black binbags at the day's end. But in country so heavily wooded and crisscrossed with roads, there was little headlong hunting. I never found myself riding in the open behind a pack of hounds in full flight and hunting a line for more than a few minutes at a time. Other people said it happened, and that it was very exciting when it did, but somehow it was always on days when I wasn't there. The country was well foxed, and they killed plenty, but it tended to be a private affair between huntsman and hounds in a wood, sometimes with the terrier man in attendance, sometimes not.

I didn't mind very much not chasing a fox about the place, because like many people who follow hounds and don't keep lambs or poultry I felt ambivalent about the kill – glad for hounds when it happened, and glad for the fox when it didn't. But I should have liked to have known what a fast hunt across country felt like, and the dangerous wasps'-nest rumbling of the politics of hunting made it seem possible, or likely, or perhaps inevitable – it was hard to tell – that I never should.

The politics was awful. It lent a sense of gathering doom to every end-of-season party and kennels coffee-morning. To my intense dismay people started asking me what I thought would happen, as though the fact that I lived five miles or so from Westminster and wrote a newspaper column meant that I might have a privileged insight into the Government's thinking. No one seemed to understand what might be going on, and there seemed a polarization of opinion, within the Ashford Valley and among hunting people generally, between those who had an almost religious faith in the Countryside Alliance's ability to secure the preservation of hunting, and those who mistrusted its combination of a grand, rather secretive manner, nod-and-wink hints at political nous that seemed not quite solidly based and frequent, insistent appeals for funds.

I found the rebarbative prose style of its Press releases – like O-level civics essays written by estate agents – hard to love, and I was troubled by its blustering responses to what appeared to be the Government's inclination – wavering, but stiffened by a need to throw something succulent to its disorderly back bench – towards an outright ban. A friend who worked at the Alliance's head office reported frayed nerves, financial muddle and an alarming lack of organization, but people I admired and respected remained convinced of the Alliance's ability to save hunting in some recognizable form.

I said to one of these people that the Alliance's public utterances reminded me of King Lear's threats: 'I will do such things – /What they are yet I know not; but they shall be/ The terrors of the earth.' He laughed and said that the Alliance knew what it was doing, and that it would not do to alienate the public and the House of Lords by violent, haphazard demonstrations. I tried to feel reassured. It was true that such demonstrations as there were by pro-hunting groups that disagreed with the Alliance were painfully ineffectual – an effort to dress up the Angel of the North in a vast huntsman's coat, foiled without difficulty by police before it had properly begun, was probably the silliest.

In September 2002 there came at last the Livelihood and Liberty march that should have taken place in March 2001, but had been postponed because of foot-and-mouth. It was a vast, well run, awe-inspiring affair of nearly half a million people, with the cathartic impact of the Last Night of the Proms, the Changing of the Guard and 'Messiah' all rolled together. Altogether a wonderful emotional clear-out, but the feeling afterwards was empty, like the emotional vacuum that comes after a furious row or a terrible crying jag. Most disturbingly, there seemed to be no plans to consolidate the impetus of the march with any further action.

I went to see the Ashford Valley's MP at the House of Commons. I waited for him in the glorious Victorian Gothic fanciness of the lobby. He was late. He arrived, full of apologies and bought champagne in a bar from whose windows you could see the Thames flow blackly past under the swagged embankment lights. 'Do you think the march will have made any difference?' I asked, and he shook his head, very kindly, like a doctor having to deliver bad news. 'Maybe if it had been a million . . .' he said. 'But no.'

All through the summer, the peculiar process continued of a consultation that everyone seemed to be pretending was real, though no one really seemed to think it was. The twin tests settled upon were those of cruelty and utility – the second of which was bizarre, given that (as David Itzkowitz points out in *Peculiar Privilege*) utility was relinquished as a serious argument in favour of fox-hunting as long ago as the nineteenth century. In fact a most powerful argument in favour of fox-hunting could be made from its lack of utility. It has a long closed season while the vixens are rearing their cubs. It is selective, targeting feeble, elderly, dim and diseased foxes, while stronger, healthier, cleverer ones escape to spread their genes around. Hunting actively encourages foxes to flourish in the wild, by persuading farmers who would otherwise eradicate them from their land to permit their continuing presence. And so on. All this lent the parliamentary discussions an Alice-In-Wonderland quality that would have been quite funny had it not been so sinister.

The question of cruelty was the serious one. Everyone I knew who went hunting had cruelty continually in mind. Everyone had moments at which they wondered whether they should go on. Mine came during cubbing, in the course of a particularly hilarious bit of holding up, with grunts and gorilla jumping around the margins of a covert. I had a prim moment of thinking that hunting was not meant to be funny, and for once I knew I was right to be prim.

It is hard to tell without objective evidence whether something that skirts the margins of cruelty – putting a fellow creature to death, whether in an abattoir in order to eat it, or in the field with guns or dogs or traps or other means – is cruel or not, particularly if your involvement is that of a spectator rather than the instrument of the creature's death. What objective evidence there was – the conclusions of the Burns report, in particular, though the Middle Way group, which campaigned for the survival of hunting in regulated form, also produced persuasive evidence about the suffering caused by shooting – on the relative cruelty of hunting and alternative methods of killing foxes offered no grounds for a ban. Yet in Scotland banning legislation was passed, and the same seemed certain to follow in England and Wales.

The questions remaining for debate should have been, is it

necessary to control the fox population at all? (I heard one anti-hunting scientist argue that it was not), and perhaps the trickier abstract question of whether one should engage in an activity whose object is the death of a fellow animal, even if one were satisfied that the means were not deliberately cruel.

But when the vote came, in the summer of 2003, it was clear that these subtleties, the nuances of logic or reason, the gradations of argument about cruelty, about tolerance, about the landscape created and maintained by hunting and the ties that bind communities together were of no interest to the House of Commons. The back benches wanted a ban, and the Government acquiesced with relief. Of the promised protests, the ones that should have been the terrors of the world, there was no sign, though the Alliance did muster several hundred hunting housewives to pin pairs of knickers to a symbolic washing line outside the Houses of Parliament, with the slogan Pants to Prejudice.

Part of me felt incredulous about this, and another part felt furious with hunting. When I was in London, I felt dully convinced that there would be a ban. When I was with the Ashford Valley – so vibrant, so passionate and engaged about their pursuit, and so good at it – I felt certain that there would be an uprising to prevent one. But ordinary hunt supporters, the ones who would have risen to protest, if the call had come, waited and waited, and no uprising came. After the disastrous end to my personal season, when my mare wouldn't jump, the dissatisfaction that I felt with my own performance began to leak into my view of hunting in general. I began to think that if the institution hadn't the vigour to save itself, it didn't deserve to survive.

There was no Ashford Valley puppy show in 2003. I was given various reasons for this, all more-or-less fanciful, all more-or-less embroideries on what I took to be the truth, that they didn't want to breed hounds merely in order to have to shoot them. Instead there was a kennels open day, to which I planned to take my son. Just beforehand, I had a telephone call from the wife of one of the Masters. In the evening after the open day, she said, there was to be a party, to which people who had made a contribution to the hunt during the year were invited. Would I like to come?

'Yes,' I said, astonished and oddly moved at the idea that I might have made a contribution to the hunt (as anything other than an object of mockery. Mind you, you could make out quite a good argument for the usefulness of that role, I supposed). Anyway, 'Yes,' I said. 'Yes, please, thank you, I would.' And then, 'Is it child friendly?' 'Not very,' said the Master's wife. 'Children are welcome at the open day, but why don't you see if you can get a babysitter for the evening?'

I did try. Nothing doing in London. Everyone was busy. I tried my son's grandparents. They were great clergy-fanciers, my parents, and quite often, if I rang to see whether they'd like Alexander to visit, we would find that some venerable pillar of the church had got there before us. So it was on this occasion.

'Oh darling,' said my mother. 'We'd love to have him, but we've got the Archdeacon coming for sherry after church on Sunday. But we could certainly look after him for a little while. Just so long as you pick him up by nine-thirty or ten o'clock.'

The grandparents' house was half an hour from the kennels, where the party was beginning at 8 p.m. I dropped him there in the early evening and drove back to Hothfield. It was June 24, old Midsummer's eve. The day had been hot, but was cooling now; the air still, with a feeling of expectancy, the sky a faint dog violet shading to indigo. Above the chestnut trees the evening star shone brightly. Rick, the whipper-in, was prodding the coals on the barbecue – his unnerving stillness, I noticed, well in evidence, even when he was dressed in a short-sleeved Hawaiian shirt with a fish-slice in one hand. There was a marquee inside which the terrier boys were doing something fancy with the disco. Later on, no doubt, we should be frolicking to that indispensable anthem of all Ashford Valley festivities, 'Hi Ho, Silver Lining'.

I was getting a little Oh-no-I-can't-I'm-driving drink at the bar when the senior Master appeared, marvellously grand, even in his hot-weather civvies. 'Ah, Jane,' said he, giving me a squeeze, 'remember that time when you over-rode me, your very first time out?' 'Yes, Master,' said I, tittering obediently. Yup, object of mockery, that was definitely my role here. The Very Novice Lady, the London outsider, the keen but hopeless oddity.

I took my little glass of white wine and water over to where Boyd and his girlfriend were sitting with a clutch of other people who had at various stages tied up my ruined jacket, passed me their hip flasks, given me leads over jumps when my contact lenses had fallen out and I couldn't see where I was jumping, and commiserations and leg-ups when I fell off. 'Sit down and kick like fuck, excuse me,' Boyd once advised, natural delicacy warring uncomfortably with his keenness to shore up my shaky nerves when the girl in front of us had fallen off over something big and scary, and he and I were the only two left on the wrong side of it.

They had lent me their clean pocket handkerchiefs, pretended not to notice when I was crying, encouraged me when something nasty was coming up, applauded if I cleared it and looked the other way if I didn't, given me advice when things were going badly, pointed out foxes, tried to make sure I knew where hounds were, given me little jobs to do, watched out for me when hard pressed themselves. Made so much room for me that I could no longer pretend to be an outsider.

I joined the queue for food in the dank marquee, its roof patched with frayed violet shreds of evening sky. Trestle tables, covered with neatly creased white tablecloths, bowls of salad, chicken legs, plates of cheese and pâté, baskets of rolls, home-made quiches, strawberry flans and chocolate cake, knives and forks carefully wrapped in napkins. A day or more of preparation and effort to celebrate a haphazard grouping of people who, as Mrs Rogers had once said, wouldn't have been friends at all if it weren't for hunting. Was it fragile or was it sturdy, the connection that bound us all? I couldn't tell. All I knew for certain was that I was sitting here, with a paper plate of quiche and tomato salad on my lap, surrounded by people who knew who I was, and would notice if I were no longer there.

Behind us the disco lights started to flash; there was a crash from the amplifiers and an answering chorus of hound music from the kennels. The sky curved over us, star-pricked mauve now, bruising to bronze and deep violet at the horizon. It would be light for a while yet, and the party would go on long after dark. But the Archdeacon's claims were more pressing than mine and I must go, before the serious business of the party had begun. Goodbye, I said, goodbye, goodbye, yes, I've really got to, I wish I hadn't, goodbye.

At the bottom of the drive, where the pale shapes of the kennels geese slept on the grass with their long necks looped under their wings, I turned and looked back at them all – the Ashford Valley, eating and drinking and flirting on Mid-summer's eve. It was dark on the road where the trees hung down and I couldn't see their faces, only their silhouettes, but as I paused there for a moment, poised just outside the circle of light and celebration, someone waved. They'd noticed that I'd gone.

Acknowledgements

Many people gave me help and advice during the writing of this book. I should like to thank Sarah Lutyens, Juliet Annan, Rebecca Lee, Michael Arditti, Damian Green MP and Alicia Collinson, Ian Irvine, Nicholas Keyes, Pip Moon, Ian McKie MFH, Mrs J. E. Tylor MFH and Sally Nicholson, Miriam Gross, Sandra Parsons, David Sexton, Anthony Sheil, Linda Southgate and the librarian and staff of the London library.

I am grateful to the Chairman, committee and Hon. Secretaries of the Ashford Valley Hunt, also to its Masters, hunt staff, mounted field and foot followers, in particular Ian and Lynne Anderson, Brian Fraser MFH, Lynette Edwards, Colonel John Parkes OBE, Neil Staines, Rick Thomson, Kate Boyd, Mike Sargent, Steve Carter, Peter Deacon, Nick and Jane Kester, Tim Laite, Lesley Moody, Richard Porter, Boyd Roberts, Mrs J. R. Stevens, Mr and Mrs Noel Watson and Mrs Diana Wharton-Tigar.

I am grateful to the staff and instructors at Rooting Street Farm Riding Centre, especially Tracey Ashbee and Tim Brier for their patience with Little Molly and her owner, and to the farrier, Gary Turnwell. My special thanks are due to Claire Wardle for driving me to innumerable meets and encouraging me over jumps that I should not otherwise have attempted; to my son, Alexander, who feels about hunting much as I do about football, but tolerates its intrusion into his life with grace and good humour; and to William Meakin, whose advice and encouragement have been invaluable. Above all I should like to express my gratitude to Jillie Rogers, without whom there would have been no horse, no hunting and no book.

335

Bibliography

While writing *The Fox in the Cupboard*, I found the following helpful.

Anon., *A Master of Hounds, The Life Story of Harry Buckland of Ashford by One Who Knows Him* (Faber, 1931)

Apperley, C. J., *Nimrod's Hunting Reminiscences* (The Bodley Head, 1926)

Baily's Hunting Directory, 2002–3 (Pearson Publishing)

Sir William Beach Thomas, *Hunting England* (Batsford, 1936)

The Duke of Beaufort, *Fox-hunting* (David & Charles, 1980)

Beckford, Peter, *Thoughts Upon Hunting* (Debrett, 1802)

Bell, Adrian, *Corduroy* (Cobden-Sanderson, 1930)

Blackwood, Caroline, *In the Pink* (Bloomsbury, 1987)

Blow, Simon, *Fields Elysian* (Dent, 1983)

Brock, David, MFH, *The Fox-hunter's Week-end Book* (Seely Service, 1939)

Carr, Raymond, *English Fox Hunting, A History* (Weidenfeld & Nicolson, 1976)

Cawley, A. C. and Anderson, J. J. (ed.), *Sir Gawain and the Green Knight* (Everyman Library, Dent, 1976)

Church, Richard, *Kent* (Robert Hale, 1948)

Cobbett, William, *Rural Rides* (Cobbett, 1853)

Coombs, Tom, *Horsemanship* (Crowood Press, 1991)

Crouch, Marcus, *Kent* (Batsford)

Dennis, Patrick, *Auntie Mame* (Frederick Muller, 1955)

Edgar, Anne, *Her Master's Voice: The Life of Betty McKeever* (Privately published, 2000)

Higginson, Henry, *Peter Beckford, A Biography* (Collins, 1937)

Isaacson, Rupert, *The Wild Host* (Cassell, 2001)

Itzkowitz, David, *Peculiar Privilege* (Harvester Press, 1977)

Jefferies, Richard, *Chronicles of the Hedges and other Essays* (Phoenix House, 1948)

Keane, Molly, *The Rising Tide* (Virago Press, 1984)

——, *Young Entry* (Virago Press, 1989)

Kipling, Rudyard, 'My Son's Wife', from *A Diversity of Creatures* (Macmillan, 1917)

Markham, Gervase, *The Compleat Horseman* (1614) (Robson Books, 1976)

McBane, Susan, (ed.), *The Horse and the Bit* (Crowood Press, 1988)

Midgley, Mary, *Animals and Why They Matter* (University of Georgia Press, 1983)

Mitford, Nancy, *The Pursuit of Love* (Hamish Hamilton, 1945)

de Montaigne, Michel, 'On Cruelty', from *The Complete Essays*, translated and edited by M. A. Screech (Penguin Books, 1991)

Moore, Daphne, *In Nimrod's Footsteps* (J. A. Allen, 1974)

Moore, Patrick, (ed.), *Against Hunting* (Gollancz, 1965)

Potter, Beatrix, *The Tale of Jemima Puddleduck* (F. Warne & Co, 1908)

Ridley, Jane, *Fox Hunting* (Collins, 1990)

Sassoon, Siegfried, *Memoirs of a Fox-hunting Man* (Faber, 1929)

Schoenberger, Nancy, *Dangerous Muse, a Life of Caroline Blackwood*, (Weidenfeld & Nicolson, 2001)

Scruton, Roger, *On Hunting* (Yellow Jersey Press, 1998)

——, *Animal Rights and Wrongs* (Metro Books, 2000)

Sellar, W. C. and Yeatman, R. J., *Horse Nonsense* (Methuen, 1977)

Sinclair, Andrew, *Death by Fame, A life of Elisabeth, Empress of Austria* (Constable and Robinson, 1998)

Somervile, William, *The Chase* (1735) (George Redway, 1906)

Somerville, E. Œ and Ross, Martin, *The Silver Fox* (Lawrence & Bullen, 1898)

Stedall, Robert, *Hunting from Hampstead* (The Book Guild, 2002)

Summerhays, R. S., *Elements of Hunting* (Country Life Ltd, 1965)

Surtees, R. S., *Handley Cross* (Lawrence & Bullen, 1898)

——, *Mr Sponge's Sporting Tour* (OUP, 1958)

——, *Ask Mama* (Methuen, 1944)

——, *Plain or Ringlets* (Methuen, 1922)

——, *Mr Facey Romford's Hounds* (Methuen, 1950)

Sutherland, Douglas, *The Yellow Earl* (Cassell, 1965)

Swift, Sally, *Centred Riding* (Ebury Press, 1998)

Trollope, Anthony, *The American Senator* (OUP 1951)

Twiti, William, *The Art of Hunting* (1327), Bror Danielsson (ed.) (Almqvuist & Wiksell International, Stockholm, 1977)

Webb, Peter (ed.), *Hunting in West Kent, An Anthology* (privately published, 2000)

White, T. H., *England Have My Bones* (Collins, 1936)

——, *The Once and Future King* (Voyager, 1996)

Whyte-Melville, G. J., *Riding Recollections* (The Sportsman's Press, 1985)

Williams, Dorian, *Master of One* (J. M. Dent, 1978)

Other Sources

Masters of Foxhounds Association Constitution Rules and Recom-
    mendations, 1 June 1999

The Final Report of the Committee of Inquiry into Hunting with
    Dogs in England and Wales, 2000

Cubitt, Guy C. Colonel the Hon., 'Riding to Hounds', Pony Club
    pamphlet, 1963

Greaves, Ralph, 'Foxhunting in Kent', Field Sports Publications,
    1958

Scarth Dixon, William, 'The Ashford Valley Hunt', The Hunts
    Association, 1930